Lincoln Christian College

P9-CQD-760

Raising
Your Child
in a
Fatherless
Home

EVE JONES

# Raising Your Child in a Fatherless Home

**A GUIDEBOOK FOR ALL MOTHERS WITHOUT PARTNERS**

The Free Press of Glencoe

Collier-Macmillan Ltd., London

Copyright © 1963 by The Free Press of Glencoe,
A Division of The Macmillan Company

Second Printing 1963

Printed in the United States of America

All rights in this book are reserved.
No part of this book may be
used or reproduced
in any manner whatsoever without
written permission
except in the case of
brief quotations embodied in
critical articles and reviews.

For information, address:

The Free Press of Glencoe
A Division of The Macmillan Company,
The Crowell-Collier Publishing Company
60 Fifth Avenue, New York 11

Designed by Sidney Solomon

Library of Congress Catalog Card Number: 62–11852

Collier-Macmillan Canada, Ltd., Galt, Ontario

301. 427
J77

# Preface

This book is for single mothers—for you mothers who must rear your child in the absence of his father.

This book is for all kinds of single mothers: those who have no marriage partners because of death, divorce, or legal separation; those whose husbands are absent for years at a time because of hospitalization, imprisonment, or employment; and those who have never married.

Essentially, this book is about how you feel and act, and why you feel and act in certain ways. It is a book about your ways of taking care of your child; it is a book about your motives, behavior, emotions, and psychological needs.

It discusses how you and your child can form a life together so that you, as a loving and intelligent mother, may be constructive in solving the major psychological problems of your developing child and of your own self.

Your ways of acting must be different from those of most parents, those discussed in most books on parenthood, for your problems and your resources are different. The first part of this book is concerned with one major source of problems that are unique for you: the problems associated with being a single woman raising your child alone. The more you know and understand about yourself, the better equipped you are to take care of your child. So this first part is called *You*.

The natural growth and development of your child is like that of all children, even though you need to react to some developments in ways that are special to your incomplete home. My previous book, *Natural Child Rearing, the Intelligent Parents' Guide to Raising Children*, deals with ordinary childhood in detail, so the second part of this book is only a brief review to provide background for your special circumstances. This second part is called *Your Child*.

23913

The main topic of this book—how to raise your child in a fatherless home—is discussed in Part Three, *You and Your Child*.

In this book, as in the earlier book, there is no information about the purely mechanical or medical concerns of child care. Your private physician can best give you this specific information.

Furthermore, there is no information about the legal matters often concerned with single parenthood. Your attorney can best help you understand how the laws of your state apply to your particular situation.

But this book does deal with some matters that involve legal or medical consideration such as the effects of support payments, of visiting privileges, and of the importance of diet and exercise, because reactions to these things play a large part in determining how you feel and act.

This book is about single mothers, not about both single mothers and single fathers, because only the single mother faces a situation which is greatly different from the one she would face if she were not single. The single father, like the married father, relies on women for the major part of the care that his child receives; his situation is different only in that he is not married to the housekeeper, aunt, sister, or other woman that he may get to take on the job of rearing his child. I hope that single fathers learn something of benefit from this book; but I believe it would have been both awkward and needless to try to extend this book to cover all single parents.

I wish to apologize to single mothers whose particular conditions of age or social and economic position are not referred to. In writing about the situation typical for the single mother who is likely to read a book about herself and her child, it has been impossible to consider, even briefly, some of the less usual situations.

I have found it convenient to refer to your child as "he." Wherever needs and reactions are different for a single mother and a daughter, these differences are noted. The differences are also briefly discussed for the ways you care for certain needs in each child if you have more than one child.

The major goal of this book is to present healthful, practical methods of living with your child; consequently, I have chosen illustrative examples from the observations I have made in nonprofessional situations—either social or personal situations. I have deliberately refrained from presenting examples drawn from professional clinical practice or from the research studies and the literature of psychology and biology, since these are often neither typical nor directly instructive.

This book is only a guide to a creative understanding of your individual situation. I make no pretence of presenting to you something that relieves you of the responsibility for interpreting and understanding your own special circumstances—I do not believe any such authority can exist.

I am thankful that it is therefore impossible to deprive you of one of your most cherished rights and privileges: being creative and individual in rearing your child.

I am deeply grateful to my editors and publisher for their help to me while I prepared this book. I also want to thank those friends and colleagues who have challenged, criticized, instructed, or praised.

My ultimate thanks I reserve to my children and their fathers. To them I dedicate this book in fond memory of much we lived through together.

# Contents

Preface      v

## PART ONE   *You*

| ONE | Over-all Expectations | 3 |
| TWO | Understanding Yourself | 7 |
| THREE | Necessary Emotions | 14 |
| FOUR | The Pressures You Face | 17 |
| FIVE | Feelings and Behavior | 42 |
| SIX | Neurosis and Singleness | 76 |
| SEVEN | Consulting Help | 88 |

## PART TWO   *Your Child*

| EIGHT | Childhood Development | 107 |
| NINE | Physical Devlopment and Reality, Responsibility, and Sexuality | 115 |

## PART THREE   *You and Your Child*

| TEN | Your Role as a Single Mother | 149 |
| ELEVEN | Providing Material Care and Protection | 159 |
| TWELVE | Providing Stimulation and Freedom for Your Child's Activity | 220 |
| THIRTEEN | Stimulating Your Child's Sense of Responsibility | 256 |
| FOURTEEN | Stimulating Your Child's Realism about Sexuality | 292 |

Index      335

Raising
Your Child
in a
Fatherless
Home

You

PART ONE

You

# CHAPTER ONE

# Over-all Expectations

You CAN most confidently approach the task of rearing your child in a fatherless home if you have a clear understanding of the general goals you may reasonably expect to achieve.

The most important ultimate goal you may accomplish is success in rearing your child to be healthy and to have as much inner capacity for finding and making happiness in his life as might a child raised by both a father and mother. You can reasonably expect this ultimate success because your child's opportunity to grow up healthy and capable of being happy is primarily determined by the direct give-and-take of emotional satisfactions between you and him. And your capacity to be sensible and reasonable in meeting your child's inner needs is not dependent on whether or not his father is with you. Alone, you can still recognize and appreciate the emotional realities of your life and of your child's life, and you can provide satisfactions for your child's major psychological wants. As you do this, you automatically prevent long-range harm to your child from growing up without his father.

But, because your immediate reality is different, you must have immediate goals that are different from those of a mother raising her child in a complete home. You must expect to cope with occasional problems that arise in your child's life outside your home. In today's world, these are not likely to be the isolation and ostracism or other realistic limitations that used to be faced by the child living without both parents. Rather, they are likely to be problems your child faces merely because most community life involves complete families. Social events may awaken occasional feelings of social embarrassment or awkwardness, even feelings of loss or of resentment. So, for example, your child may be saddened by not having his father present to watch him receive his scout badges. But events like these do not arise often; and a healthy youngster is unlikely to be seriously hurt or disturbed when such special happenings occur. Just be sure to distinguish between the problems that arise in almost all parts of society and the ones that come about because a particular child suffers from inner difficulties that truly are related, not to the fact that his father is absent, but, instead, to the fact that his mother has failed to help him learn necessary emotional attitudes. With his basic needs satisfied as a result of the life you and he lead together, your child can easily and with a minimum of pain or embarrassment be helped to take occasional inconveniences or disappointments in stride.

With only one major exception, your child can learn all important psychological attitudes in the course of living only with you. This one exception, discussed in detail in Parts Two and Three of this book, is the psychological orientation toward sexuality that develops during a limited period of childhood. In the complete family, this development takes place in a way and at a time that is difficult to arrange in your incomplete home; so you must expect to take necessary steps that let your child learn to handle it satisfactorily.

Every other aspect of growing up can be accomplished by your child even in the absence of his father. You can successfully help your child learn the important characteristics of independence and control; he does not need a father to teach him these basic psychological strengths. If he has difficulties with other people that are not the minor sort mentioned previously, you can be certain these difficulties are connected to some failures that actually need not have occurred. If in his life outside of home he shows discomfort that is due to problems concerning self-assertion or temper control, for example, such problems would probably still exist even were his father with him. A child who feels deeply troubled because he cannot boast his way out of a clash with a playmate by shouting, "You leave me alone or I'll tell my Daddy on you," would not be genuinely better off, so far as learning to gain respect from friends is concerned, if his father were at home to be called out to fight the child's battles for him. This child still is one who has not learned independence and control.

All of these conclusions emphasize that your child's ability to be healthy and to cope with his few social inconveniences is primarily dependent upon his obtaining from you the basic satisfactions he needs.

In giving these to him, you can certainly expect that your being single creates special circumstances that make you go about mothering in ways different from the ways used by other mothers. But though your daily life is different from that which you would expect if your child's father were sharing the everyday complexities of a family, the over-all effect can still be the same. As Part Three shows, you can still accomplish the good results that a sensibly mature mother always can. All you actually need to concern yourself with is the extent to which you can be flexible and aware of the altered circumstances of your life. Being a single mother is a harder job than being a mother in a complete home, but it is still a job that can be done well.

Because you can conclude that your child's welfare is mainly dependent upon how well you satisfy his needs, and you can feel confident that you can meet his needs if you are flexible and realistic, the most important over-all consideration becomes the question of how you are affected by being alone.

Is it possible for a healthy, mature woman to avoid being greatly troubled as a result of being single? Can a woman who is not emotionally immature or disturbed live a life alone without developing serious inner difficulties?

The answer is that the difficulties of living alone can be met and handled; they are not problems you must simply suffer, unable to solve.

But they are not minor problems. They can easily trouble even a stable woman who otherwise is in no way emotionally upset. They must, in fact, trouble any woman. Thus, they are not like the problems connected with direct social consequences for your child or like the difficulties involved with changes in details of mothering.

Fortunately, though considerable, these problems can still be handled and solved as you face them honestly, with careful thought and controlled action. They do not require magical qualities of supermaturity or inordinate power.

It is not always easy to appreciate how the major sources of difficulty for a single mother caring for her child lie in her personal problems as a single woman. Because of the very nature of the problems that being single raises, you may occasionally lose sight of the fact that your characteristic feelings may be largely a product of your particular situation. You may have become accustomed to believing, instead, that your feelings are a product only of your own inner personality. You may blame yourself too much in your efforts to avoid what you consider the irresponsibility of claiming that your circumstances have any part in creating your troubles.

In addition, you may have become unnecessarily resigned to the idea that there is no way to keep your child from being forced to participate in your own inner unhappiness, whatever its cause. You may believe that your feelings must automatically carry over to your child and cause problems for him; and, although you do not wish to share your misery because you neither blame nor seek to hurt your child, you may believe you cannot prevent it.

These defeatist attitudes are unnecessary. They interfere with your functioning well as a single mother; so you must pay particular attention to keep from developing them.

The following chapters of Part One are devoted to helping you know your strengths and vulnerabilities and know the special problems you must handle because you are a woman living alone. With additional confidence as a woman, able to take creative action to fulfill your own life, you can avoid creating for your child the hazardous pattern of living that leads him to difficulties both in immediate daily life and in the future. You can take for granted the basic assumption made at the beginning of this chapter, an assumption this book is written to support: though singleness alters your ways of acting and though it affects your child's life, it does not require the ultimate sacrifice of your child's well-being and health.

# Understanding Yourself

IN ORDER to allow a self-analysis to be a profitable venture, rather than a waste of time and effort, you must exercise and practice three helpful personality qualities. Each of these qualities is one you possess and practice daily, but it is useful to distinguish them clearly to yourself.

The first quality is your *honesty* in deciding to discard all pretense that your life is perfect. By making this decision, you open the way to learn new things about your life. As you thoughtfully approach yourself with the idea that you want to discover your unsatisfied needs and your limitations, you take the first step toward being constructive and efficient in getting these needed satisfactions and in extending yourself past your present limits.

The second quality is your *forebearance* and *courage* in suspending value judgment. This enables you to consider your situation without becoming involved in the pointless, disturbing conclusion that it is somehow bad to be forthright with yourself. Because you need not waste thought and emotion in defending yourself against your own self-judgments, your entire task of self-analysis is made much easier and more productive.

The final quality is *self-control*, an inner brake you put on action that carries out the emotions occurring within you. As you curb yourself, as you seriously think through your situation before acting impulsively, not only do you gain more from your self-analysis, but you also strengthen one of the prime qualities that enables you to carry out your vital task of rearing your child without complicating his life through your actions.

Being single increases the amount of self-control you must exercise, because you meet greater direct pressures in your single life and you do not have available some of the external checks and props for your self-control that other mothers find in day-by-day living.

Chapter Four discusses in detail the pressures, the different kinds of insecurities and frustrations, of your life: the social and economic insecurities and the emotional and sexual frustrations. In addition, you face an implicit demand for extra self-control because your life does not contain the limitations and aids to self-control that the daily presence of a husband provides to other mothers. You are free of interference, untouched by the necessities for compromise and justification of your way of acting and taking care of your child and for handling your own personal needs in coordination with another adult. Although your day-time life is not much different from that of most mothers with preschool children—for they, too, are home without a husband during the days of the work week, without a husband to examine, question, challenge, or contradict their actions—you do not have a constant adult male companion relieving your relative emotional deprivation of the day during the evenings. You cannot look forward to having surcease from isolation and responsibility by sharing your adult feelings in an intimate, easy manner; there is no one to call your attention to what you are doing, reminding you that a short-lived spurt of temper or complaining or teasing is probably related to some subsequent unhappiness or disturbance in your child. You are the boss, single and unlimited. And it is not easy to be a responsible boss, wise and controlled, since no one else gives you the moral encouragement, rewarding praise, and emotional support that you deserve for keeping your temper, confining your complaints, and keeping yourself from bothering your child. The only compensation is that, because you are alone, you alone set the goals and make them possible, you alone gain directly in self-respect and pride each and every time you exercise self-control.

In controlling yourself, you are preventing yourself from

doing something psychologists call *acting out*. As you carry out your self-analysis, clearly differentiate between acting out, which merely releases inner tensions connected to underlying emotions, and *expressing* your emotions through appropriate and, usually, constructive behavior.

Acting out lets the way you feel about one situation dominate the way you act in another situation. Acting out is behaving inappropriately, for your acting out typically has very little to do with the actual, overt situation you are really facing. Consequently, acting out is seldom constructive and problem solving. It is also seldom straightforward, because it usually represents only the false and superficial emotional façade that covers both your genuine emotional needs and desires and the conflicting anxieties you feel about expressing these basic needs. Thus, it often either aggravates the discomforts that are already present or precludes obtaining some other pleasures from the current or future situation.

It does relieve some immediate tensions, of course, otherwise no one would behave in this manner, for all people strive to be free of uncomfortable tensions. But the few tensions that are released and relieved are usually only the superficial ones caused by your conflicts or by some additionally troublesome pressures that your conflicts cause. Acting out is frequently, but not always, related to neurotic conflicts, conflicts that are connected to childish and confused attitudes about basic personality needs. So, by being alert to your acting out, you can obtain valuable information about the possibility that you may possess deeper neurotic conflicts. By exercising self-control, you at least keep from complicating your life. You may still feel the anxiety that is part of the neurotic conflict causing acting out, and you probably still experience neurotic distortion and symbolization of your underlying emotions; but you save yourself and your child the additional problems that your acting out can create. You are keeping your troubles limited to yourself, as much as possible.

Much preferable, certainly, is expressive behavior. The following chapters of Part One are designed to help you increase your expressive behavior. Expression of emotions involves forthright, direct representation in action of your basic, underlying feelings. When you express yourself, you expect to accomplish something beyond mere release of some inner pressure. You expect to solve the immediate problem with which your emotions are connected. So, when you are expressing your emotions, you can fairly easily figure out what you are feeling and what you are doing and why; there is little alteration, distortion, or symbolic representation to confuse you or others, as there is with acting out.

This does not mean that expression is always conscious and deliberate behavior. Healthy people—who are the people expressing themselves—are spontaneous and confident individuals who do not necessarily plan every step they take. But they know what they're doing, primarily because their behavior is directly related to the immediate situation, and they can check their realistic evaluations of the immediate situation to learn more about their inner emotional reactions.

Unlike acting out, therefore, expressive behavior does permit genuine release of underlying pressures without creating additional ones. To the extent that it frees you to make plans for problem-solving behavior and provides motivation for constructive action based on these plans, expressive behavior actually leads to a remedy for a bad situation; to the extent that it lets other people know how they are contributing to your problems, it also helps establish a healthy climate in which differences and misunderstandings can be reduced or eliminated.

Even when the immediate situation prevents you from openly showing your emotions, expressing them to yourself lets you gain some lasting relief from the problem causing you to react. Your inner strength is increased when you let yourself get next to yourself; and every increase in strength makes your problems relatively smaller. (You accomplish some of this inner strengthening merely by controlling your acting out, but to a lesser extent.)

By expressing your feelings to yourself, you also gain valuable clues to situations that you may well be able to avoid or prevent. Chapter Four provides many illustrations of situations that typically call forth troublesome emotions; as you express to yourself what you feel in these or similar situations, you open up constructive possibilities that would not exist if you were to persist in not expressing your emotions to yourself. In a psychological sense, you must remind yourself that your shoes are tight before you can take action to remove them.

As a single mother, the most important consequence of your emphasis on expressive behavior and control of acting-out behavior is that you thereby avoid causing any serious and lasting conflict or loss of healthy gratifications for your child. It is only when a parent is acting out, and so operating blind to the real, objective situation with a child, that the child's needs may be disregarded, unmet, or unnecessarily confused and complicated.

By controlling your tendencies toward acting out and by making sure that you are honestly expressing at least to yourself your own emotions without necessarily translating them into action, you avoid letting your unhappy feelings or inner conflicts trouble your child. You make sure that you are not acting toward your child in a way that is genuinely appropriate only to some other, unseen, situation. You keep yourself from forcing too much of something on your child or preventing him from getting enough of something; you keep your emotions from causing real behavior that might hurt or deprive your child. The action you do not perform is the kind of activity that promotes and fosters neurosis by thwarting healthy psychological gratifications in your child. So by self-control, you prevent these unfortunate consequences.

Keep in mind that, even when there are severe emotional pressures, you only need to feel your emotions; you do not need to show them or let them lead to action. There is no truth to the popular misconception that everything that affects you must ultimately affect your child. It is a mistaken notion, because you can keep your feelings from bothering your child simply by controlling your actions. By all means, discard, once and for all, any ideas you may have that, since you are bound, willy-nilly, to show your emotions, you might as well show them full force and without any control or attempt to brake yourself. This is a poor excuse for lack of control; were it valid, there could be almost no hope that you or anyone might benefit from past experience and, through thoughtful and deliberate self-control, might keep from transmitting each and every hurt previously experienced on to the next generation. A book like this would be completely pointless; it would be asking you to do the impossible.

Clearly, so long as it is possible to control emotions and keep them from leading to actual behavior, it is nonsense to conclude that only by being completely mature, emotionally, can a mother save herself and her child from pain. You will find it easier to control yourself if you let yourself know what you are feeling, and if most of your feelings are not based on neurotic difficulties; but it is always possible to stop yourself from acting out your feelings with your child if you are firmly resolved to limit matters to your own internal struggles.

Self-control not only lets you refrain from getting your child involved in the problems of your private life, it also saves you the waste of time and effort that invariably arises because your child *cannot* truly be of real help to you with your adult problems. Your adult needs must be expressed to and with another adult in order to be met and understood and shared. In the absence of anyone else, telling yourself of them still provides some of this. But if you were to make your child your audience and involve him in your problems, you would only expose your needs, yet receive no genuine help or understanding. Your child clearly cannot perform the impossible and be or become an adult; he must remain a child, with a child's understanding and limitations. By self-control, you keep your child from trying to respond to the implicit demand that he act as if he were an adult, instead of a child, and then try to share, understand, and respond to your adult ideas and feelings. You keep him, and yourself, from the additional confusion that easily arises because your child lacks experience and has a relatively poor capacity for getting a sure notion of what he is supposed to do. You prevent his needing to wonder when he is supposed to act like a "pretend-adult" and when he ought to behave like a child again.

Because even after an acting-out pattern has begun there is no one else in your household to step in and call your attention to the problems you are creating, you must rely upon your self-control far more than even a highly neurotic mother in a complete home. You must face one final extra demand upon your self-control, too. You must exert self-control if you are to keep from overwhelming your child with your personality, if you are to provide him with privacy to be and become himself. In a home with both parents present, a child can obtain relief and respite from one parent by turning to the other; he can still enjoy the unself-conscious, easy intimacy that is found only at home, while he is thereby escaping from one parent's point of view. By your conscious, deliberate efforts to ensure a balance of how close to him you become and how open you are about expressing your views, you let your child have privacy at the same time that he can obtain a sense of belongingness. You let him feel free in his own home. You reduce to a minimum the conditions that so often lead a child living with only one parent to feel either depressed resignation or frenzied resentment over a lack of individuality and privacy.

All in all, though it is a most difficult task, your exercise of self-control, of intelligent interest in what is right and what is wrong, and of tolerance without self-prejudice lets you be creative and constructive in your life. Your reliance on these inner strengths lets you limit your problems of being a single woman and lets you forestall the development of problems in and with your child. In short, the same qualities that the following chapters call for from you, the same qualities that let you benefit from the self-analysis the following chapters guide you to engage in, are the very qualities that enhance your life with your child. In your efforts to understand and fulfill yourself so that you can accomplish best the task of being a single mother, each and every accomplishment produces a multitude of rewards.

# CHAPTER THREE

# Necessary Emotions

THE EASIEST way for you to begin analyzing your own feelings is to consider which emotions make up an ordinary, full, happy life. Once you know the feelings needed by all adults to feel happy and satisfied, you can compare your own state of mind to this model and determine how complete your emotional life is. This chapter provides a guide to you in making this comparison.

## *Positive Feelings*

The emotional satisfactions that make up an over-all feeling of well-being and contentment, happiness and joy, are needed by all adults, male or female, single or married. Without them human lives are incomplete and drab, if not downright miserable and painful. Though people differ as to how much desire for a particular feeling exists within them, a minimum amount of the following feelings are necessary for all adults. These feelings arise when basic, healthy psychological needs are being satisfied; so, by recognizing what you feel, you automatically learn how satisfied you are.

(To reduce the confusions that words for emotions often cause, consult the current Merriam-Webster dictionary; the terms

used for emotions in this book are all used in the sense of the
dictionary definitions.) When your emotions are positive, you
feel:

Loved and loving
Independent, with a sense of self-determination
Proud of your skills and accomplishments and of receiving
    concomitant prestige in the eyes of people you know
Self-controlled, with a sense of relaxed authority as you re-
    ceive respect for your status from others
Comfortable in a material and physical sense, and secure that
    your possessions and privacy are reasonably safe
Hopeful and optimistic about your plans for the future
Self-esteemed because you are living up to your own self-
    chosen ethical standards
Trusting and acceptant of others, with a sense of belonging
    to a compatible group
Spontaneous about living, with a cheerful sense of having
    chosen your major responsibilities

If you usually have most of these feelings, you usually feel
self-respect and love and respect for others.

## Negative Feelings

Safeguarding how accurate you can be in deciding that you
do or do not feel certain positive emotions is the fact that the
threat to some satisfaction or the absence of certain pleasures
automatically calls forth a whole group of other feelings, defensive or negative feelings. These are usually troublesome and
easily noticed by you. So check your first analysis of positive
emotions by reviewing the negative feelings that are related to
them. When your emotions are negative you feel:

Angry and hating
Incompetent and dependent upon others for help and mercy
    in not ridiculing you for needing their help
Afraid of losing control over yourself or over those people—

especially your child—who are properly subordinate to
you

Anxiously worried about your health and comfort and property

Guilty and ashamed of yourself for being less than you believe you ought to be and can be

Despondent, with a sense of futility

Estranged and misunderstood and lonely

Exhausted and hemmed in on all sides by the burden of your
life

Each of these negative feelings may be easily promoted in
even a mature, sensible woman if she lives alone. Many of them
are frequently felt by all single women, not just single mothers.

Sometimes, though, these negative feelings are not just a
natural result of the kind of life that a single woman leads; they
may be, instead, feelings she has even though her current life is
not directly promoting them. Or it may be just coincidental that
what is really happening to her is the sort of situation that
typically calls forth the emotional reaction she is feeling. And
it also may happen that she actually creates the conditions about
her to give herself an ostensible excuse for having her negative
feelings.

It is vital for you to determine which is your condition. You
can do something about altering your emotions if your situation
causes direct reactions; this is constructive, problem-solving action.

If, however, you have some personality characteristics resulting from past experiences that now make it very difficult
or perhaps impossible for you to react to even the best of circumstances without feeling underlying negative emotions, you
must make changes in *yourself* before you can expect to decrease
your discomfort by altering your external situation.

The next chapter provides illustrations of situations that ordinarily exist in the life of a single mother and usually make her
feel unhappy. Before you conclude that your primary problem
is circumstantial and easily changeable, or internal and less easily
remedied, compare your reality situation to the ones that ordinarily generate negative feelings.

# CHAPTER FOUR

# The Pressures You Face

ALTHOUGH MANY PRESSURES you face are faced in common with all single women, whether or not they have ever married, your particular circumstances are highly colored by your motherhood and by the reason for your being single. So, in analyzing your actual stresses and pressures, it is primarily necessary for you to reflect on the appropriate unique features typical of the lives of the various major kinds of single mothers, with special attention to yours.

Use this chapter as a starting point for your own thoughtful speculations about your life; use it as a *guide*, not as a pronouncement of pressures you absolutely must be reacting to. If you have been fortunate and have avoided some of these typical pressures, you need not do more than check your reactions against the ones described in Chapter Five. And even though your analysis reveals that you are operating with many of the typical pressures, remember that they can be withstood and reduced; as Chapter Five indicates, you need not merely suffer in reaction to them.

## Divorce and Separation

If you are divorced or separated, you belong to the largest group of single mothers with young children. Thus your life contains most of the pressures thought typical of the life of a single mother. Some of these pressures are intimately bound up in the reality that your child's father is still tied to him, financially or through visitation rights; Part Three of this book considers these special pressures. This section considers mainly the pressures you must face because you have divorced or agreed to a legal separation.

As you review these pressures, be sure you do not reflect toward yourself the attitude that is typical of the subtle form of scorn society often directs at a divorced or separated mother. This scorn is less extreme than that heaped on the mother who is known to have borne her child out of wedlock; and it is not the contempt that is often mixed with the pity shown to a deserted woman who has no knowledge of her husband's whereabouts; but it is still destructive, whether it is directed toward you by others or felt by you about yourself. In essence, this attitude is the unsympathetic retort, "Well, you're the one who let yourself get divorced, now put up with it."

The objective fact that you may have participated deliberately and actively in bringing about your single state cannot and ought not prevent you from realizing what your single state is like. Whatever pressures you face cannot be dismissed merely because you have helped to create them; your well-being cannot be increased just by efforts to be stoic as a kind of self-punishment for having made the mistakes you think you made. Remember that only by being dispassionate and self-forgiving in analyzing your emotional state can you achieve the desirable goal of increasing your comfort and contentment and of being able to rear your child healthily and well.

Marriage generally is a product of a many-faceted emotional and practical relationship shared by a man and woman who love each other. In the course of your former marriage, events led you to believe that marriage no longer afforded you the chance that being single might once again give you to avoid pain and gain pleasure. So a divorce was obtained.

But what effect do such events have on love? What happened to the love you felt toward your husband when you married him?

Typically, feelings of love and consideration are destroyed by the happenings that lead to a decision for divorce. The conflicts and dissatisfactions of the unhappy marriage arouse negative feelings that supplant or outweigh the positive feelings. You end up hating, not loving.

If the word "hate" is too strong for the emotions generated by the breaking of the moral, emotional, and practical contract of your marriage, your hostile feelings may be more exactly defined as contempt, disgust, annoyance, or irritation, sometimes screened behind feelings of boredom, pity, or indifference. But whatever they are, they are not so important in themselves as the reason they have come about. A major pressure affecting your life is your reaction to the fact that you can no longer love your former husband without ambiguity and ambivalence—if at all.

The reasoning that usually is given for the development of hatred within a marriage which has not worked out well often takes the form of: "After we were married, I found out that he was———(fill in the blank with the appropriate word: irresponsible, lazy, thoughtless, cruel, and so forth) and I got to hate him so much for that, that I couldn't put up with the marriage any longer."

But the bad quality named is seldom discovered only after the marriage. Most troublesome characteristics are fully recognized before the marriage but are discounted and viewed as negligible, either because they seem to be related only to the courtship, or because it seems so "obvious" that they will change quickly and easily in the warmth of marriage. Since you tolerated the behavior before marriage, the behavior itself cannot be of prime importance in the development of subsequent discord and hatred. If you truly disliked it, you would not have been attracted even at first to a man who exhibited the behavior you later selected as the source of your marital troubles. To take an extreme example, a woman who genuinely dislikes people who drink to excess does not continue to date a man who habitually drinks to excess. She dismisses such a man from her list of acquaintances long before there is opportunity to form a love relationship with him. Thus, the woman who marries a drinker with the hope that he will stop drinking for her sake is not really so disturbed by his drinking as she later insists. It also happens that a quality that is singled out as the reason for the development of hatred toward a husband is a quality that does not greatly trouble you in other relationships. Friends, relatives, co-workers—people with whom you spend many waking hours—may exhibit exactly the same characteristic and yet be tolerated and well regarded.

So it must be concluded that the personality quality as such is not the source of trouble. And, unless some very complicated assumptions are made about the quality of your love in the first place or your motives in marrying, the most obvious source for your hatred is that it is related to the love you originally felt. As you may recognize yourself, you would not have hated your former husband if you had not originally been in love with him.

In order to trace the basis of your hate, go back to the time when you were in love: you felt wonderful; you thought that being able to love someone was the greatest of good fortunes. And if, at the time, you were disconcerted by occasional facets of your loved one's personality or of your own, you just assumed that they were not powerful enough to withstand the force of the great love between you and your suitor.

In a sense, at the beginning you and the love you felt were indistinguishable. You felt good because you loved, and you believed your love to be all-powerful. So, of course, you, too, felt powerful. Such a sense of well-being and power, however, is usually short-lived, even when no severe marital conflicts ensue, because much of it is based on inner reactions that cannot continue once there is greater intimacy, knowledge, and contact.

This sense of power evaporates even more quickly when there are marital problems, for it runs hard up against the fact that people do not change fundamental attitudes or characteristics easily.

So, although originally you may have thought that your power of love could alter a troublesome characteristic, once you were married, you found instead that the characteristic did not change. You were faced with the evidence that your love is ineffectual, faced with the evidence that you could not get your husband to "love enough" to be willing to make changes in himself. You then needed to defend yourself against the awareness that neither you nor your love is all-powerful.

Usually the defense consists of counterattacking feelings, hostile feelings, directed toward the person who has defeated your love. In short, you develop hatred or other hostile feelings toward your husband because he has shown you that your love could not "conquer all."

You cannot automatically do away with your angry feelings just because you are no longer married. If they were directly related only to the way you were treated, they would disappear quickly once you freed yourself from the marriage. But connected as they are to your own feelings about yourself—for all people like to feel that they can succeed—they continue to bother you and cause you to react bitterly until you finally learn to forgive yourself for being weak and human.

Accompanying these frustrated and hostile feelings is a feeling of impotence and lack of control. Part of everybody's inner equipment is the capacity to imagine how things "ought to be." Translating these ideas and images into concrete reality usually involves persuading, coercing, or even forcing changes in things as they have been. You can probably recall many occasions when you attempted to preserve your marriage by trying to make things more closely approach your image of what they should have been. Yet your divorce is proof that you were unable to exert sufficient control. This, in addition to the proof that your love has been powerless to effect changes, can result in severe insecurity. The feeling of insecurity is further accentuated if your child possesses the behavior characteristics that were the focus of attention and efforts to make changes in your marriage.

In addition to these forces from the past, the objective pressures you face in the present accentuate the problem of maintaining control, as Chapter Three pointed out. If your material welfare depends upon your continued working outside of your home, or if your divorce settlement has stripped you drastically of material possessions, it is natural to devote a large portion of your energies to coping with problems of control and with anxieties about health, property, and security.

Like anyone, you feel most secure when you know how to deal with the situations that are most likely to occur, especially if you know you do not need to exert a great deal of self-control in order to handle them. But you face a life in which there are many situations that present new challenges to you, ones you cannot cope with by recourse to tried-and-true methods; and many of these situations require a great deal of self-control. For example, you face more direct invitations to take part in casual sexual adventures, yet you cannot defeat seduction by recourse to the same protections you could easily use as a never-married or securely-married woman. You cannot say, "I don't know what you mean," or, "I could never think of doing something like that to my husband." For you, as a divorced woman, there is only the simple situation of being propositioned by a person who knows you know what he means and who knows you cannot hide behind assumed loyalties to others. Often, apparently because you have a child, men assume you are more eager for sexual adventures than a divorced woman who is not a mother. And it is easy to believe these propositions are a result of some fault on your part, so that you feel additionally insecure, not sure of what you are doing wrong. The only successful stop comes from saying, "No," and meaning it; but this requires a great deal of self-control if you are not to show the anger, shock, or uncertainty that is more likely to excite than to inhibit advances. All in all, such stern tests leave you feeling insecure and worn-out.

Another set of factors causing negative feelings after divorce are the many examples of how dependent and unskilled you are.

Like every single mother, you are forced to be aware of the basic, unchangeable, and inescapable fact that you cannot be both parents to your child—you must admit to yourself that you need others to supply for your child actual examples of how men act and how they look on life.

In addition to this generalized pressure that increases your dependency, there are other areas of incompetence that may seem objectively trivial, but still cause considerable anguish. You may never have considered that sheer physical size and strength are skills until you discover that you are unable to perform some tasks without a great deal of effort and trouble. For example, carrying in the groceries, assembling toys, and playing rough games with your child are all activities that take strength most women lack; yet you must perform these tasks because your household requires it. The never-married woman and the once-married woman with no child, both, of course, still relatively weak women, do not need to cope with as many chores as a single mother.

Too, your special social position keeps you from asking and receiving help from the husbands of neighbors, for they often regard friendly help as an indication that they approve of divorce.

Even when you change your residence, so that your neighbors are strangers to your former marriage, help is difficult to obtain because, as Chapter Five indicates, you are regarded by married women as a peculiar threat to them; the wives strive to keep their husbands from helping and thereby making what may be regarded as chivalrous overtures.

The implication that friendly help from a single man signifies deeper and more involved emotional relations makes it awkward, too, to obtain help and counsel from male friends who are not married.

All in all, your life contains many minor pressures increasing your dependency, thus making it additionally likely that you may aggravate matters by overtaxing your strength in your efforts to decrease your dependency. Many times, the security and health of single persons are endangered by the immoderate activities that can easily be engaged in: eating a relatively poorer diet, paying less attention to aches and pains, and generally striving to avoid letting physical limits be recognized. Physicians recognize a direct connection between being single and being relatively less healthy physically. Because you have the additional responsibility of your child, you must be careful to let things go occasionally, to take it easy and be kind to your body, otherwise the pressure of ill health can further increase your insecurities and feeling of powerlessness.

As time goes by without any measurable and foreseeable relief of your loneliness and insecurity, it is easy for you to become subject to feelings of hopelessness. However despondent you may have been at the time of your divorce, there was probably a strong feeling within you of hope and eagerness to approach a life that would be relatively free of strife; you looked forward to a new life as a bigger and better person. And as your new life fails to keep the promise you sought in it, your feelings of futility increase.

The fact that you are not married is a most important subjective factor that also plays a part in making you feel futility. Like most women, you probably spent much of your youth looking forward to marriage, visualizing it as the embodiment of all fulfillment. With its breaking up, go many hopes and convictions about yourself and life.

Thus, both in your plans for yourself through marriage and in your plans for yourself through divorced, single life, you find planning almost pointless, for plans have been shown to miscarry.

Remarriage, of course, begins to loom larger and larger as the solution to the problem of futility. And as soon as this happens, as soon as remarriage becomes a goal in itself, it also becomes a pressure. It leads to an increase in every negative feeling described so far, for it keeps the present from having importance—only the future can be regarded as possessing possible positive values. Then, too, if instead of being divorced, you are legally separated, this possible solution, remarriage, is objectively recognized as un-attainable, though your thoughts may still stray to it.

The loneliness of your life needs special recognition; though rationality tells you that you cannot be lonely if you have your child as company, to the extent that you exert the self-control spoken of in the previous chapters, your child is unavailable to you as a true companion. So you can easily feel lonely.

Your loneliness is not just aloneness in a home lacking a hus-band with whom to eat and sleep and talk about your child or with whom to do any of the social and personal things that are part of marriage. Loneliness is also produced by the disruption of your relationships with most of the people who were your friends before the divorce.

Most of the social life of a married woman is in groups of other married couples—often associated through the mutual in-terests of the husbands—and divorce causes a loss of the common status and friendship with these married people and business associates, not necessarily out of hard feelings or scorn, but just because of concern about possible "scenes" should the divorced couple meet. In the social circles where the men and women group off, you constitute an intrusion. If you go to a party alone, you are slightly alienated from the group of women who are discussing, not just their jobs and children, but also their hus-bands and their property. You cannot talk freely about the dress you just bought—other women are too likely to react by com-menting enviously or contemptuously; yet neither can you freely complain about not buying a dress recently—other women are too likely to react with impatience. If you bring an escort to a grouped-off party, you lose him to the group of men discussing their affairs, find yourself still not quite a part of the group of women, and thereby fail to have either an enjoyable date or a good time at the party (although your competitive position as a female is better than if you had come alone). Only in social circles where the men and women do not form separate groups can you easily maintain sociable relations.

Loneliness is caused, too, by the disruption of friendships with unmarried people. A long-standing but casual friendship with a man is difficult to maintain once you are single, in part because you usually expect and hope for greater intensity and permanence, and in part because the man finds it difficult to disregard these wants and to dismiss the social implications of a continued friendship. And during the years between twenty and forty, ties between single women are highly competitive or masochistic, depending on whether the women concerned have maintained or given up their interests in marriage. Most women this age are married; their friendships typically focus on their children or their husbands. Close friendships between single women exist most easily before marriage, during adolescence, or in the later years of life when both women are elderly. So your friendships with other women, single or married, are likely to be highly tense and frustrating.

Adding to the sense of loneliness is the fact that your divorce probably broke up some of the older, childhood friendships you had sustained during your marriage. People tend to take sides, sometimes violently, about divorce. And however reasonable a woman you may be, you probably cherished the hope that all who knew you and your former husband fully understand how sorely tried you were, what a saint you were, and how pressured and forced you were to do the few wrong things you may have done during the marriage or while obtaining your divorce. Along with such a shameless hope goes the automatic expectation that all former friends will stay friends after the divorce. When this does not happen, when some people actually sympathize with your former husband, you naturally feel misunderstood, rejected, betrayed, and lonely.

If the friendships were just acquaintanceships based on your former husband's occupation, you can shrug off their loss more easily; but the objective fact remains that you are alone, even though you are able to defend yourself better against feeling betrayed by these losses.

Beyond the self-condemnation that may or may not be based on what really went wrong, there are other factors that pressure you to feel self-blame. One of these is related to the fact that marriage fulfills many different ideals about the self. These fulfillments cease, of course, at least in part, when the marriage ceases. Thereafter, it becomes necessary either to alter the ideals or else to find other proof that these ideals are being realized. The part of the self that insists on what a person ought to be is not a part easily satisfied with past proof of having once been attractive or having once been loved. So, until you muster new and current proof that you are what your conscience and ideals dictate you ought to be, you are prey to punishing feelings of futility and unworthiness—and you readily tend to blame yourself.

However high the divorce statistics may be or become, our culture still holds that marriage is good and divorce is less good. Because you have grown up in our culture and believe in its standards, yet have betrayed the standards, you feel bad about yourself. Apprehension that you may hurt your child by depriving him of his father serves to increase these bad feelings, even though you may know, sensibly and reasonably, that such feelings are not fully warranted.

These subjective elements combine with the depression caused by loneliness and insecurity; and together they augment the tendency to berate the self for not being sufficiently worthwhile to have avoided all such pains.

They also pressure you almost to welcome, as punishment, the actual discomforts and other miseries of being divorced. Thus you are made additionally vulnerable to all the forces that make you feel pinned down and acutely limited: the social limitations, added responsibilities, and decreased resources. Instead of impatiently resisting these pressures, you tend to tolerate them and thereby make them more effective in causing you trouble.

Your responsibility and sensitivity also make life more difficult than it need be. In the same way that heightened sensitivity increases your perception of the nuances and hidden facets of life, yet also makes your awareness greater of its crassness and monotony, so, too, a heightened sense of responsibility can extend joy in parenthood, but also heighten your realization of the limitations set upon your life by your situation as a parent.

One of the crucial limitations is connected with the possibility of remarriage. Able to surmount the day-to-day difficulties you face, you may yet still feel immobilized because you are by no means sure that you can marry again. The statistics are on your side, but these only show that most women who divorce eventually remarry. The statistics do not reveal anything at all about how good the second marriages are or how children may be regarded by second husbands.

Wanting to be the "most" you can be, thinking of how marriage helps stretch a personality to its fullest, you may earnestly hope you haven't lost all chance of this. But you can recognize that you now have more discrimination; having truly profited from past experience, you now have a fuller idea of what you need in a husband, marriage, and family life. So, as you contemplate remarriage, it is easy to doubt that it is possible to meet the man you know you need and have that man be willing to chance the hazards of raising a child not his.

After all, parenthood is a way of self-perpetuation, of continuing a person's flesh and blood into the future; and the child of a divorce is still the embodiment of this kind of self-perpetuation for two people—not just for his mother. The man who would step into the role of father to a child not his, a child who may still have many emotional and real ties to his actual father, is a man who must forfeit some of this primitive self-perpetuation in exchange for something more abstract. He must give up other things, too, like the right to start out fresh, creating his own wife from an otherwise untried woman and making a mother of her, as he develops a new role for himself while forming his own family.

As you contemplate the essential contradictions between what marriage means for the mature man and what must be involved in the reality of marrying you and living with your child, you may easily conclude that remarriage is difficult or unlikely, especially when you add the factor of your greater selectivity. Even though you know perfectly well that you compare equally with other women who have not yet married or who have no children, you may not be able to overcome the tendency toward feeling immobilized and limited.

Remarriage, though helpful, is not the most reliable avenue for escape from the predicament of lacking opportunity for self-enhancement. But the other main channel, gainful employment on a job, is also greatly affected by the reality of your being a mother. Career commitments are necessarily less complete for you or any mother than for a woman without children; any job you take must be a job that can withstand occasional interruptions when your child needs your presence at home, else you will forfeit some of the most meaningful aspects of your role as a mother. And as a single mother, you face additional pressures that cause still other difficulties, compared to those of the married mother: You cannot be so discriminating about taking a job, for example, because you need your salary immediately just to make ends meet. You cannot afford to accept low starting wages for a position with a good future. Flexible hours often cannot be offered by you, because the nursery school closes or your sitter needs to leave at a specified time. You cannot easily secure new training or further training, because you have neither the free time nor the relative economic independence.

Even compared to other single mothers, you still face more pressures. The attitude of people toward a widow's going to work is different, for example, than the attitude you customarily face. The working widow is granted a tolerance that is not shown to you for occasional absences and lapses because people take the attitude noted at the beginning of this chapter: they regard you as a person who has made a bed she must now lie upon. The widow receives, "Poor thing, it must be tough to lose her husband and have to support a ten-year-old kid alone." You are met with, "If she can't handle the job, I don't see why she doesn't stay home and live off her alimony, and stop taking a job away from other people who could manage it." The objective reality that most widowed mothers receive funds from personal or public sources that are roughly equivalent to the alimony and child-support funds paid to divorced mothers by former husbands is to no avail. The prejudice remains, and you must work within it.

In almost every area of your life, you face conflict-laden conditions. Unless you recognize and admit your unique pressures, you cannot take constructive action to reduce them; you must instead suffer inordinately from feelings of being constricted and hurt.

## *Widowhood*

Widowed women actually head the largest number of fatherless households in this country; but, since their children are not mainly in the younger age groups, fewer widows than divorced women face the problems of being single mothers of growing children.

If you are a widow whose married life was good, you carry within yourself many fine memories that are of great help in your task of fulfilling your own life and of rearing your child.

But if your marriage was marked by increasingly frequent discord and strife, and if only the accident of death kept you from joining the group of divorced women and separated women, then your problems are complicated mixtures of the situations previously described for the divorced mother and those that follow in this section.

You, yourself, know the true circumstances of your own past married life; be careful to seek for suggestions from the appropriate section.

All the elements contributing to the divorced mother's feelings of dependency are also present for you. Perhaps these feelings are even slightly more intense, because you can say to yourself, rightfully, that you never "asked" to be alone. In addition, the real problems involved in settling an estate may very well tax to the utmost your limited understanding of your husband's affairs and of the legalities involved in such matters.

In no way is the folly of human endeavor brought so sharply into focus as by the death of a person who is intimate and dear. Every factor that contributes to the sense of futility in the divorced mother is further accentuated for you as a widow.

Bewilderment about the meaning of life is sharply increased; you feel more intensely the pointlessness of planning. Your love and desire for your husband are not counteracted by feelings of hostility directed toward him for deliberate pain. Without these feelings that are typical of the divorced mother, you are left emotionally much married to your former marriage partner. By yourself, you must withdraw the emotional investment you have made; and as you do this, you suffer a period of loss and emptiness.

Dependency is increased as the result of the role you are expected to play. Society, particularly in a small town or closely-knit community, practically dictates that a widow with small children not show great eagerness to fend for herself. This notion that a widow's life is seemly only if she spends a suitable time in regrets and immobility makes it difficult for you to behave like an independent woman, bring your grief under control, and get down to the business of creating a life for yourself and your child. If you do not demonstrate suitable dependence, you risk creating the impression that you really may not have cared much for your husband.

Even after the acceptable period of mourning is over, the different status of the widow constitutes a problem, for you are almost forced to accept special favors and thus become additionally dependent. In contrast to the associates typical of the divorced mother, your friends are eager to go out of their way in order to help you out; and it is difficult to reject friendly offers of help just in order to assert independence.

Anger may seem like a strange and unexpected reaction to the loss of a husband and father, but deep and intense anger is often a problem if widowhood is faced suddenly. The pressure that brings it about is not the kind of transformation of love that is characteristic of the divorced woman; nor does it seem to be caused by outrage against the husband who so cruelly and thoughtlessly left you alone and exposed. Instead, it is a transitory reaction to the proof that you are weak and human, unable to control what happens to you. Once you have had a chance to tell your bitter thoughts and cry out against your fate, reason and common sense come to your aid, and you cease to feel singled out for special misfortune.

To the extent that this feeling has been buried and repudiated, however, it continues to exert a hidden force upon your life, making you more easily exasperated with imperfection, making you more insistent on attaining other ideals. It may even lead to extravagant mourning and long-lasting depression. In either case, it increases the likelihood that you will face other frustrations in your life; and so, ultimately, it tends to increase your over-all load of anger.

The actual circumstances of death often superimpose another source of anger. When a person has paid for his mistakes by the loss of his life, it becomes impossible and meaningless to condemn him for having made his mistakes—yet the reactive anger is still aroused. For example, terrible conflict at the time of her loss is easily felt by a woman who is confident her husband might have been alive had he heeded the advice of his physician, or by the woman who tried, but failed, to get her husband to live more safely before death resulted from carelessness. This kind of anger, being more objective in nature, is more easily understood—but still not any more easily discharged and reduced.

Though many external factors eliciting insecurities are the same for you as for the divorced mother, many subjective or semi-objective factors are not present. You do not, for example, need to feel afraid of losing control of yourself, for your marriage didn't stop because you were impulsive or otherwise lacking in self-control. And typically men are more hesitant about making illicit propositions to you than to a divorced woman who does not have, in a sense, a man watching over her.

But though these demands upon your self-control are reduced, you can easily feel insecure because you have faced the ultimate proof of your impotence: you have met death and learned how powerless you are in the face of its coming.

Although social and community life provide more comfort for you than for the divorced mother, you cannot avoid feeling terribly alone, of course. Social expectations constitute pressures that can force you into additional loneliness in much the same way that they make it difficult for you to be independent. After the initial mourning period with its rush of condolence visits, you are expected to avoid company, so that you may be alone with your memories. The major avenue for social stimulation available for the divorced mother—meeting men and accepting invitations for dates with them—is thereby closed to you for a considerable time; friends hesitate to introduce men to you for fear of being considered tactless, impolite, or cruel; you may even be considered improper for wanting to go out. Until you do, until you demonstrate to the social group of married people who are your closest friends that you are seeking social stimulation, your loneliness is intense. When you do get back into circulation with your friends, fortunately, you are less estranged, compared to the divorced mother, and more unbegrudging efforts are made by your friends to provide suitable partners to you.

Since pity and concern, not scorn, are shown to you, you are generally able to feel hopeful about your own personal future; and so you can feel less frenzy about your immediate unhappiness. A job, as mentioned before, is more easily an avenue for self-fulfillment for you. And in the second major area of life, marriage, you also face fewer conflicting pressures. You can more confidently imagine being able to marry again. A possible new husband does not need to cope with the problem of sharing with another man, even if only during brief visits and vacations, the role and title of father. Unlike the divorced mother, you are free to dream of meeting a man who will want to cherish and protect your fatherless child—not only if the man lacks sufficient energy and will create his own family, not only if the man guiltily sacrifices a portion of his manhood and birthright, but simply if he's big enough to love two people, you and your child.

The entire meaning of remarriage is thus greatly different; when a widow remarries, the man is viewed by many people as a new father; when a divorced mother remarries, the man is more typically viewed as her new husband. (More widowed mothers than divorced mothers do marry again, perhaps due to these differences in attitudes.) Aware that most widows remarry even while their children are very young, you can believe in your future more confidently and so feel less immobilized. However tied down you may be in your present state, you need not suffer the same feeling of being doomed to loneliness that often haunts the divorced mother.

The major subjective pressure causing negative feelings within you is your own internalized sense of guilt that both springs from and causes a host of emotional discomforts. Unlike the divorced woman, you cannot easily assuage bad feelings about arguments and difficulties that existed in your marriage by recalling to yourself the harsh words and mistakes of your husband. You find it hard to forgive yourself for having made his life with you anything less than perfect, or you condemn yourself for being so unforgiving and relentless as to recall these past troubles, for, in a sense, your husband's death more than punished him for any of his failures.

Added to this pressure is the complicated self-condemnation that arises from your inner urges to cease mourning and take up the threads of life creatively again: wanting to date and to remarry, feeling sexually attracted to living men, or otherwise wanting to live though your husband is dead.

Another problem, so seldom discussed that you may have had little opportunity to learn how common it is, is the upsurge of love and excitement your memories may provoke.

Most women re-sense desire and happiness when they recall some past event that was especially thrilling. Such associations constitute an important source of happiness to a woman and tide her over temporary depressions when life is unrewarding. Usually, because a woman continues to love only a man who is with her, but has ceased to love a man with whom she has had the typical bitter experiences that lead to divorce, desertion, or separation, the only man a single woman *thinks* romantically about is the man who is with her, with whom she is in love.

But as a widow, you are in the peculiar position of still loving a person for whom you have what constitutes a positive balance of emotion—there isn't the intervention of strong negative feelings to counterbalance and wipe out this deposit of love. Only time erases it. And so it is likely that thoughts of your husband evoke a flood of inner warmth. This natural self-arousal easily causes tension and shame, because it is difficult to learn that it is not strangely different from the experience of other women. You may find yourself feeling more guilty, more disturbed, by manifestations of sexuality connected with your lost husband than by such feelings connected with a man still alive. Surrounded by the silence that prevails about the continued existence of sexual desire in women not immediately being aroused by a man, you cannot easily relieve your anxieties by turning to other women to question them about their reactions. You instead may easily develop so much guilt that your feelings of depression may increase in the unconscious thought that this pain, real enough, will make up for some of your faults.

In short, of the pressures you face, your own unrealistic conscience may well be the greatest.

## *Illegitimate Mothers*

Probably only a few of you women reading this book are illegitimate mothers. Because it is unlikely that you have flaunted your past in the face of your immediate circle of friends and acquaintances, your *objective* circumstances are likely to be ones resembling those of the divorced or the widowed mother. People regard you in either of these two roles, so, despite the unrevealed fact that you have never married, the preceding discussions apply in part to you.

About the only objective circumstance that may be quite different for you is one related to your having moved from your former home. But living in a location where your past doesn't play an important role in your daily life with other people, comparative strangers, is not wholly a relief or a burden. You do not face such pressures as conflicts in loyalties of friends, warmhearted but confining sympathy, or loss of status and prestige; but you do face the burden of starting your life anew.

And a major item in this burden is connected with the constant effort you must put into maintaining the story you tell about yourself. After you have moved to a new city, taken a new job, or cut off all friendships with people from your past, you need to present to new people a story about yourself that satisfies their curiosity—lest by creating an air of mystery, you provoke speculation that you are not the widow or divorced mother you present yourself to be. And you also must withstand fear and insecurity about the possibility that some unlucky happening may disclose your real past.

These pressures all result from your need to function in a society that does not look with kindness upon the illegitimate mother. You face *internal* pressures, therefore, because you seek to avoid the worse pressures involved in being known as an "unwed" mother.

Several additional sources of internal pressure arise because of social circumstances—not ones directed at you, personally, or even having to do with your state as an illegitimate mother. Rather, these are the changed societal attitudes regarding the sexual behavior of American women. Despite the changes that seem to indicate a more tolerant attitude toward extramarital sexual activity—an acceptance of the fact that a majority of women are not virgins when they marry—your pressures are not reduced, but are instead increased.

The two striking changes in societal attitudes are, first, an altered attitude toward the "double standard," and second, a radically changed attitude toward reporting the findings of studies of human sexual behavior.

When the double standard was the accepted thing, men and women were expected to keep their own secrets. A man did not tell his prospective wife about his past indiscretions; and, if a woman had some skeletons in her closet, she firmly shut the door against them and bore her burdensome memories alone.

But with the acceptance of the reality that most women have had some sexual experience prior to marriage, the double standard has disappeared; a woman no longer is expected to have to try to lie about her past experience to her proposed husband. While it still remains foolish and needless to provide extensive details about her past to her husband, she is expected to trust his love for her and his sense of realism enough so that she can marry him without resorting to outright lies about her life before her marriage. Marriage has taken on new qualities of equality and sexual frankness and honesty, however unchanged other characteristics of an ideal marriage, like sexual continence and sexual loyalty, may remain.

When you contemplate marrying a man you have met in your new setting, you must decide what to do about divulging the truth of your past. If you attempt to meet and fulfill the current concept of what ideal marriage ought to involve, you put yourself in the position of admitting, not only the fact of your child's parentage, but also the fact that most of the façade you have presented to your intended husband is a fiction built by consistent distortion of facts.

Your past cannot be changed by sharing the truth about it with your prospective husband; and telling him your true story may be the equivalent of handing him a weapon to be used cruelly in arguments arising in the future course of the marriage. Yet the alternative is to go against all belief and conviction within you that a good marriage must not and cannot be based on massive dishonesty or withholding of the truth. If you keep your secret, your feelings of guilt can seriously interfere with the spontaneity and freedom that are now considered essential to a good marriage.

Whatever decision you make about sharing your past with your husband is one that requires a great deal of strength and courage; you must work very hard and withstand many pressures.

This first alteration in attitudes about sexuality—the altered attitude toward the double standard—is related to the second change in the current attitude toward learning and widespread reporting of the factual truth about human sexual behavior. Both changes impose additional pressures on you, the "unwed" mother.

In the past ten years, many well-conducted studies about sexual behavior have been reported. Most of these studies report that there is a wide disparity between the conventions our society is supposed to be pledged to uphold and the actual sexual behavior of most of the persons within our society. These reports have appeared, not just in relatively obscure professional journals, but even in daily newspapers or magazine reports on what sociological experts have learned when they have studied human sexual behavior. So this information is generally well known.

Before this publication of information about sexaul behavior, the illegitimate mother could find a peculiar kind of comfort by comparing herself to what she believed other women were like. She could think—and evidence did not contradict or challenge her conclusions—that there was just something "wrong" with her, and she was different from the women she saw enjoying motherhood in marriage. She could believe that she lacked certain self-control, she was by nature or fate different. Whatever was the difference, she more than made up for her original sin by suffering as she did in her unwed motherhood, so she did not have to do further penance by feeling guilty.

Today, of course, you can hardly avoid learning that most women have had sexual adventures before their marriages. You are forced to recognize that the major difference between you and other women—women who also had premarital sexual adventures but did not become pregnant, women who became pregnant but did not have the child, or women who had the child but became married—is a difference connected to extrapersonal factors, usually. Differences cannot be said to consist of differences in capacity for withstanding sexual temptation, for few women seemed possessed of this capacity. You can only attribute your state to lack of know-how, to failure to practice contraception or commit abortion, or to some other aspect having to do with the extent to which you could control the external situation. All such conclusions are harder to take than the conclusions of a mother a generation ago.

In contrast to other women who did not become unwed mothers and who, therefore, could easily dismiss from their minds the memories of past indiscretions, your child, the living proof of your past, chronically reminds you. Only by constant exercise of strength and honesty with yourself can you combat the loss of hope and sense of freedom that tend to accompany your difficult life.

To the extent that you can avoid remembering past events, you can keep them from provoking negative feelings; but to the extent that you bury rather than accept, evaluate, and then put away thoughts of your past, you promote underlying tensions. It becomes additionally necessary for you to take an honest and whole look at your past.

You must be especially careful to investigate your current feelings about your past experience. Whatever the reasons or circumstances, the reality is that you were deserted; you did not agree to and permit the departure of your child's father—as do most divorced mothers—and you did not face the uncontrollable fact of death—as does the widow. (Deeper motives that may have been operating are not being considered. Although it is possible that every deserted mother unconsciously has sought desertion, the ostensible fact is that most "unwed" mothers have not openly

declared that they sought this state.) Left in an unpleasant position, left there by a person toward whom you felt positive emotions, you must have begun to question whether it was passion or
love that was felt. You need to explain to yourself why the pre-
sumed love did not lead to your being claimed and acknowledged
in marriage so that the product of the love, your child, could receive his father's protection and affiliation. Even if there were
mitigating circumstances like being below the legal age for
marriage or prior marriage, you must still reconcile these with
your desire to believe that genuine love was shared and exchanged.

Because it is often impossible to reconcile the two, many mature women grant that love either never existed or was very short-
lived. So, reveries about the past tend to increase feelings of anger
and frustration. It is difficult to avoid agreeing that it was fool-
hardy to trust; the actual circumstances of having your child out
of wedlock challenge such faith. Self-esteem and pride are lost in
front of the manifest desertion; and self-determination and self-
control can be retained only by trying to pretend that the unen-
viable and inglorious situation of illegitimacy was deliberately
sought out—an argument that falls flat.

## Deserted Mothers

Many of the pressures that exist for the illegitimate mother are
also important to a deserted mother, a woman whose husband
leaves either to turn up periodically for short visits and then
leave again or else to vanish without trace or return.

If you are a deserted mother, you do not face the moral difficulties that beset the illegitimate mother; but you are precluded
from being able to plan and control many facets of your life.
Thus, your feelings of being immobilized are probably the greatest of all single mothers'. Until you become willing and able to
take advantage of the legal rules covering your status, you are
subject to most of the pressures previously described for other
single mothers, though you are kept from the few benefits they
may enjoy. You also face special pressures like problems about life

insurance payments, social security benefits, pension fund payments, and property ownership. You cannot escape the reactions of friends and neighbors by moving, for you are naturally hesitant to leave the surroundings your husband might return to. Hence, your feelings of dependency lead to intense anger, frequently.

Even this anger, though, is subject to complications, because you cannot be certain you are not a widow; this uncertainty makes it difficult to keep from vacillating between mourning and rage over having been deserted and also leads to troubles in helping your child reach conclusions about his feelings toward his father.

Because the pressures are so many, yet so undefined, you must live a blend, a multitude of lives, in part similar to all other single mothers. Be sure, therefore, to exercise great caution in making decisions about the causes of your negative feelings; be careful to investigate thoroughly the guides offered in this chapter, so you may gain maximum help.

## Other "Single" Mothers

Objectively, the term "single" doesn't apply to you married mothers who know where your husbands are when they periodically or temporarily live away from home. But you share many pressures in common with other single mothers. In many respects you are like the widow and have high social status if your husband is a serviceman, a man who works for a company in a foreign country, a man hospitalized for a chronic medical, non-infectious disease, or a man whose occupation takes him away from home for more than just the working days of each week. In many respects you are like the divorced or deserted woman and have low social status if the reason for your husband's extended absence is imprisonment for criminal activity or hospitalization for mental disease or an infectious disease.

You may easily obtain many positive gratifications like the feeling of being loved and trusted to be responsible and independent, the good accord of neighbors and friends, the prospect of the future when the family will be together again, the moral protection and financial support your husband provides—if you are a high status wife. But you must still feel lonely, for you are alone. You must feel that your load is greater than that of many other women, for you have no husband helping you. Your feelings of being happy about independence are complicated by guilt and shame aroused by anger and loneliness. Often, you exhaust yourself by efforts to sustain the kind of homelife that will not make your husband feel like an intruder on his infrequent stays at home. So your positive gratifications tend to become less significant, while the reality of daily life promotes negative feelings. Thus, despite the official existence of your marriage and your husband, you must learn that the day-by-day life that is meaningful to you is a life containing the pressures other single mothers face.

If you have low social status, many of the positive gratifications disappear as the pressures leading to negative feelings become accentuated. Shame and guilt, especially, become great, even though you may have had no control or responsibility in determining your husband's state. Many times you suffer from deliberate social castigation and scorn, and suffer additionally as you see your child being reacted to unfairly because of his father's difficulties. You face unique internal problems of conflicting loyalties between respect for the law and affection for your husband, if he is imprisoned; or conflicts between your anxious fear of sickness, insanity, and strangeness and your affection for your husband, if he is hospitalized.

Whatever the objective cause of the separation may be, if you are one of the single mothers who are "married-yet-single," you have more in common with single mothers than with women who share life daily with their husbands.

## Maintaining Emotional Stability

It is obvious that any single mother has a hard job maintaining her emotional equilibrium. Your pressures are great, and you are forced to react to many of them with more negative feelings than can comfortably be borne. It is vital that you decide on how much of your emotional discomfort is the product of circumstances that are ordinary in the life of a single mother. If you decide your tensions rest on deeper, personal, and internal conflicts, you may still obtain some measure of help from taking constructive action to change your daily life. But to the extent that your feelings depend on past experiences that are not represented in the things really happening to you now, such changes cannot serve you so successfully as changes made in your basic personality structure.

And even if your reactions are quite in keeping with the actual pressures you face, you must learn how to express your negative feelings in a constructive way, so you can promote your own sense of well-being and keep yourself doing a good job in taking care of your child. The next chapter provides guides to constructive ways of expressing negative feelings and signposts to unproductive ways that lead to further complications and bad feelings.

# CHAPTER FIVE

# Feelings and Behavior

As YOU REFLECT upon the actual circumstances of your daily life and compare them to the ones described in Chapter Four, you can determine how likely it is that circumstances evoke the negative emotions you recognize as yours on the list provided in Chapter Three. If you decide that it is likely your reality situation is causing you troubles, the following sections of this chapter can provide a guide to you in the corrective measures you can take, ones either geared to alter your situation so that it becomes less pressuring or else geared to alter your behavior so that it becomes genuinely expressive of your negative feelings. Eliminated or expressed, your negative feelings cannot create further problems like the ones connected with acting out. So that you may clearly distinguish between expressive and acting-out behavior, descriptions of typical acting-out behavior are provided in the following sections, too.

Because acting-out behavior is usually connected with emotional conflicts, you can further check on your emotions by interpreting your behavior. Regarding yourself as if you were another person that you are judging only by the way she acts, not by the way she tells you she feels inside, you gain vital information about your own deeper, usually troublesome, emotions. You avoid some of the inaccuracies that can arise when you merely regard your emotions introspectively, looking for them as if they were real and tangible things. Reasonably certain about what you feel, you can take steps to search more deeply into the sources of your emotional conflicts. Examples of some common sources are provided along with the examples of nonexpressive, acting-out behavior so that you can more easily use this chapter as a guide to further self-knowledge.

From your own experience with others, you have learned to connect certain kinds of behavior with certain underlying kinds of emotions. To do this, you start with a stereotype of how people behave when they feel certain emotions; and when you notice a person behaving according to your stereotype, you assume that the appropriate emotions are being felt.

For example, when you observe someone turn red in the face, clench his fists, and swear, you generally do not hesitate to conclude that he must be angry, even though he has not said so exactly. And you are usually correct in making this assumption.

Sometimes, though, the connections are not so clear and straightforward. The person described above may be only embarrassed and angry at himself for blushing. Or he may deny that he is angry, and he may genuinely not be aware of it within himself.

Of course, most of the time, you need not bother to get exceedingly involved in figuring out exactly what is being conveyed by another person's behavior; in fact, if you were to start to guess about inner strong emotions in others, if you were to begin practicing curbstone psychoanalysis, you would probably upset yourself and them or waste your time and effort. Most of the time, you have reasonably long-standing and ordinary contacts with the people for whom you care enough to wonder about, and you can wait and see how they act over a long period of time; when you need to figure out how a given person is likely to act about a current situation, you can count on what you remember about past interactions. Even with a casual acquaintance or with a person you are meeting in a certain capacity, like a guest at a party or a potential employer, you can depend upon ordinary, commonsense courtesy in behavior, and you can assume there are typical, obvious feelings behind the behavior. Unlike the psychologist, you are seldom thrown into intimate contact with a person for limited periods of time under highly artificial or unusual circumstances (by all means, "psychologize" rapidly if you are stuck in an elevator with a stranger or if you are called upon to help out in some emergency).

In short, do not use the following guides to help your understanding of other people, because psychologizing is unnecessary most of the time and it can often be misleading or disturbing.

This precaution, however, is not necessary in regard to your analysis of yourself. Clearly, you must know as much about yourself as you can, and you also must be sure that your behavior directly demonstrates what you are feeling. So, it is necessary for you to resort to the methods developed by psychologists for interpreting what a person feels from how the person acts. It is especially useful for you to use these methods to discover negative emotions revealed and represented by behavior that is more acceptable and less threatening than behavior that exposes basic feelings, but not completely expressive. You can do this ing than behavior that exposes basic feelings. You can do this safely with yourself, because you have a built-in regulator that keeps you from discovering more than you can handle adequately. You can avoid the slight possibility of misleading yourself, jumping to an unwarranted conclusion, by thoughtfully substantiating a new hunch with the evidence you already have about yourself. Remember that you have an inner knowledge about yourself that is greater than you will ever obtain about anyone else, a knowledge that you can rely upon to tell you whether an idea is helpful or not.

Getting next to yourself, discovering how you are behaving in ways that are not appropriate to the ways you actually feel, and discovering your deeper emotions by interpreting your behavior are integral parts of being and becoming a fully self-confident, mature person.

There is not always an exact correspondence between behavior and emotions, of course, so the following descriptions are useful only as *guides* to the connections commonly demonstrated. While using them, keep in mind that the final proof that you have reached absolutely reliable and valid conclusions comes from your success in changing your behavior. If you are expressing your inner emotions relatively directly, you can alter your circumstances and thereby change the way you feel. But deep emotional conflicts are not easily changed and removed; they are generally associated with suffering that continues even when circumstances or behavior change. Aim not just to suffer or to translate suffering into acting out; aim to make your life satisfying and rewarding, to create the situations that permit healthy emotional expression.

## Freedom and Responsibility

You are most happy and satisfied about freedom and responsibilities—both necessary features of a healthy emotional life—when you are able to do well all that you want to do, and when you want to do all that you have a legitimate necessity to do. In this happy circumstance, your activities are expressive, problem-solving, and satisfaction-gaining.

When, instead, you cannot do most of what you want to do, you suffer secondary feelings of being immobilized; and these feelings can only be relieved by problem-solving, expressive ways of behaving, so that the immobilizing situation can be eradicated, the negative feelings can be expressed, and you can get back to gaining satisfactions.

If, though, you want mainly to be irresponsible, you behave in ways that demonstrate your impatience with the restrictions of reality. These acting-out ways seldom are effective ways of relieving your invalid feeling of immobilization; usually, they create further problems. The only way this kind of complicating situation can be relieved is to alter your original goals. Until your wants are realistic, you cannot satisfy them. Until your feelings of immobilization are warranted by the realistic facts, you cannot correct reality and relieve your burdens. So expression often hinges on the elimination of unnecessary duties or restrictions, while acting out usually involves rejection of a legitimate duty.

Thus, a crucial question arises: How can legitimate duties be differentiated from unnecessary ones?

In general terms, genuine and legitimate and necessary responsibilities are ones that cannot easily be taken over by automatic or mechanical or impersonal means, though most unnecessary duties can be satisfactorily substituted for or replaced by mass-produced or purchased helps.

The mothering woman shows her interest in what something means to her child by responding sympathetically and with interest to the disjointed "talky-talk" of her child when he reports on the things he has been doing and wondering about. As she does this, her child is made to feel loved, noticed, and appreciated. No machine currently available can replace her spoken reflections or her changed facial and body expressions. Only another interested, mothering person can replace this aspect of mother's role.

In contrast, thoughtless comments like perfunctory *Oh*'s and *Really*'s and *My*'s could well be put on tape or on a record—a child listening to such noises from a recording machine would probably feel no more human warmth than he does when the same remarks are voiced by a preoccupied mother or babysitter.

So, for a short rule to tell you as a responsible parent who loves her child the difference between what you ought to do and what you need not do, just keep in mind that genuine parenthood is not a series of mechanical tasks involving the physical care of a child.

You cannot substitute a handsmocked dress for openly-shown, loving attention to your daughter as she prattles on about getting her first stamped and mailed "real" invitation to a birthday party. Nor can getting the doctor immediately when your son develops a sore throat make up for dealing perfunctorily with him after the doctor has given him his medicine and left. Home-baked pies are fine, but not if the baking claims your attention so completely that you give no time to listening and reacting to your child.

True parental responsibilities involve emotions, intangibles; these are expressed through action, of course, but not through actions that are mechanical and empty. Sometimes you can let your child know you love him by baking a cherry pie or by buying him a cherry pie—but only if you manage to let him know that the pie stands for what you feel for him. All the pies in the world will not make him feel loved if you give them to him as a substitute for loving attention.

To learn whether the way you are living is the way to promote optimal feelings in you of freedom and responsibility, start by comparing what you must do with what you want to do.

Make a list of all the detailed activities that make up your usual day from waking until bedtime. Note down, next to each item, how successfully you believe these activities meet the responsibilities you feel are rightfully yours, note down how free and satisfied you feel about assuming or discharging these obligations, and also note down, as a kind of P.S., the activities that you are certain you ought to be engaged in but don't want to. Call this your "reality list."

Then make another list, an "ideal list," of the activities with which you would like to fill your day. Make room for notes about items on your reality list that either are not accomplished or that you wish you did not have to do. For example, if in your real life you must carry out the garbage, but you do not like to, be sure to put down on your ideal list the item, "Seven o'clock, do not need to empty garbage." Or, if in reality you know you should read to your child, but you do not, put down on your ideal list an item such as, "Eight o'clock, enjoy reading with my child."

Sit back and compare your two lists. The more closely they resemble each other, the more your ways of acting are likely to be ways by which you achieve a sense of freedom as you discharge your day-to-day responsibilities. The further apart the two are, the more likely it is that you suffer from feelings of being pressured, burdened, and unfulfilled.

To feel happy, free, and responsible, therefore, you must be able to claim that your ideal list and your reality list are identical, and that each contains all the activities appropriate to your legitimate tasks as a grown woman and as a single mother.

Your comparison shows you where to get started making constructive alterations in your behavior so you can accomplish those parts of your ideal that are realistically possible. It also makes it easier for you to see clearly where your expectations are quite out of line and unrealistic, because no feasible changes in the way you act can lead to fulfilling these unrealistic expectations.

By far the easiest point at which to start is to eliminate the tasks you neither like to do nor need to do. You are not subject to any guilts or other problems as you drop these activities; you can just feel free and on your way toward making a better life for yourself and your child. Drop them right now.

Next, about all the tasks you still have on your reality list aside from those clearly necessary and legitimate parts of parenthood, ask yourself a few questions: To what ends are such actions directed? Who or what demands that these actions be carried out in the particular way they have been?

Several activities you have been taking responsibility for are likely to be no longer particularly enjoyable, and they may actually take your efforts away from more rewarding ones. Since you face so much extra demand on your energy just by virtue of being a single mother, you must be careful to eliminate those unnecessary tasks that end up being over-all burdens.

To change your behavior in order to eliminate these activities, act like a psychologist. Assume that connected with the unnecessary act is something you feel guilty about, else you would not have continued to punish yourself by burdening yourself. No one does anything unless it either satisfies him or relieves some internal pressures from negative feelings like guilt or shame.

Look for your guilt; follow up on the ideas that come to your mind till you discover something that you feel guilty about. You know the heavy feeling that guilt consists of, so you can recognize when your ideas—however far off the track they may seem —make you re-sense the burdensome feeling of guilt.

Often your guilt lies in something outdated, an activity that can only be dignified by the term "traditional." Usually, you can recognize both how unnecessary it is to continue to feel guilty and how pointless it is to continue activities that actually do not get rid of the guilt, but only succeed in wasting your time and effort.

For example, a mother may have assumed many responsibilities simply because she wanted to please her husband who liked what she accomplished by her efforts. She may have made sure to arrange her schedule so that her children bathed while she prepared supper, and then so they dressed while she set the table— all this because she wanted to present an attractive picture of clean youngsters, warm food, and a well-set table to her husband.

After she is widowed, she may continue this tradition even though she receives no husband's praise to make up for her added tensions as she juggles supervising the children and doing the cooking, and as she strives to conquer her fatigue and irritation produced by the extra effort and cost of the extra laundry. She may not even realize that she could easily accept some help in setting the table, and that her children would enjoy a different routine that would permit them to assume more responsibilities.

She may feel guilty about her husband's death. The old pattern may be continued out of a misplaced desire to keep things as they had been before she became a single mother—although other, far more meaningful facets of her life have been radically altered—so that the discomforts punish her and in this way diminish her inner feelings of guilt.

Once she acknowledges to herself the possibility that she is feeling guilty, she is free to realize that her guilt is misplaced and that, anyhow, it truly is not expiated by the continuation of a daily, burdensome routine. She can change her ways, enlist the help and company of her children during meal preparation; and, more rested and peaceful, she herself can genuinely reconstruct the quiet air of contentment that actually was the important quality of former meals with her husband, and that she had believed was the goal she sought by carrying out the tiring tradition. Permitting her children to gain a sense of their importance to her and learn to take and enjoy the responsibilities of helping out, she actually provides herself with ample justification for being alive, not dead like her husband, and she thus needs to feel less guilt.

Such elimination of habits that no longer comfortably suit your situation as a single mother can have a sizable effect on relieving your feeling that life consists of just an endless series of activities from which you get little emotional return. Just as you know better than to try to make a big dinner every night to prove you love your child, start making real efforts to avoid chores that leave you unable to relax; strive to put your efforts into the things that really count to you and your child.

Your inner sense of freedom is directly expanded also as you take the constructive action necessary to fulfill those parts of your ideal—especially those parts connected to major emotional gratifications—that are realistically obtainable.

So you have a duty to yourself to check all discrepancies between your two lists where you want to do something that is not in any way opposed by a necessary task of parenthood or by ordinary reality.

Many times, some activity passed over as an idle dream, beyond possibility of realization, becomes possible through assumption of a few additional responsibilities that are not burdensome because they are freely chosen means to a desirable end.

To be free to recognize available possibilities, you must come to grips with any inner emotions—usually guilts—that have kept you from seeing the possibilities. Take another page from the psychologist's book. Assume that if you are failing to do something you think you want to do, something that is neither hurtful nor unrealistic, it must be because you feel guilty about something connected to it. Ask of everything that comes to your mind when you start wondering about guilt, "Is this what is keeping me from going after a pleasure?" Start the doubly rewarding process of getting rid of the unnecessary guilt and of obtaining the sought-for pleasure, now.

For example, suppose that your ideal list contains the item, "Spend an occasional evening with people who enjoy good books." You may regard this as an impossibility because you do not know enough people who will come to your home and talk about books, you think you cannot get your child to bed early enough to be able to meet with friends without interruption, you do not have enough extra money to provide refreshments, or it would be difficult to keep the talk centered on books—many other excuses and rationalizations may come to mind.

But once you make the interpretive assumption of guilt, once you decide that for some foolish reason you don't want to enjoy yourself, you can start searching for the reason. It may turn out that you feel guilty about taking away time and attention and money from your child; you may discover that you feel guilty about feeling resentful attitudes toward your child (perhaps his birth marked the end of cosy intellectual evenings with your former husband); you may feel guilty about wanting to have a pleasant evening.

Whatever the ultimate basis of the guilts may be, it is usually something unchanged by continuing to forego the pleasure of meeting with people to talk about books. Once you see this, you can get around the realistic aspects of the excuses you professed. Emphasizing the book discussion part of your desired activity, you can take steps to locate and join a book study group that meets on a night when a sitter is available, and you can cheerfully tolerate the sacrifices required if you are to pay the baby-sitter. No longer pointlessly punishing yourself because of some guilts over misplaced resentments or other reactions, you can come to grips with your inner feelings, forgive yourself and your child for the previous mixed-up feelings, and make a better relationship possible with your child as you increase your own pleasure in life through your new activity.

As you set about finding practical methods for actualizing your ideal, you expand your inner sense of freedom because you come to terms with and usually eradicate the guilts that kept you from fulfilling your ideal. Your self-confidence is increased. You have renewed vigor with which to approach the somewhat more difficult task of recognizing other negative feelings.

You must analyze what is and what is not efficient about the ways you use to discharge your negative feelings. You must strive to alter your behavior so that you truly discharge your negative feelings by expressive methods which clear problems up and enable you to increase your sense of freedom even further. Only by obtaining satisfaction can you be left with sufficient strength to start assuming the legitimate duties you may currently be neglecting. The first step toward learning to like what you must do is accomplished as you do what you want to do (if not hurtful to anyone), and the second step is accomplished when you freely acknowledge to yourself, if to no one else, that you hate doing something you must but do not want to do. Typically, when you confront your feelings head on, you recognize how childish it is to go through complicated personality shenanigans in order to avoid some trivial duty. You quickly eliminate the emotional involvement and end up taking a matter-of-fact attitude toward the task.

Then, finally, tackle the responsibilities that are legitimate but that are being shifted by you on to others or neglected entirely. Start by asking yourself why are you really basically angry at yourself? Why are you hurting yourself by trying to make your life more complicated and burdened with the extra guilts or other added pressures that are the inevitable consequences of neglect of necessary responsibilities?

You, but only you, most of the time, can see your irresponsibilities and small private acts of neglect; only if you are grossly irresponsible can your failures be noted by others easily. So you must rely on your own conscience to tell you how adequately you are carrying out your legitimate responsibilities. Guilt can easily be compounded by you as you seem ostensibly to be living up to your responsibilities; when the details of your activity are examined and the natural cause-and-effect basis for your activity is taken into consideration, many of your responsibilities can be seen to be neglected.

Suppose, for example, you work to support your child and pay for his care in a day nursery. Tired and rushed after a day's work, you may pick up your child and take him home, showing little interest in listening to him or asking him much about his day away from you. Eager to get into more comfortable clothes, you may place his supper before him to eat by himself—or you may let him suffer through his crankiness caused by fatigue and hunger until you change from your work-day clothes and prepare a meal for the two of you. Ready to eat by yourself or eager to clean up after your meal together, you may put him into the tub to play and wash by himself, or you may, instead, rush through the bathing without giving him a chance to enjoy the water. Striving at last to have some of your evening free for yourself, you may put your child to bed without spending any leisure time with him.

You may operate like this without any conscious desire to hurt or neglect your child; you may merely be trying to cope with your many pressures. Yet, in reality, since you are doing little with your child, you incur guilts and you get few satisfactions from your life with him. You are discarding your present almost completely as a time during which you can find any great joy in living except for the relief you obtain from sitting down to read or watch television or from leaving your home for the evening.

By foregoing all opportunity to play a meaningful role in your child's development, you have also sacrificed a prime opportunity to be creative and to receive the intense pleasures that come from watching your child imitate and identify with your personality.

Many examples can be given of mothers who really fail to be mothers despite all outer appearances. Some are the mothers who spend a great deal of time away from their homes, engaged in social or community activities. Some are the mothers who pay only superficial attention to their school-age children, letting homework, extracurricular activities, books, and television serve as screens or barriers to close interactions between them.

With any kind of rejection of responsibility, guilt feelings accumulate and increase the negative feeling of being overburdened. Mere release of pressure through careless neglect of a legitimate responsibility cannot be long effective.

Irresponsibility and carelessness can be eliminated, and relief and expression gained, by the thoughtful assumption of legitimate responsibilities and the intelligent rejection of unnecessary duties and habits. No healthy and mature adult woman needs—or wants—to get rid of sensible responsibilities for more than a brief and occasional rest period.

Ask yourself what your negative feelings are that lead you to be negligent. Are you angry because you are in a situation that forces you to cope with most responsibilities by yourself? Are you envious of other women who are not in such a predicament? Do you blame your child for your misery?

Cry. Call yourself and everyone else names. Have a full-scale tantrum. Get your anger into the open where you can see it, instead of trying to pretend that you really want to assume all your responsibilities, but you cannot manage everything. Then use the steam you have built up inside of you, as you have labored under pressure, for constructive purposes, to remedy the bad situations in your life that result in sacrifice of some rightful pleasure or neglect of some gratifying responsibility. Decide, right now, you are not going to put up with hurting yourself or your child by your negative feelings.

Take the example previously given, and see how simple it is to turn the entire sequence of events into gratifying interactions: Arrange to have your child take a short nap late in the afternoon so that, when you call for him, he will be better able to tolerate delays of dinner and bedtime. A light snack is a good idea, too, for him, and an after-work coffee break helps you, as well. Share the routine of getting out of daytime clothes, let your child help you put away the clothes from work and select others. Let your child participate in some of the patterns of meal preparation—not necessarily the cooking, but at least the table setting and getting out the bread and butter. If you tighten up other budget items, you may be able to arrange to have your child cared for at home;

you then have more time in the morning to spend in leisure with him, and the evenings are less hectic. In addition, the relief from housework may well compensate for the added pressures caused by the increased expenses. In either case, whether your child is cared for at home or away from home, you can talk about your day's work and make conversation with your child about what he has been doing. Constantly strive to draw from every experience the maximum amount of shared pleasure—always making certain, of course, that you are not expecting your child to respond as if he were an adult. Remember that you must be giving to him, not trying to take.

Similar approaches are open to a nonworking, socially active mother or any mother. Aim to convert into a sharing experience with your child some of the activities you have engaged in primarily for their personal rewards to you. If your child shows that he might enjoy such closeness, for example, substitute scout work or room-mother work for something like hospital volunteer work; your child can then join in with you to a greater extent, even if only in knowing the teachers whose names you mention or in knowing which troop meets at certain meeting places. If you tend to withdraw into quite private pursuits like reading or painting, make deliberate efforts to "convert" part of your activities to shared ones. Your child can paint along with you; you can portray him or his things; you and your child can read a book together at regular times each day. Sometimes, rescheduling is all that is needed to let you keep up the same activities, but at times of the day that will not interfere with your participating with your child.

Whatever your individual situation may be, analyze it thoroughly, eliminate unnecessary mechanical acts, expand your satisfying and constructive activities, and emphasize the meaningful mothering acts you perform. You can thereby avoid most burdensome feelings of loss of freedom and responsibility.

## Love and Discrimination

It is important to you, as it is to anyone, to feel confident that you are living up to your own standards of taste and morals. As you increase your self-respect because you are fulfilling your responsibilities, you are, of course, increasing your feeling that you have lived up to certain standards within you. But inner standards are not only related to what your conscience tells you you must do. There are also meaningful standards of taste and of style, standards of likes and dislikes, that contribute to another feeling within you, a feeling of zest and pleasure and being in love with life.

The negative feeling that is produced when standards of taste are frustrated or not upheld, when discrimination is not or cannot be exercised, is a feeling of forlornness. Rather than feeling eager and interested in the daily acts of living, the person who has failed to exercise the discrimination that healthy inner standards require feels bewildered and hazy about what to do next. In another way, the person whose standards are unrealistic is also unable to feel joyous—sensitivities too often hurt become blunted. Even worse, the overly sensitive person sometimes denies the life about her in favor of her unreal images of perfection, so that almost all zest for living is lost.

Because the "kick" you get out of living is dependent upon fulfilling your standards of taste—or modifying them if they are unrealistic—you need to be sure that you are recognizing and satisfying your standards.

Use the same technique of preparing a list in order to begin the analysis of your standards and their fulfillment.

First, list your likes and dislikes. Do not confine yourself to activities as you have done previously. Get involved with values: the things you like, the people you like, the way you like other people to behave, the qualities you dislike and want to avoid. This is your ideal list; if you could live in a world with these values paramount, you would be contented or living in total joy.

Of course, the world does not follow your ideal, and it is important for you to see where and how it fails. But before even considering this aspect of external frustration, you need to take a thoughtful look at the internal sources of conflict and frustration that cause anxiety and unhappiness.

By making a positive choice of any sort, you usually are also making several implicit negative choices; love for one object often involves discrimination against other objects. Very often, because your standards are set at different times of your life and in different ways, one of your standards may call for liking something that another standard makes you despise. Some cherished "like" may actually involve your acceptance of some despised "dislike." Or a clash may exist between a goal and some standard; for example, you may want to be noticed by others, yet hold as virtues being shy, retiring, and demure.

Whatever they may be, such clashes impose on you a necessity for tolerating either frustration or ambiguity, they keep you from fully enjoying whichever aspect you choose to satisfy at a given time.

The internal conflict that is produced when this happens is a major source of frustration. Take a good look at your list to discover such conflicts. Draw a line connecting all the likes and dislikes that are mutually contradictory; these are sources of trouble for you. The more such sources you can identify, the more fully equipped you are to do something constructive about reducing such conflicts.

Since you are happier if you can reduce such internal clashes, you must examine the standards that promote these clashes. If you suspect any particular standard is an outmoded relic of your childhood, a rigidly unrealistic or inhuman concept, make a real effort to think it through and discard it. Or, if you suspect that some positive choice is only caused by a temporary affiliation or conformity to current fads, examine why you have linked yourself to the fad the way you have; if you do not have a truly sound reason, stop just going along with the crowd.

Once you have analyzed the internal consistency of your ideal, take reality into consideration. Check off all these aspects of your ideal that can be easily and enjoyably realized in your day-to-day life. The items left over—assuming that they are based on healthy standards—are hungers, wants whose unfulfillment leaves you empty and yearning, at first, and then later frustrated, anxious, angry, and eventually forlorn.

If the proportion of such hungers is very small in comparison to the gratifications, your standards are being well met. If, however, there are great demands upon you to tolerate ambiguity or frustration, you must examine your behavior to see how you may be acting out these tensions.

It is relatively easy for the single mother, frustrated in her need to love and like and to have these feelings returned, to become anxious lest she fail to find the things she wants and lest she abandon her standards. In her frantic search for escape from this anxiety, she may take nonconstructive action that leads either to overconstriction or to undiscriminating reactions. As contradictory as these two pathways may seem at first, each succeeds in temporarily resolving a portion of the dilemma, but each eventually increases the inner reactions that promote forlornness.

Many single mothers constrict themselves and their life space, refusing to try to make satisfying adult ties. In so doing, the divorced and illegitimate mothers are demonstrating, in effect, attitudes that say, "I've been shocked and hurt, and now I'm just going to trust my child and not bother about other people." The widows more typically justify constrictive reactions with attitudes that say, "I've had one big love, which was more than I can ever hope for again, so now I'll be content with my child and my memories."

The damage that the constrictive reaction inflicts on a child cannot be exaggerated; the child has no such unrealistic ties to his short past, and he knows only that he cannot enjoy his current life. But this is not the only pain that this kind of acting out causes, for the single mother, too, suffers additionally as she works to keep her life constricted by rejecting the world about her.

Perhaps if life could ever be perfect, rejection of all subsequent experience could be accomplished without pain. But no single mother can manage without pain to run away and refuse to accept new experience and new life, yet honor the reality of her past, not tampering with her memories, not changing her history. The past has not been perfect—neither perfectly horrible, as some divorced women might contend, nor perfectly wonderful, as some widows might contend. In order to sacrifice the present and future to a memory, the memory must be colored. The single mother must compose a fiction about her past; she must contend with her own capricious recall of events that do not fit her fantasy, and she must alienate herself to guard herself, for she is vulnerable to attack by old friends who may confront her with the truth. Although she may want to bury herself in her memories, she must end up by destroying the real memories of her past in favor of her fantasy; and it is in this fantasy alone that she buries herself.

Thus, in her efforts to keep alive the past and use it as her justification for denying the reality of her present, the constricted single mother actually accomplishes the distortion of her past.

This process of rejecting further experience in life also acts to cut the single mother off from the contacts with reality that her dependencies require. Thus, she creates additional anxiety within herself and makes it even harder for herself either to live in her memories or to shake herself free of her fantasied self-sufficiency so that she may seek satisfaction in an on-going life of reality.

The pattern of constriction and rejection of current reality is less likely to occur today than formerly; but you must be alert to any signs that you are following such a pattern, even in small ways. Be especially careful to look at your ideal list with an eye toward asking yourself: Do I like this because I genuinely enjoy it, or do I like it only because I used to enjoy it when other things were different? In the same way, examine your dislikes. Experiment to see if your tastes have changed; deliberately expose yourself to a small dose of some dislike—be it turnips, historical novels, or German expressionist art—and discover your current, unprejudiced reactions. Be sure, too, to check to see how much you impose your constrictions on your child.

The opposite acting-out pattern is shown by the mother who throws herself into the world in the hope of finding meaning and purpose outside of herself. She greedily embraces every possible source of love; she joins. She constantly accepts people or situations that are not exactly what she feels she wants, but that are all that is available. And, for jettisoning her standards, for compromising with them, for betraying her inner likes and dislikes, she incurs additional guilt. She, too, has destroyed her past; she acts as if her experience had left and could leave no trace.

Sometimes she demonstrates this tendency by casting herself into an acquaintanceship enthusiastically, hoping that the people she meets will like her and want her for a friend. Ordinary precautions of privacy are thrown away in a sudden intimacy that, it is hoped, will ensnare the other person into friendship, into perfect friendship. Usually, so demanding a relationship wears thin quickly, and then the single mother has neither the friendship she has hoped for nor the consolation of knowing that she has been sincere and true to herself. Fortunately, aside from loss of shared time, her child is not hurt much by this reaction.

Sometimes these very intense but short-lived associations depend on the single mother's constant contributions of complaint about her life. When she gets tired of supplying the other person with material for a private soap opera, she discovers there is nothing to talk about, and the other person is shown up as a minor sadist who enjoys hearing only about misery. The single mother again has lost the relationship, along with her personal dignity.

A single mother, like any lonely person, may throw herself into a cause, rather than become involved with people. Charity and church work does provide her with the occupation she needs to keep from becoming more frantic, and it does give her a chance to be helpful and satisfy her feelings of duty. But she is bound to be disappointed in such a source if she hopes to find love and gratitude through it. If she chooses fanaticism of any sort, she must deny the common sense that tells her no dogma is perfect. And usually, she hurts her child greatly by imposing fanatic standards upon him.

Another unfortunate way of acting out the need for love is the sexual affair, especially one that is entered into with the stated idea that "no one is going to get involved." The single mother trades the use of her body and also a great deal of compassion and care and dignity in exchange for a man to cook an occasional meal for, someone to dream about, someone to take to parties, someone to go to bed with, and someone who possibly will bestow upon herself—or upon herself and her child if she is so foolish as to permit her child and her lover to spend much time together—a small amount of guilt-laden sentimentality. In the long run, such an affair usually ends with the gratuitous advice to the mother from her opportunistic partner, "Next time, look for someone who loves you, so he won't hurt you." Yet it is the very fear that she must not wait till someone loves her—for she may wait forever—that prompted her to dismiss this sound advice when it came from within herself at the start of the affair. The results of the affair are pain, disappointment, and guilt about discarding her own inner standards. To the extent that her child has been involved, or neglected, he has been hurt, too, and she feels additional guilt.

Examine your ideal to see how much of it is governed by your haste to accept whatever is available in the hopes that you will learn to "make do" with it. Be alert to the possibility that you may be attempting to use some transitory enthusiasm in order to obtain gratification for a real need. You must discover which aspects of your ideal you may have sold yourself on for one poor reason or another.

Wherever your behavior is conditioned either by a need to preserve the tottering remnants of your past or by the need to escape the isolation your standards impose on an inadequate reality, wherever you either constrict or fail to discriminate, you are acting out the negative feelings related to love and discrimination. Recognizing your acting-out behavior, take steps now to express your negative feelings in constructive activity. Unless you make a deliberate attempt to satisfy the self that is developed already, you cannot rid yourself of the worry that you have lost yourself, and thus made yourself even more lonely.

So notice the powerful and painful feelings that develop when your need to love and be loved is frustrated; permit yourself to feel them, intensely, so you cannot and dare not just give up and accept emptiness or superficiality. Let your pain impel you to search for the things you need to love.

Refuse to permit yourself to engage in any of the self-damaging behavior that is acting out: imitation, self-castigation, yearning, suppressing inner demands, or blunting sensitivity. Be sure that you attempt to learn new things, develop new tastes, meet new people, and make new friends; but, in such an extension of yourself, keep from tossing away your own recognition of your reactions. Keep in mind that learning a new taste is not the same thing as imitating an enthusiasm demonstrated by someone else; emulating another person whom you esteem is not the same as following a fad in an undiscriminating, promiscuous, and agitated way. Be sure you do not require yourself to hide those characteristics in you that have already been developed and found to be gratifying.

You know by now the sorts of persons you really like and respect. And you also know the sorts who will reciprocate your respect with genuine acceptance. So, rather than hurt yourself by accepting substitutes because they are available, search for the people whom you can accept happily as friends, and accept the small amount of suffering that comes as you wait and bear with your loneliness.

It helps if you keep in mind that the kinds of people whom you like and who are like you are people who tend to do the things you like to do. So, by making sure that you spend your leisure time doing the things you like to do, you are increasing your chances of meeting people with whom you have tastes in common. Even a pastime like reading can be the basis for joining a book-discussion club or visiting the reading room of the library where the librarian may be able to make introductions. Think creatively about your likes, and figure out how to enjoy them in public gatherings; seek music at concerts instead of on records, enjoy plays at the theater instead of in a book, obtain financial advice from an investment club instead of from a newspaper column.

Few things you do with people depend upon whether they are friends rather than just acquaintances. There are lots of things that are more fun if you do them with friends, certainly, but you are seldom limited just to friends, particularly if you live in a big city.

If you keep your values straight and distinguish between the bridge game and the bridge talk, for example, you can usually join a bridge club and there find people with whom to play bridge, even if you do not find people who become intimate friends. Many respectable groups exist only because lonely people exist; you can join these groups—like your local Y, church groups, school associations, and special recreation groups—without needing in any way to feel uncomfortable. It is no admission of personal worthlessness to be alone and to seek company.

Give yourself a moderate chance to get acquainted with the people you meet at these activities; but do so safely. Trust your first impressions if they are bad—you are not a baby; as a grown woman, you can usually recognize traits that disturb you at first meeting. And if some later behavior turns up that you do not like, speak up about it—the fact that you met someone somewhat casually does not mean you must let yourself in for embarrassment or annoyance. You have a right to say how you feel; express your legitimate negative feelings openly. Remember that you are not worthless; your feelings require your attention and care.

Do not behave as if you were a young adolescent girl just starting to meet the world. Whereas it makes sense for a young girl to accept invitations from many sorts of people to gain experience and learn more fully exactly what she really does and does not like, it is a waste of time for you, a mature woman, to try to alter your deep convictions about people or yourself. (If your convictions are based on neurotic conflicts, of course, they ought to be altered; but rubbing yourself against the grain is hardly likely to be an effective way of altering neurotic attitudes. Even if you think you are "sick," be kind to yourself and honor your standards.)

It is unlikely that you will meet a compatible person at an event holding little interest for you, so attendance at such events is a waste of your time. It is even more a waste of your time to miss an evening with your child.

So pay no attention to the adage, "Go on, go, even if you don't like the fellow you're going with or the affair you're going to go to, you may meet someone that you do like." It is a poor guide for action for an adult woman whose tastes are fairly stable and well developed. You do better to remember the adage that birds of a feather flock together. Stay away from people or activities you know you do not enjoy.

Everytime you succeed in doing something you want to do, without sacrificing your standards, you are gaining pleasure at no loss. If you do this consistently, you can develop for yourself a satisfying life which involves a minimum of anxiety and anger. You may still be living alone with your child, but you do not need to feel lonely.

## Respect and Tolerance

One of the most important positive feelings needed by a healthy person is an over-all sense of security, the knowledge that things are going right and according to regulations, that material

comforts are safe and assured, that social requirements and courtesies are being honored and respected, that painful situations do
not have to be tolerated but can instead be remedied. Much of
this feeling of security is bound up with complicated intangibles
like social standing and self-confidence, but part is connected to
feeling relaxed about the basic security of very real and simple
things, like life, limb, and property.

As a single mother, you may often find yourself uneasy and
insecure, worried about threats both to your safety and your
social standing. Defensively, you may become angry or hesitant;
worried about self-control and control of others, you may release
your anxieties in habitual doubt or irritation. You can easily
develop nonconstructive patterns of behavior, going around with
a chip on your shoulder and so provoking the attack you basically
are fearing—or backing away in self-doubt and confusion from
all contests that might establish what you will or will not put up
with.

If you are sure to express your natural reactions to threat—
your doubts, fears, and angers—you can use these powerful moti-
vators to eliminate or reduce the causes of your insecurities. Part
Three of this book considers many examples of interactions concerning your child's father that cause trouble; but for purposes
of illustration here, assume you are divorced, and consider the
example of your feelings of insecurity when your former husband fails to turn up on time for his appointment to see your
child:

You may hesitate to react and express your insecurity; you
may therefore pretend you are not troubled and made anxious.
You do nothing to remedy the situation by this nonexpressive
behavior; by your assumed indifference, you almost invite a
reoccurrence of similar happenings in the future. To the extent
that your former husband actually prefers to have a pleasant
relationship with you, you are not being fair to him by your
silence; you are not calling his attention to a source of difficulty
between you that he can, if he wants, take constructive action
about.

You may, instead, be unwilling to express your insecurity
but more than willing to express the reactive hostility you feel as
a result of your insecurity; thus you provoke an angry scene

that spoils a part of the visit. You may also deal with your anger in a less open way, making sarcastic remarks about your former husband to your child or failing to have your child ready on time when your former husband shows up for his next visit.

Constructive and forthright expression of your reactions can work toward clearing up the difficult and trying situation: "Next time you notice you will be late, please let us know, because we both get extremely tense waiting for you, and that makes the whole visit less enjoyable."

Neither a hostile nor an uncertain remark, clearly letting him know what you are feeling and why, and what you suggest as a way of preventing similar feelings in the future, this form of remark is both expressive and constructive. The steam power of your inner feelings provides the push or drive you need to make such a statement.

In a similar way, strive to use other tensions—angers, fear, or doubts—to work toward solution of other problem situations. Do not act them out through counterhostility, pointless hesitation, and self-questioning or fearful reticence.

Check yourself closely, for many small ways of acting out hostility are used by people who are ordinarily thought of as responsible and self-controlled. By taking things out on innocent people or objects, by breaking laws or customs, people act out their desire to get back at a world that has caused discomfort. Outright pilfering and vandalism are common not only among juvenile delinquents—grown women engage in these acting-out ways, too. You can fail to stop at a stop sign, you can bump a car deliberately because it is taking a parking space, you can fold or mutilate a punch-card received as a bill—these are all small ways of showing contempt for the law or striking back at a bothersome world. Gossip, bigotry, and prejudice also serve as handy channels down which to pour venom and hate. Many times, no overt punishment results when hostilities are acted out in these ways.

But to the extent that you share and believe in general ethical codes of our culture and society, you provoke an inner sense of tension and guilt each time you utilize one of these acting-out methods. Thus, not only is the acting out unsuccessful in itself, but it also leads to additional tension. The tension, in turn, often leads to guilt that undermines whatever security may exist—the whole reactive cycle tends to constitute a vicious one.

Chronically submissive behavior—also viewed by psychologists as a common way of acting out underlying hostility and fear—is also useless so far as increasing genuine security is concerned, although it has the superficial recommendation of controlling the extent to which the acting out provokes counter-hostility from other people. (It even, at times, may exhaust and wear down the hated or feared person; but this kind of victory is by no means sure or simple.)

In this civilized world with established personal freedoms, most of the time it is realistically purposeless for you to engage in any of these ways of acting out covert anger. It might make sense to be devious about either anger or fear if you are stalking a tiger in the jungle or if you are absolutely imprisoned by a cruel conqueror—in each case, presumably, open fear or anger will make attack more likely. But in the ordinary world of today, with personal mobility permitting a wide choice of acquaintances and friends, there is no benefit to be gained by keeping hidden from yourself the negative feelings aroused in you by some wrongful and hurtful behavior in another person. You must maintain your self-respect, and this is absolutely dependent upon your making sure that you neither hurt yourself or anyone else nor permit another person to hurt you. Work to develop stable feelings of security; take steps to eliminate those relationships and activities arousing legitimate anger in you.

List for yourself the situations that you react to with consciously felt anger, fear, doubt, confusion, dishonesty, irresponsibility, or rudeness. (It does not matter, for the time being, whether or not you believe these feelings are brought about because of the way someone else acts or because of the way you are already set to react. It also does not matter if you do or do not customarily betray your inner feelings by your behavior.)

After you have listed the times you know you feel these negative feelings, jot down ways to put these feelings to constructive use in similar situations in the future.

Resolve to nip annoyances in the bud—use the first flickerings of irritation to spur you to mention your feelings casually and without heat. Do not pretend that you are invulnerable or have the composure of a saint who demonstrates no wrath; if there are some people who customarily annoy you, take realistic precautions to avoid them. It is much harder to control your reaction than it is to avoid the provoking situation in the first place.

Combine an inescapable but disliked activity with an activity that is pleasurable to you. For example, if writing to your former mother-in-law each week annoys you, write about a topic enjoyable to both of you: her grandchild. If you absolutely must spend time with people you dislike, keep the meetings from being only exhausting or bothersome: introduce topics that may be rewarding because they are of mutual interest. Do not wear yourself out by discussing meaningless topics; do not hurt yourself by becoming emotionally involved; do not offend your standards by lying about your activities and reactions or by being rude. If you can do nothing more, make the meeting a profitable excursion for you into the realm of self-control and diplomatic, politic manner—practice saying nothing smoothly and well.

Deliberately refrain as much as possible from dwelling on thoughts of people who have wronged you. Once a source of hostility is recognized, it is pointless to continue to devote idle thought to it. Hating an evil without constructive thought toward disposing of it is a vice in itself; and hating an evil over and done with is utterly wasteful. Huxley has called those who enjoy thinking about their hates "adrenaline addicts"; stop stirring up your liver, act positively or not at all—do not let yourself be an adrenaline addict.

Prejudices and dishonesty usually mask some reactive hostilities that cover up even deeper fears of a characteristic you are not willing to accept within yourself. Deliberately seek to understand your prejudices and think over what you lie about. Learn what it is you are afraid of. Let your mind wander and seriously consider the thoughts that arise as you consider whatever behavior you engage in that shows lack of respect for the rights of others or for fundamental truth. Remember that respect for others is part and parcel of self-respect; prejudice and dishonesty show fear or doubt about your rights and your responsibilities.

Irresponsibility, too, indicates similar underlying reactions. Often it leads to feelings of anger within you directed at the person you have been irresponsible toward; and the anger leads, in turn, to more irresponsibility and hostility. Self-respect and security eventually take a terrible beating, so put an end to your irresponsible behavior.

Even if you cannot always act constructively, be sure to save yourself from the ramifications of guilt and anxiety by apologizing, admitting your error. Or if you know there is some activity that you are often unreliable about, forewarn other people who may be involved. You at least take a share of the responsibility when, for example, you tell a friend that you are careless about being on time for a shopping trip; she can take precautions to avoid being inconvenienced if you do show up late.

When your behavior is consistently honest and responsible, without much meekness, belligerence, or superficiality, your feelings of self-confidence are high; thus you can manage to regain equilibrium when small amounts of anger or fear or doubt are produced in your daily life. Your own intolerance for these negative feelings and for the conditions that produce them gives you the courage and the control you need in order to make things right again.

## Admiration and Originality

In addition to the feelings that have been discussed up to now, you must be able to feel pride—the feeling that you are important as an individual with unique, original, noteworthy characteristics and patterns of behavior that are recognized and remembered, no matter how slight they may be.

Adult pride is based on skills that take training and learning to develop. Only childish, defensive feelings—mixtures of shame and false pride—are demonstrated when a person claims prestige because of things, like family background or natural good looks, that have not required any individual effort, training, or skill.

You obtain your greatest feeling of pleasure from pride when you base it on something original you have done and done well. This can be anything from making new kitchen curtains to writing a prize-winning novel.

The married mother can always obtain some pride from the

mere fact that she is important to her husband and her marriage. In the absence of this secure source of prestige, you must not forget that you, too, need to establish your individuality and importance in the eyes of the people you know. Hurt, ashamed, perhaps even convinced, in part, that no one really cares if you are alive, you open yourself to pain; your anxieties blind you to your basic need to feel successful and competent; worse yet, they may cause you to behave in ways that are likely to lead only to additional loss of pride in yourself.

Put your anxieties to work for you, instead of against you. First of all, identify for yourself what you really feel proud about and seek recognition for, what you can rightfully and happily, but modestly, claim a measure of fame for, however small. List your skills and talents. Then make opportunities for yourself to exercise and practice them. If, for example, you take pride in your cookie-baking abilities, do not let your reducing diet stop you from showing off your talent. Donate to cake sales, to orphan homes, or just to the neighbors. Let yourself enjoy the compliments you win; and be sure, too, to practice often. You cannot enjoy being good at something unless you prove, frequently, to others and to yourself, that you are still as good as you ever were.

After you have taken constructive action to be sure your pride is being sustained, analyze the shames that you feel defensively tense and anxious about. Shame is felt when you have an inner conflict about a potential source of pride. Once the shame is eliminated, you can get to work on developing that underlying pride and thereby increase your over-all joy in yourself.

Shame is hard to discover, because it is natural to hide the fact that you are ashamed—and the shame itself hides a conflict. So you must take the psychological route to discover your shames, the round-about route. Make a list of all the situations in which you act in one of the following ways: bragging, boasting, provoking by teasing, flattering too much, ridiculing, challenging, apologizing without sincerity, making fun of yourself, or making excuses for behavior that others say you need not excuse yourself for.

These are the main ways psychologists identify underlying

shames. So you can call this list "situations in which I feel shame for something within myself."

Now, get going on your discovery of the inner shame. After each item of where and when and with whom you behave in one of these shame-indicating ways, list your hunch of what is troubling you.

Most people are ashamed of only a few things, although they may react in many different ways in various situations that remind them of their shames. You may, therefore, only have a few repeated notions.

For example, consider the following list constructed by a divorced woman who lives in a college town and who quit college after one year to marry the man she later divorced:

| WHAT | WHEN | WHY |
|---|---|---|
| Flatter insincerely | When I talk with Professor Brown | Lack of education |
| Apologize insincerely | When I check out library books | Lack of education |
| Make fun of myself | When I meet Dr. Mary Smith | Lack of education |

With this insight, she can discover that she is trying to avoid ridicule from her old friend Mary who concluded her college and medical education before she married Bill Smith and settled down to practice medicine. In addition to stealing the punch this way, she may discover she is also keeping herself from demonstrating any jealousy of Mary for her success in marriage. The insincere apology can be viewed as a way of calling attention to the fact that she does read a lot; it forces a compliment from the librarian. And flattering Professor Brown lets him know that she keeps up with intellectual matters and knows he has just published a new article.

Seeing what she is doing and why, she can alter her behavior, so it forthrightly demonstrates her justifiable pride. Acknowledging that she does, indeed, read a lot, she can start to discuss books with the librarian or with Professor Brown when the opportunity arises. Knowing that she has little in common with Dr. Smith, she can either keep their meetings down to brief exchanges of social courtesies, or else she can strive to reinstate a genuine current friendship by inviting Mary for a visit during which self-ridicule and false humility are absent and the give-and-take between friends is present.

Even though the amount of time and effort you waste on your defensive actions may not be very significant, analyze your behavior and get rid of your shames. It is likely that you will discover that most of your shames are not sensible and meaningful in the light of your realistic, grown-up world and your standards for yourself today. This is one of the startling things about shame: it is often related to failures or differences that are quite childish and trivial—like being left-handed, not being able to dance well, being the only girl in a large family, or having big ears. Once you bring into focus these silly vanities, your adult, sensible standards will not condemn them; they will be forgiven and forgotten.

Of course, not all sources of shame are easily dismissed as trivial and unimportant. But usually the remaining shames are about things that are completely unchangeable, in reality; so the best thing to do is to strive to bear with them or rise above them. If your father was the town drunk, for example, your experience was neither trivial nor unimportant. But your shame doesn't help anything, anyhow. You might more sensibly take pride in having kept from following in his footsteps.

It is easier for you to stop yourself from acting out your shames if you recognize that, like most acting out, there is a basic core of guilt underlying your shames: You feel guilty for wanting to be an individual, and you become ashamed to prevent yourself from ever trying and thus challenging the guilt.

As soon as you can acknowledge, fully, that you have every right to be a separate person with your own tastes and desires, your own skills and strengths, you can stop feeling guilty and be free to eliminate shame.

Do not rationalize when you seek to explain to yourself the why and what of your actions. Explain; do not distort facts. For example, consider the following rationalizations offered by various single mothers with regard to why they are single, not remarried:

A divorced mother says, "I'm just not the kind to stay content with one man forever."

An illegitimate mother says, "Listen, I don't care if I live to be ninety and no man ever talks to me again."

A widow says, "Well, it's awfully hard for a man to step into a ready made family, and anyhow, I wouldn't even think of marrying again."

These rationalizations can be turned into genuine explanations by only a small amount of attention to reality:

"I'm afraid I'll make the same mistake over again."

"I can't really trust a man anymore."

"I don't feel right about wanting to get married again, not yet."

Be especially careful not to rationalize in order either to copy other people or to hide your own qualities. No one can gain a real sense of pride by copying the attitudes or mannerisms of other people; and, in the adult world, it is seldom necesssary to hide individual qualities and to copy other people to avoid unpleasant reactions. You can be yourself, so long as you let other people be themselves, uncriticized and not despised by you.

For example, do not rationalize that you must keep quiet about your home and child when talking with your fellow workers because these topics are out of order in the business world. You do not need to feel guilty about having a fuller life than some of your fellow workers; they are unlikely to reject you for it.

If you really want people to know and value the real you, do not hide your light under a bushel. After all, you are not a high school girl who needs to be afraid of being liked if she can win at games often. Your acquaintances are grown up and quite able to accept your competence and your unique background.

The easiest way to reduce your entire load of shame is to develop your good potentiality to the fullest, letting your shame over past failures spur you on to correcting your faults. Decide what you want to be good at, what you have good potential for; try out and practice new skills; get specialized training if some skill requires it. Once and for all, throw away the false pride involved in worrying that others will ridicule you for trying something new; the only behavior deserving ridicule is envying other people who have enough gumption to try something new, yet never testing out how much you have. And avoid inflicting your learning efforts on others; do not become an exhibitionist. If you try something and find you do not have enough natural talent for it, give it up and try something new, or confine your efforts to private or with people who are no better.

By acting this way, by accepting yourself and fully assuming responsibility for being what you are, you are choosing the best way to go about being a proud, independent, and capable individual. You may very well be the product of your past, much of which was uncontrollable; but you are also the person who is in the process of becoming tomorrows' person. You can affect what you will become, and you can thereby alter the ultimate effects of your past.

One area of living in which it is more difficult for you than for other women to act naturally and spontaneously, without shame or reticence, is the area of male-female relations. In the eyes of men, you start with a handicap; in the eyes of women, you start with an advantage. So, in the race for male attention, you must take special care not to act out, for this will only increase the realistic difficulties you face from the reactions of the people around you.

Acting out shame about wanting male attention is often shown by flirting and teasing. As a woman with experience in relating to a man, you can easily realize how unnecessary, how unproductive, and how sometimes unsafe it is to flirt and go overboard in trying to prove you are in no way made tense by a male-female relationship. You know that a man who wants to be attracted will search out a woman to be attracted to—he does not need to be goaded into noticing her if she is around and is ordinarily pleasant and attractive. You also know he wants a woman to be alert to his maleness when he emphasizes it—he does not appreciate her having so matter-of-fact an attitude that she laughs it all off. But he also does not want her to be insecure.

Because there is always a steady undercurrent of natural competition with women, you can expect greater success in forming pleasant relations with men than with women. This is intensified because your singleness provokes additional competition from other women. Some of this is due to the slow death of the youthful concept most people have that "Life Should Be Fair." Women who have not yet had their chance at marriage tend to think it unfair for a woman who has been married once to do anything about getting married again. They regard her relationships with men with more antagonism and suspicion than that with which they might view the same sort of relationship between a man and a never-married woman. Childish though this reaction may be, do not seek to rationalize it away; accept the idea the other women will naturally be jealous of you, and it is your responsibility to keep from arousing added jealousy.

You are probably better off if you keep your personal dating life away from the attention of women friends. Do not seek to draw the pack to your scent; only a person with great insecurities needs to try to conquer such additional difficulties. Of course, do not go too far in the other direction. Do not avoid letting yourself be naturally attractive; do not play down your spontaneous response to the attentions of men. After all, in the competitive race for men, you do actually have some extra advantages; use your added skills and experience to make it easier for yourself to win. Remember that it is impossible to secure genuine friendship and acceptance from other women unless you and they are acting like full-grown women; never try the impossible, the attempt to reassure other women that you are no threat to them, competitively, with regard to men. The most this can obtain is acceptance from women who are not, themselves, mature; therefore, the friendship is heavily tinged with shades of contempt or pity.

By controlling acting out of shame, by increasing your skills through practice and exercise, by increasing your personal feeling of pride in yourself through forthright acknowledgment and acceptance of yourself without rationalization and excuse, you are taking the necessary steps toward securing extra admiration from others. You are making it easy for the people around you to value you for your own original qualities. Thus you are acting in a constructive way to obtain a major psychological gratification.

## Patterns and Combinations

The different kinds of behavior described in the foregoing section are only a few of the many sorts of actions that can express or release negative emotions. Exactly how you behave depends on many factors, including the relatively unchangeable ones like your age, vigor, natural supply of energy, intelligence, curiosity, and educated thinking habits—all operating in your own special life situation, socially and economically limited.

Psychologists find that some patterns of acting-out and release behavior are shown consistently by certain types of people, whatever may be the peculiar individual, social, and economic conditions.

Check yourself against the following descriptions of these types to get additional clues as to how you may be behaving in nonexpressive, nonconstructive ways:

*The type that just gives up*—she apologizes for herself, lets other people boss her around, yearns for many things but fears to ask for them, complains because she never gets what she wants, is confused about how other people manage, and wonders why she is treated the way she is.

*The kind that refuses to participate*—she criticizes and puts up objections until there is nothing she can feel confident about doing; she backs away from help and almost dares people to try to overwhelm her and make her want to be happy; she resists every challenge that might lead to giving up her conviction that life is unrewarding.

*The kind that is destructive*—she ridicules people who can do things she cannot do, condemns people who do things she does not want to do, and despises people who can do only what she can do; she forces and shocks others into associating with her, and she delights in ruining their joy whenever she can get the upper hand.

*The type that is demanding and exhausting*—she leans and begs, pleads, questions and nags.

*The kind that is assertive*—she boasts, preens herself, tries to manipulate people and situations so she can get the most from them, and greedily takes everything that comes her way without hesitation or feeling the need to reciprocate.

*The charitable type who is "too good"*—she protects everyone, praises and flatters, encourages and tolerates, with never a hint of desire for recognition of her own wants.

*The kind that fights*—she argues and challenges; she stubbornly refuses to relax and let things ride; she cannot face and accept conclusions.

All these types reflect negative emotions in ordinary behavior. You can easily see the hostility involved in being destructive, assertive, and aggressive; the other types also can be seen to take more than they give or to give nothing at all. Even the ostensibly charitable type manages to be destructive because she fails to appreciate the outstanding qualities in others and instead dwells on their mediocre facets; for example, she compliments you on how nice your old dress looks as you bring in a dessert you have spent hours preparing.

If you recognize your resemblance to one of these types, try changing the way you act to the kind of behavior that genuinely expresses negative emotions in a problem-solving way. Stand up for yourself and go after what you want. Spend more time and thought on how to get along with people and less on how to back away from them. Do not let yourself do anything that is only destructive; do not say or do anything unless it is both true and kind to others and yourself.

Try your new way of acting, a day at a time. See how much easier it is to be alone when you can review a day that has been spent mainly in being constructive—or, at least, not destructive. If you deliberately and consciously resolve to limit your acting out, you can save yourself much trouble and obtain many new pleasures.

# CHAPTER SIX

# Neurosis and Singleness

MANY GENERALIZATIONS have been made about the relation of neurosis to marriage, neurosis to divorce, and neurosis to other states of being single. Some of these generalizations can be of help to you as you make sure that you are not too ready to assume that all your problems are situational or that everything is neurotic.

Remember that merely labeling problems "realistic" or "neurotic" accomplishes little aside from providing a kind of shorthand notion of the relative ease with which you can solve your problems. Neurosis is a disease—it cannot be cured by the psychological equivalent of turning the patient's pillow over, although some superficial, temporary relief may be felt after such a maneuver. Only realistic, situational problems are eased by simple changes in daily life.

But be sure to keep in mind that neurosis is only a disease. It is not a term of moral condemnation, not an insult, not a punishment. If you eventually decide that your problems are neurotic, you are not thereby declaring that you as a person are less worthy of respect, affection, or consideration than someone who is not neurotic. Nor are you making your problems into imaginary ones. You are only stating that your problems make it difficult for you both to accept and provide the important psychological gratifications of love and respect.

Keep in mind that your fundamental purpose in seeking to determine if you are or are not neurotic is to let you take the most effective course of action possible to make yourself happier. Calling yourself neurotic neither cures nor hurts. Do not let yourself be led astray by the label; it is the meaning that counts, and what you do about it.

In evaluating yourself by referring to generalizations, you need to keep in mind the distinction between immaturity and neurosis. Up to now, "grown up," "mature," and "healthy" have been used as if they were always synonymous. But they can only be used as meaning the same state of emotional development *if* they are being applied to an adult, to a person past the age of twenty, approximately.

Those terms are not synonymous when used to describe people who are still in the process of growing through childhood and adolescence; these young people are called "immature." They may be neurotic, they may be healthy, but they are still immature. They see life through the lenses of youth; they are unable to bring to bear on life's experiences the information and the personality strengths developed only after years of practice and exercise of judgment and responsibility. Thus, an immature girl, though healthy, easily may make serious errors of judgment. Because of her inner limitations in emotional resources and experience, she may be hurt greatly by her errors.

But though the young may be foolish, though healthy, the adult cannot be immature, yet not neurotic. The tasks of living that are accomplished when emotional maturity is present are all tasks that can ordinarily be fulfilled in the first two decades of life. Thus, every person who is chronologically an adult has had ample opportunity to mature *if* neurotic blocks and conflicts have not been developed. So, if emotional immaturities are still present past the teen-age years, neurotic emotional conflicts must be assumed.

As you generalize about yourself, therefore, it is important that you determine if you are still making childish, immature errors of judgment, or if you are still being childishly hurt by events. If your decision is that you are still being immature in many ways, you must give careful attention to the possibility that you are being neurotic. (Only if you are still not fully adult in years can you disregard the implications of immature behavior.)

This distinction becomes especially meaningful when you consider one of the important valid generalizations about marriage and mental health. This is that a healthy adult is typically married and happily so; marriage is advantageous to an adult who is emotionally healthy; the adult gratifications and securities necessary for good mental health can be most conveniently and efficiently obtained within marriage.

As an unmarried woman, therefore, you must question yourself: Am I unmarried because I am immature, hence neurotic?

The connection between marriage and maturity and health comes about because the healthy person is usually operating at maximum efficiency in obtaining needed gratifications. In fact, every increase in the amount of effort required to obtain a gratification decreases over-all efficiency and so decreases the likelihood that good mental health can be achieved easily. And though almost every healthy adult gratification and security afforded by marriage can also be obtained outside marriage, the effort involved in gaining them outside marriage is much greater; consequently, marriage provides these gratifications more efficiently, and marriage is therefore considered a "healthier" state than singleness for an adult.

The married mature woman can look to her husband and her marriage for most of her gratifications; the price she pays is only the extra work in her home connected to caring for her husband, and this is often only slightly more than a single woman puts into the daily routines of homemaking. She can also legitimately use her husband and her marriage as vehicles to express discontents or aspirations, because she provides a steady deposit of affection and care against which to draw when she is bad-tempered or when she expects her husband to make greater efforts to provide vicarious satisfaction for some of her ideals and goals.

The mature single woman, however, in gaining the gratifications and securities that are viewed as natural to adulthood, must engage in much planning and maneuvering, must withstand or overcome many limitations of social customs, and must settle for an added degree of artificiality and frustration. If she is to go against the tide of her circumstances and achieve a sense of being worthy and positively valued and loved, she must actively develop her social contacts, her job, her hobbies, and her daily routine into meaningful and reliable channels for and sources of positive emotion. She cannot casually or without planning, control, reticence, and judgment assume that her available channels for pleasures will become meaningful and reliable; she must be thoughtfully calculating about the amount of tolerance she expects and grants, about the favors she receives and provides. And since friendship or social relations cannot long be maintained in the face of one-sided demands or complaints, she often must tell her troubles to her hairdresser, dressmaker, or a trained expert in human relations, rather than burden her friends who may not need to reciprocate by expressing unhappinesses.

All this is more work and effort; it returns to her, at best, only the same gratifications that a married woman finds more easily.

Because they can reasonably expect marriage to be a boon, mature people are willing and able to expend the effort that is required initially in surmounting the obstacles involved in finding a marriage partner and in adjusting to the demands that married intimacy and growth together entail. The good marriage between two emotionally mature and healthy people more than makes up for the original extra efforts to make it good.

Your attitude toward marriage can be examined to provide information about your emotional health. If you really don't value marriage, if you sincerely believe that being single is actually the best way to be, if you regard marriage as more demanding and less satisfying than being alone and as not worth the effort it requires, you are demonstrating attitudes that are not justified by an examination of the relative merits of marriage and singleness. These emotionally prejudiced attitudes are out of line with realistic evaluations; so you must entertain the suggestion that some underlying neurosis is causing them. (Only if you are chronologically not an adult is it realistic to view marriage as having few psychological advantages.)

Another important and valid generalization about maturity and marriage is that a man and woman who are both emotionally mature when they chance to meet and decide they like each other can usually create a successful, healthy marriage. They make their marriage; it doesn't descend upon them, fully formed, from heaven.

Chance does influence when people meet and whom they meet; but simple fortune alone is not usually the major force causing the meeting of two people with the characteristics desired by each in a good marriage partner. Instead, mature people, to a significant extent, create their own circumstances; they make and explore wide opportunities for themselves to meet people. They select for close association some of the people they meet as they move through life; then select for friends and for sweethearts only people who satisfy certain of their needs and ideals; finally, they select for partners in marriage only those they are reasonably certain can satisfy the needs they consider most important in marriage.

All this active selection, choice, and decision-making takes away most of the importance of luck alone. About the only room left for luck, most of the time, is the extent to which it is possible to exercise intelligence or choice with regard to a specific partner; not all people who might be selected are eligible; and mistakes in judgment can occur, because no one can know another person fully.

So, as you review your past marriage in the light of this generalization that mature people create what they have and generally create a marriage that is satisfying, and as you examine what you think about the possibility of marrying in the future, be careful to weigh how much importance you attach to luck. If you still insist that good luck is a major missing item in your life, that bad luck is the force primarily responsible for the lack of a good marriage, you are attempting to shift from yourself the responsibility for your own actions. Such behavior suggests that neurotic fears of responsibility are operating within you.

You can also learn something about yourself by considering the connection between marriage and neurosis. The most important valid generalization about marriage and neurosis is that marriage is seldom advantageous for a person who is severely neurotic. Despite the prevalence of marriage among neurotics, the emotional price paid for the emotional gratifications available to the neurotic person from marriage is exorbitant. Many marriages involving neurosis are broken by separation or divorce because of the pressures exerted by this high price. You cannot generalize about neurosis simply on the basis of which person sought to break up the marriage; sometimes both partners are neurotic and both seek separation; sometimes only one partner who is neurotic seeks surcease from the demands of intimacy; and occasionally, when one partner is mature, the mature partner seeks separation because the emotional gratifications available from the neurotic partner are too few and too highly priced, emotionally.

All marriages involving neurotics are not invariably broken, of course, and all marriages that endure are not invariably ones between people who are emotionally healthy. Many neurotic couples exist within marriages that, far from being good unions, are only neurotic compromises enabling the partners to bargain about and trade certain tolerances for particular opportunities to act out. And neurotic marriages are also often held together because of reality pressures like religious scruples and financial considerations.

Although two neurotic people have small likelihood of creating a good marriage, occasionally a marriage that was initially based on neurotic needs becomes a firm and good marriage after the two partners manage to struggle toward their separate maturities at roughly the same rate and before each has hurt the other so much that the fabric of the marriage is rent by accumulated pain.

Ordinarily, very few healthy adults end their marriage. These few are usually partners in marriage with a person who is discovered after the marriage to be highly neurotic; occasionally they are people who became healthy adults after marriages that took place when they were either immature or neurotic.

In short, you cannot decide anything about your own state of health merely by reviewing how you have come to be single. Healthy people seldom stay single as adults, but they may marry or divorce; neurotic people may stay single, or they may become married and stay married or become divorced—unless they grow up and develop healthy personalities, they remain neurotic through all these changes.

Take special care, therefore, to consider fully your own circumstance. Being divorced doesn't automatically indicate being neurotic, but it is more often associated with neurosis than with health.

In many ways, the connection of immaturity and marriage involves the same generalizations.

Most immature, healthy people who marry do not have, at the start, genuinely good marriages; they have immature relationships legalized into marriages. Sometimes they have pleasant relationships that gradually change from a let's-play-house, going-steady type of marriage into one that is based on emotionally mature ties—such marriages become good adult marriages. Or they may have a pleasant romantic tie that changes into a cat-and-dog conflict, as intimacy strains emotional development and needs are not gratified—such marriages become either neurotic marriages or divorces.

Some immature marriages take place because the partners are not prevented from acting on the basis of their immature judgments. Once the impulsive act has been completed, other reality pressures may contrive to keep the marriage together until it settles down into either a healthy or a neurotic pattern.

But most immature marriages involve at least one, usually two, youngsters who are not fully secure and healthy. Some psychologists insist that only emotionally disturbed youngsters seek escape from the tasks of adolescent development through impulsive flight into marriage; this writer generally agrees, but makes exception for some marriages forced by pregnancy that results from an isolated episode of acting out sexual impulses.

If you married young, whatever your state of mental health may have been at the time, your important consideration now is whether or not neurosis is still present. Probably the best indication that your personality has matured healthily can be gained from a review of your teen-age behavior and desires and fears; if you can recognize significant differences between then and now, you may well have left behind whatever immaturities or neurosis may have been present previously.

The connection between illegitimate motherhood, immaturity, and neurosis has been generalized upon by many psychologists. If you were an illegitimate mother, the conclusions made by some of these psychologists, including the writer, are pertinent and require your careful attention.

The largest percentage of illegitimate mothers are immature; in fact, half the births out of wedlock in several large American cities are from girls who are fifteen years old or younger.

Despite the prevalence of neurotic problems among these girls, many of whom were studied before they became unwed mothers, there are also many of these girls who had no neurotic problems, but who were just extremely immature, uninformed, impulsive, and unprotected. Their immaturities and vulnerabilities, in many cases, not only contributed to their becoming pregnant, but also led to their decisions to keep their childen; in their ignorance and simplicity, they believed it not too difficult a task to rear their children alone—an older and more experienced woman would not have so optimistic a view.

So, the illegitimate mother who became pregnant during her adolescence is not able to draw automatic conclusions about her state of mental health at the time she conceived; she may not have been neurotic, she may only have been highly immature. If she is still, in her adulthood, much the same, though, it is very likely that she is a neurotically disturbed woman.

Many psychologists, including this writer, believe that there is, however, a definite connection between being neurotic and becoming an illegitimate mother as an adult. If you became an illegitimate mother in your adulthood and you have chosen to keep your child with you, take several extra looks at yourself, because the probability is that your reactions at the time were decidedly neurotic.

The connection is made between neurosis and illegitimate motherhood, not because of puritanical viewpoints (all moral evaluation is essentially outside the province of psychology), but instead because of conclusions reached by analyzing evidence and by examining the question: What can possibly be healthy or neurotic about the decision to engage in nonmarital sexual intercourse? These conclusions have implications, not just for the illegitimate mother, but for all adult women in this society.

Psychologists start by stating what is healthy and what is neurotic. You remember from former chapters that a major characteristic of a healthy woman is that she does not willingly ask to be hurt; she does not risk or sacrifice her basic personality gratifications unless she must do so in order to avoid getting terribly hurt, or unless she seeks to protect the people she is responsible for. If she must jeopardize her psychological peace of mind and happiness when other imperative needs are involved, she does so with the inner resolution to stop her pain as soon as possible; she does not joyfully seek to increase her conscious anxieties.

If the need for sexual release through intercourse were the same kind of need as your need for food, water, and oxygen, a lot of psychological trouble and pain might be endured in order to satisfy this imperative need. If the absolute security of another person were involved, intercourse might be engaged in to protect the other person. But, since the need for sexual pleasure is not an imperative need for you or for your partner, as a healthy woman you do not place yourself in avoidable jeopardy merely for sexual pleasure.

An immature girl may not fully understand the jeopardy involved in nonmarital sexual intercourse. But an adult woman does. She has had ample experience and instruction in the ways of the world, she understands that nonmarital sexual intercourse involves many anxiety-provoking hazards like loss of social standing, impregnation, chronic concern and need for precautions against either of these, guilt about moral and practical-legal transgressions, curtailment or interruption of the sustained companionship that is part of love and of loving, and interference with spontaneity because sexual activity must be planned for and almost contracted for.

Knowing all these hazards, an adult woman does not put her head in the buzzsaw. Only if she succeeds in kidding herself that these hazards are not real and probable can she willingly engage in nonmarital intercourse; usually, she can rationalize and deny to this extent only if she is operating neurotically.

Her neurosis is not established by the fact that she gets "caught," and becomes an unwed mother, or by the fact that she has to coerce the father into marrying her, if she is like many teen-age married women, or by the fact that fornication is against the law. Her neurosis is established by the simple fact that she is not facing up to realistic considerations—she is trying to convince herself that she is a special case—because underlying neurotic difficulties are forcing her to act out by engaging in nonmarital sexual intercourse. (No single neurotic conflict can be separated out as the fundamental conflict; sex can serve as the vehicle for acting out each and every possible kind of neurotic conflict.)

Every woman who has once had an affair when adult need not automatically conclude that she is still neurotic; but she does need to take an exceedingly careful look at her current reaction to determine if she is now being more realistic.

She may find that the affair was a last fling of immaturity. Because the last task of emotional maturation is integrating sexuality into the whole personality and getting it controlled by realism, a sexual escapade can often be used by a woman who is slightly delayed in growing up as a last acting out of the remnants of her immaturity. She can learn and grow from this experience, so that she comes out of the affair a mature woman, no longer a slightly neurotic girl-woman. Usually, she enters the affair with a childish view of sexuality that makes intercourse equal to a fine game or a good meal—devoid of emotional overtones—or a view that requires a "test" or "proof" of what marriage will be like. In the case where she leaves the affair a wiser woman, her harsh experience teaches her that her former views do not make sense. She ends up deciding that healthy married couples can form enjoyable and satisfying patterns of sexual behavior without testing, that healthy marriages are not based on guilt or obligation, and that healthy adult women can no more dissociate sex from love than they can fly.

So the connection between illegitimate motherhood and neurosis is made, basically, because of the connection that psychologists see existing between nonmarital sexual intercourse and neurosis. This connection is farther supported and confirmed as psychologists examine the evidence in the light of the question: What can possibly be healthy or neurotic about the illegitimate mother who decides to keep her child and rear him, alone?

Psychologists have learned that most healthy people do not like to be reminded of past errors. They have also learned that the illegitimate mother is often acting out guilt, shame, and her need to punish herself by continually reminding herself that her child is a symbol of a past mistake; the healthy female desire to keep her child seldom appears to be of prime importance in her considerations. By contrast, the adult woman attempts to retain or regain health and maturity of attitude and seeks to avoid subjecting her child to the avoidable pain that society often imposes upon the mother-child relationship or the child when there is no marriage. So she generally does not decide to keep her child with her alone. She usually sacrifices her own healthy desire to keep her child to a consideration of her child's needs, and places her child for adoption.

(Indeed, were it not for other considerations, it could be argued logically that every husbandless mother ought to insure her child against future pain by putting him in a home where he could have two parents, not one. One of the realities that makes this argument foolish is that most women—except for the illegitimate mother or the woman whose child is born after she has become widowed or divorced—have built up loving ties with and through their child and husband, all interconnected and symbolically meaningful. Thus, the disruption of these ties would hurt the child more than the pain of growing up without a father. And another reality—one this book is dedicated to demonstrating—is that a single mother can do a good job of rearing her child if she is but careful to remedy major emotional difficulties that cause acting out.)

Psychologists, therefore, conclude that most adult women who choose to keep their children born out of wedlock are acting out some highly neurotic conflicts. This writer believes that occasionally there are exceptions to the general rule, especially in the low-income sections of this society where illegitimacy and government-sponsored financial aid to dependent children are not viewed with strong social disapproval and where adoption is unlikely. The illegitimate mother in this setting who keeps her child rather than subject him to institutional living is probably choosing the better of two unfortunate realities; the only evidence of neurosis within her must rest on other behavior, particularly on her reasons for failing to get married.

Even if you conclude that you were neurotic when you conceived your child, or when you decided to keep your child with you, you need not assume that neurosis is still operating. You need not assume that neurosis is still operating if—like most women—you have ever had an affair. But you must examine your reactions to sexuality and motherhood *now*.

Because of the difficulties connected with nonmarital sexual intercourse, the healthy single adult woman finds intense sexual tension uncomfortable and disturbing; so she takes steps to reduce the likelihood that certain people will arouse her sexual desire, and she strives to contain her desire within reasonable limits that do not include overt release through nonmarital intercourse. If you can subordinate sexuality in this manner, yet still retain your capacity to respond within appropriate limits, it is unlikely that you are reacting neurotically about sex.

## Decision-Making and Action-Planning

All these generalizations and considerations suggest that no condition of life automatically proves that a specific person is neurotic. Some conditions, though, often are connected to either a current or a past operation of a neurosis.

In deciding, therefore, what you need to do and what you can do about constructive and remedial goals, you need to analyze your specific situation and your specific reactions.

You will undoubtedly conclude that many of your problems are situational. Go ahead and work out a solution to these, think creatively, and take reasonable, common-sense, remedial action in the appropriate aspects of your everyday life. By changing things for the better, you automatically prove your problems to have been situational.

However, if some of your problems are based on neurotic conflicts, do not expect common-sense action to be easily or lastingly effective in solving them. You can still confidently expect to solve neurotic problems, eventually, but you will probably find it advantageous to obtain professional help. The following chapter contains information to guide you in seeking such professional help.

# CHAPTER SEVEN

# Consulting Help

In solving problems based on neurotic conflicts, you can seek help from many different professional people and services. To find help efficiently and economically, you need to consider some practical and material aspects characteristic of the services of different facilities or professional workers.

## Where to Go to Find Professional Help

In narrowing down available choices, you must give thoughtful attention to the practical and emotional advantages or disadvantages to you of obtaining treatment through an agency, clinic, or hospital outpatient service or through direct private practice. These are the settings in which professional people work who treat emotional and mental disturbances.

You can obtain the names of reputable nonmedical therapists by writing to the national organizations of the mental health professions. Among these are:

> The American Psychological Association
> 1333 16th Street, N.W.
> Washington 6, D.C.

National Association of Social Workers,
Psychiatric Section
95 Madison Avenue
New York 16, New York

The American Psychoanalytic Association
36 West 44th Street
New York 36, New York

The National Psychological Association
for Psychoanalysis
66 Fifth Avenue
New York 11, New York

The American Orthopsychiatric Association
1760 Broadway
New York 19, New York

Your private physician or the local medical society can provide information about available medical specialists in private practice and can help you locate the nearest treatment center. For additional information about medical facilities and personnel, you can obtain help from:

The American Medical Association
535 North Dearborn Street
Chicago, Illinois

The American Hospital Association
840 North Lake Shore Drive
Chicago, Illinois

The American Psychiatric Association
1270 Avenue of the Americas
New York 20, New York

The quality of service and treatment in a reputable treatment center is professionally equal to the service and treatment you can obtain from a therapist engaged only in private practice, so you need not be concerned with this factor. In fact, most therapists who spend the majority of their time in private practice still devote a portion of their practice to public service.

But in choosing between obtaining treatment in a public setting or in private practice, you must consider if you can obtain treatment at the time you seek it. Although he may not have time available to accept you for treatment immediately, the therapist in private practice can often arrange his schedule flexibly, so that he has time for an initial interview to determine if treatment is advisable; then, if he believes it is warranted, he can usually refer you to another therapist who does have open time. Many clinics, however, have waiting lists even for the first appointment; also, it is often more difficult for treatment center personnel to estimate when openings will occur than for the private therapist to judge his schedule.

Some centers also have definite treatment interests or limitations on the religion, age, income, or race of those who may be treated; the private practice therapists ordinarily have no such rigid standards. Inquire about clinic acceptance procedures when making an appointment for an initial interview; and if all near-by centers are closed to you, be sure to ask about obtaining private practice care from staff members who may be maintaining private practices.

Most centers and most private therapists have a sliding scale of fees, so that people with low incomes pay a smaller fee for service than do people who have less limited budgets. Generally, you can more easily obtain treatment at a reduced fee from an agency than from a private therapist, because the private therapist must ensure himself a reasonable income and has fewer low-fee hours available—the agencies can provide more low-fee time because they usually make up a major income deficit by appealing to community funds. In either setting, be certain to present your financial picture openly. Although the therapist may not be able to reduce the fee, he often can modify billing procedures and defer part of the fee until treatment is terminated. In several communities, your therapist can help you to get financial assistance from the government or other sources to pay for treatment.

Another important deciding factor to be candid about is your own attitude toward obtaining help for your emotional problems. You may believe, most sincerely, that mental and emotional problems are no different from physical problems, yet still feel some hesitation about having several people know you are seeking treatment for an emotional problem. Although this kind of feeling usually ceases to be significant after treatment has been going on for a while, it can present a disturbance to the initial phases of treatment. If you attend a clinic, this feeling is likely to be intensified. Of course, in a well-run treatment center, personal information bearing on your problems is generally kept in files that the nonprofessional staff has no access to—your record is not a tidbit for gossip—but there is a necessary lesser degree of anonymity to clinic attendance than there is to keeping an appointment with a therapist in his private office. The enrollment procedure at most large centers usually involves giving information about your problems to several different staff members; only after a diagnostic council has discussed the results of these different interviews are you assigned to a particular therapist for your regular treatment appointment. If your therapist is not one of the people who conducted the preliminary interviews, you may find yourself with still another stranger; and after all these contacts, as well as the necessary ones with file clerks, cashiers, and other administrative workers, you may feel that everyone in the center knows you are seeking help. Knowing that only your private therapist sees you at your regular visits to his office may be sufficiently relieving so that you feel more free to seek help under these circumstances.

Knowing how long treatment is likely to continue is necessary, not just for budget considerations, but also for other matters like job assignments and leases. Ask the professional person responsible for you to estimate how long treatment is likely to take; but remember that this estimate, based on experience with similar cases, is only a rough one and can only be determined after initial interviews with you. Because some clinics have policies about providing treatment to patients whose treatment is likely to extend past a set time, you may risk going through the preliminary procedure at a treatment center only to be denied treatment. These clinics customarily make referrals to other treatment centers where no time limits operate, however, so the procedure is seldom completely pointless. In a large treatment center, where therapists receive advanced professional training for limited periods of time, you may also find it necessary to change therapists during the course of treatment. By comparison, once a private therapist has decided to work with you—a decision he usually makes after a few meetings—he commits himself to continue treatment with you until the emotional difficulties are understood and solved, or until he feels treatment is no longer appropriate. All therapists, certainly, have the same dedication and commitment, but the private therapist has a greater amount of control over his own course of action.

Wherever you go for treatment, you can be confident that your therapist is bound by professional ethics to continue treatment with you while it is worthwhile and productive. He will seek consultation or supervision if he feels it is necessary; frequently, a therapist in private practice will ask for a diagnostic consultation at the very outset, and you will be asked to meet with a colleague for an additional interview or for testing.

In the professions concerned with the treatment of emotional problems, the ultimate safeguard for the patient is the professional training, reputation, and ethical concern of the therapist. Thus, the initial decision of choosing a therapist is often the most important decision the patient makes. Once you have obtained a therapist whose training has been thorough and whose professional conduct is responsible and ethical, you can wisely and safely permit your therapist to make further decisions regarding the course and conduct of treatment.

## The Mental Health Professions

In deciding where to go and whom to see, you may need to become involved in understanding the differences between the professions engaged in mental health care. Just having a clear idea of who is called what and who does what is helpful, especially if you attend a clinic and meet with several different people at first.

Although psychology is the science that deals with the mind, so that every professional person involved in mental health care may be considered a kind of psychologist, this term is usually reserved for members of the profession of psychology—one of the three professions that are usually responsible for treatment. In addition to psychology, the other two professions are medicine and social work. Together, these three professions contain most of the people who treat emotional difficulties by talking with the patient; these therapists are called "psychotherapists." Therapists who treat emotional difficulties with drugs or other physical agents must, by law, be members of the medical profession; often they are people with specialized training in the branch of medicine called psychiatry, and are called "psychiatrists."

The difference between members of the three mental health professions is not how well qualified they are in psychology and psychotherapy, but rather *how* they have been qualified and which specialized kind of academic information they have studied during their university and postgraduate training. Each comes equipped with a slightly differing emphasis upon some of the important areas of living; each learns some skills that are not regularly learned by the others. But, any therapist who is professionally trained and affiliated meets certain qualifications believed necessary in order to treat patients; each profession has proved it contributes important and worthwhile skills.

The clinical psychologist usually has a Ph.D. degree, received when he completes about three years of advanced university work beyond a basic four years of college, when he has spent two additional years in training as an intern in a mental health facility where he obtained professional supervision of his study and treatment of emotionally-disturbed patients, and when he completes an independent research project on some aspect of human behavior. He is called by his title, doctor. He has specialized training in testing human behavior and in making diagnostic reports, so he is frequently consulted by other psychotherapists to conduct tests of intelligence, personality, aptitudes, and vocational abilities of a patient and to provide a report about the strengths and weaknesses of the patient. If he is conducting a research project, the clinical psychologist may see patients of other psychotherapists in order to obtain research data.

The social worker who has studied social service as connected with mental health problems is referred to as a "psychiatric social worker"; training requires about the same number of years of university work and supervised clinical experience, but usually the psychiatric social worker has a Master's degree, not a Ph.D., because several years are spent in university training that is not focused on psychological matters. During these years of basic training, the psychiatric social worker learns specialized information about how particular groups of people live and becomes especially knowledgeable about the agencies available for help in such matters as providing financial support to needy people, providing medical care and vocational opportunities, and obtaining membership in church or recreational groups. The psychiatric social worker is often consulted for help in obtaining these kinds of assistance for a patient.

The psychiatrist, like all physicians, has completed four years of medical school after three or four years of college and has spent one year in general practice training during his hospital internship. Although the law of most states permits a physician to practice as a specialist in mental health problems without further training, usually the physician takes further supervised training courses as a resident in a hospital or clinic where he specializes in treating patients who have emotional and mental disturbances. In order to be certified as a specialist in psychiatry by a national medical board, he must complete three to five years of a psychiatric residency and also pass a comprehensive examination. By virtue of his medical license, the psychiatrist is permitted to prescribe drugs, and he is also able to take legal responsibility for hospitalizing a patient for severe emotional difficulties when this is necessary. If other kinds of psychotherapists think commitment is necessary, they always consult a psychiatrist. In practice, though he is qualified, the psychiatrist does not conduct physical examinations of his patients when he is a psychotherapist. Like the psychologist and the psychiatric social worker, he refers his patients to other physicians for medical care.

The three major mental health professions are alike in their common concern for the welfare of patients and in their common interest in mental health problems; but members of each profession are also alike in having particular viewpoints about personality and methods of treatment. These viewpoints, called theoretical orientations, often make for greater similarity between members of different professions than exists between members of the same profession who have different orientations. This is especially striking when a psychiatrist employing methods other than talk and thought is compared to a psychiatrist who uses only psychological methods.

If you know only that a therapist is a psychiatrist, you cannot determine without further information if he uses physical treatments like electroshock, neurosurgery, insulin coma, hydrotherapy, tranquilizers, or other drugs that influence mood and attitudes. (Be sure to check to ascertain that a person using these methods is medically licensed; *immediately leave* a therapist employing these methods who is not a fully licensed physician, and report him immediately to your State's Attorney, for he is breaking the law and may be dangerous.)

The different theoretical orientations of psychotherapists may concern you if you are intensely interested in obtaining treatment only from a specific kind of psychotherapist; you may also care to be able to label and describe your treatment to others. So it is helpful to know your way around the several terms that describe these orientations.

Any psychotherapist—whether psychiatrist, social worker, or clinical psychologist—who practices according to special techniques and theories of personality called "psychoanalytic" is called an "analyst" or is called a "psychoanalytically oriented psychotherapist." (Any good library usually has several excellent books that discuss the specific differences in the theory and treatment methods of the various psychoanalytic orientations developed by such important leaders as Freud, Adler, Jung, Rank, Horney, Sullivan, and Fromm. This book is based primarily on Freudian principles.) Some Freudian analysts see a patient several times a week for treatment sessions that mainly involve analyzing and interpreting the patient's dreams and free associations; these analysts are given a special name, "psychoanalyst," and the treatment is called "psychoanalysis." Other forms of treatment are frequently referred to either as "treatment" or as "psychoanalytically oriented psychotherapy."

Most analysts have had specialized training in analytic theory and technique and have experienced personal analytic treatment by trained analysts. Because training requirements are very extensive and time consuming, and because membership requirements are very exclusive, many excellent psychoanalytically oriented therapists may not be members of a formal training Institute or of one of the national psychoanalytic organizations. Thus, though membership practically guarantees that a given therapist is well trained and experienced in a particular psychoanalytic method, nonmembership is no proof of lack of equivalent training and experience; this is particularly true in those parts of the country where a local training Institute does not admit psychologists, social workers, educators, or any other professionals except psychiatrists for training. Ask a local member of The American Psychoanalytic Association, The National Psychological Association for Psychoanalysis, or The American Orthopsychiatric Association for a well-informed opinion about other local therapists who are not members and who claim they are analytically oriented.

Common to all analysts are basic ideas about how people behave and why. All the different theories hold that personality is molded mainly during infancy and childhood, that both healthy and neurotic attitudes are the product of early experience; each different theory has a unique view of what are the molding forces. All analytic theories agree, too, that neurotic conflicts are symbolized, so that a person has difficulty in thinking directly about how or why he is troubled neurotically. Thus, all analysts believe that symptoms and neurotic behavior must be interpreted and analyzed to be understood.

Because many childhood experiences must be remembered and interpreted, then related to other events and to present-day reality in the course of analytic treatment, treatment is usually a long, drawn-out procedure. It is also usually expensive when obtained on a private basis, because the analyst sees only a few patients a week, and he must insure his necessary income from a high hourly fee to allow for losses when a patient is absent on vacation or ill.

Aside from the analytic forms of psychotherapy, there are other, nonanalytical psychotherapies. The best known is based on methods and concepts originated by Dr. Carl Rogers; it is called Rogerian treatment, "client-centered therapy," and sometimes "nondirective therapy." Its methods and concepts differ radically from the analytic ones, particularly in the lessened emphasis upon the childhood origin of neurosis and upon the symbolism of neurotic complaints. In treatment, called "counseling," the patient, called "client," does not free associate to bring up childhood memories and does not interpret his dreams to understand symbolic meanings. Treatment is conducted as the counselor, assuming the frame of reference of the client, helps clarify the client's feelings by reflecting these back to the client. Sessions typically are less frequent and treatment goes on for fewer months or years. Training in client-centered therapy is conducted mainly in university departments of psychology. You can obtain referrals by asking help from your nearest university or by writing to the American Psychological Association. Either source will help you avoid becoming involved with a person who may have had some training in this form of treatment but who lacks other full professional qualifications.

## Checking on Your Choice

Wherever you go to obtain help, be sure to ascertain that professional standards of qualification are being met. Unfortunately, unethical practices in mental health care do occur—but only when patients fail to assume and discharge their responsibilities for insisting on learning whether or not a given therapist is operating ethically. You are being sensible and responsible, not out of line at all, in requesting that a therapist reassure you he is meeting his ethical obligations.

You can be reasonably confident that a therapist or facility is professionally responsible if you have obtained the referral from any of the professional organizations, for they have set at least minimal training requirements for their members and deny continued membership to anyone guilty of serious misconduct. If you use other sources of referral—advertisements, solicitations, or just picking a name out of the phone book—be certain to check with the national societies to see if a given therapist enjoys a good professional reputation.

All this may seem like a lot of trouble and concern, especially as you compare it to the relatively easy task of selecting a dentist or physician. But remember that it is not easy for you to determine progress in treatment aimed at solving complicated emotional problems; you have few psychological counterparts of a lingering toothache or rash to let you know that your illness is getting no better and the therapist is not helping you. Also, because state law typically does not license people in the mental health fields, quacks can open offices and present themselves as having professional qualifications, without incurring criminal liability. So you *must* resort to checking the credentials of a given therapist; if he is fully qualified, professionally, you can reasonably assume that he conducts himself in a responsible and ethical manner.

Remember that inadequate standards occasionally exist even within large institutions; poorly trained people and quacks do not confine their activities to private practice. So be sure to reassure yourself as to a particular therapist's training and credentials, even in a clinic. Of course, an unseasoned therapist in training can be doing excellent work even though he isn't fully professionally qualified; but you certainly have the right to know that he is a trainee, and you have an obligation to yourself to make sure that he is receiving appropriate supervision from others who are professionally qualified. Because all personnel in the mental health field are in heavy demand, you may occasionally find a good therapist, not yet professionally qualified, working without supervision; in this case, you often can reassure yourself about your treatment by asking for more information from the administrative authority of the center where he works, or by questioning him directly if he is in private practice. Every ethical therapist will willingly provide you with information about his education, training in therapy, affiliations, and other pertinent details. Your private physician is usually able to give you his professional opinion of a given therapist to whom you have been referred by another source.

You may also obtain help in arriving at a final decision by following the recommendation of a trusted friend or associate who has been in treatment. This is far from reliable because the judgment is usually highly subjective, but it may provide some valuable guideposts.

You can easily check on one therapist's opinion regarding the advisability of your entering treatment by consulting another therapist for his opinion. This requires several meetings with each therapist, but the added expense may be warranted if you gain reassurance.

In a city with many therapists, you can usually learn who is outstanding for his professional ability if you request referrals from three or four therapists picked at random from lists of those with full professional qualifications; usually, one or two names will be referred to by each of those whom you contact, and these are mainly the names of people with excellent, not just minimal, abilities.

If you are faced with a choice between no help at all or help from a person who does not meet full professional qualifications, request an advisory opinion from the appropriate professional organization listed at the beginning of this chapter. Write and explain your circumstances: the problems you are seeking help with, the source of your referral to a specific individual, the fee he is asking, how often he proposes to see you, and what he has said to you regarding methods and duration and outcome of treatment. If he is considered reputable, proceed into treatment without further qualms. If he is considered a charlatan, however, remember that you are more likely to get hurt than helped by consulting him. Inform your local medical society, State's Attorney, Better Business Bureau, or Mental Health Society; and have nothing more to do with the quack.

Do not let the fact that you are unhappy and emotionally disturbed shame you into silence about a charlatan. You are not just flying off the handle, neurotically, in notifying public authorities that a quack is operating; you are performing a public service. Remember, too, that a quack may have had some professional training; steer clear of the private practice therapist who is a psychologist, with or without a Ph.D., but who has not completed a two-year internship in clinical psychology; avoid the social worker who has no specific training in psychiatric social work and psychotherapy; do not consult for psychotherapy the medically trained person who has not taken at least a year's internship. Unless highly extraordinary circumstances have been present, most people without these experiences of minimum training are working ethically only under strictly supervised conditions in a clinic, hospital, or other treatment center agency.

In short, seek to locate a qualified therapist; usually he is a person with a deep and sincere belief and understanding of a widely accepted view of how people behave, what causes them to be unhappy, and how they may be aided in recovering good mental health. He can help you.

## Getting Maximum Benefit from Psychotherapy

To obtain maximum benefit from treatment, you must approach it fully willing to assume certain responsibilities, and be free of incorrect expectations that are easily picked up from television, moving pictures, or even friends who have had non-professional associations with psychotherapy. Although the helpful attitudes are eventually developed in competent treatment and the unhelpful attitudes are discarded, you can save yourself effort, time, and money by starting with the correct frame of mind.

Discard ideas that suggest the therapist has some magic means through which to clear up your neurotic difficulties quickly and without inconveniencing you. Even the therapists who use drugs and other quick-acting physical methods of treatment agree that these do not provide instantaneous cure—at best, their methods quickly work only to ameliorate some of the symptoms. Remember that it took years to develop your neurotic conflicts during your childhood, and it has taken years of steady practice to develop your adult neurotic attitudes and ways of behaving. Changing all this is unlikely to be accomplished in less than many months or several years. The talk and thought involved in psychotherapy take time.

Another misconception you must discard is the idea that your therapist knows all about you, but is waiting for you to learn some vital facts that then will magically remove your neurosis. Your therapist probably knows a lot about other people who have been his patients; he probably knows a lot about patients discussed in the professional literature; and he probably has some reasonable ideas about what your problems are connected to. But no one can know more about you than you do yourself. All your therapist's knowledge is but sheer guess and speculation applied to you until you confirm it by your reactions. And no single event has created or can destroy your neurosis; you are wasting your time if you try to placate and please your therapist so that he will give you

hints about where to discover the source of your misery. He
cannot. Treatment is a consistent, steady practice at being
thoughtful and reasonable, at governing your actions by realistic
evaluations.

Be sure, too, to get rid of notions that your therapist is engaged
with you in a series of lessons, advisory sessions, or indoctrination
lectures. He is not trying to instruct you in particular terminology
and theoretical concepts, to convince you that his form of treatment is the only good method. He is not trying to convince you
of anything except the fact that you can understand yourself and
control your actions. So do not waste time arguing about concepts
of psychotherapy; if you are seriously interested in psychology
as such, enroll in an academic course and argue with your professor.

Because your therapist cannot know you or your objective
circumstances and inner reactions better than you do, he cannot
provide meaningful advice to you about how to live your life,
how to meet a crisis, or how to carry out your day-by-day
routine. He can only call your attention to special aspects of your
situation and to possible alternative ways of acting. He can only
analyze with you the tensions you are releasing unconstructively
in acting-out behavior. He can only discuss decisions with you
before you take action on them. At times, he can only provide
you the comfort that comes from knowing that he is there for you
to go to when you may feel that no one else is willing to listen to
you. But always—before, during, and after treatment—your
life is yours to lead. You are responsible for yourself and your
decisions, no matter how neurotic the problems or how com-
pelling the neurotic pressures; only if you are so incapable of daily
functioning with this personal responsibility that you require confinement to a hospital or commitment to a sanitarium can you expect other people to take over the task of directing your life.

Along with discarding expectations that your therapist will
take charge of your life, discard notions that being in treatment
permits you to do neurotic things without suffering the consequences. You have no guarantee that the decisions you make
while in treatment are all wise and leading to success. If you make
mistakes and if you act out while you are in treatment, you are

Lincoln Christian College

just as likely to suffer as when you acted this way before starting treatment.

Many therapists believe that almost every patient, in the neurotic part of his personality, does not really want to get well. This neurotic self is believed to develop all sorts of expectations of magical relief and misconceptions about treatment in its effort to resist treatment. Of course, if this neurotic self continues to dominate long after treatment has started, your therapist is ethically bound to inform you that treatment with him at the moment is a waste of time, money, and effort. If you are going to derive benefit from treatment, and if you are to be permitted to continue in treatment, you must strive to control and eventually undermine your neurotic self.

However dominant may be the neurotic part of you, keep in mind that you also have a healthy self. And remember that the healthy part of you wants all of you to become healthy, so that all of you can be creating happiness for yourself. This healthy self has ideas, too; its ideas are likely to be ones that aid the course of treatment. So emphasize your correct expectations. Continually reassure yourself that it is possible to solve your problems, but it takes work and time, patience and tolerance, self-control, honesty and intelligence, the willingness to suspend judgment, and just plain guts and gumption. You have these qualities, however submerged they may be by neurotic mannerisms and inhibitions; you must draw upon them and permit your therapist to summon them. Therapy does not develop new drives or talents where their seeds were not present before treatment, but it does help you bring into play your strengths and resources. Wanting to become healthy, working with the skillful help of a competent professional mental health expert, you can overcome your neurotic tendencies.

## Other Sources of Help

In addition to the formal psychotherapy and psychiatric care described so far, many other sources of help exist that you may use in your search to make your life less troubled by neurotic difficulties.

Religious leaders, always concerned with how man conducts his life here on earth and usually sympathetic toward human misery, often can provide emotional support and advice to a troubled person. A religious leader with special training in the clinical approach to human problems is also usually able to provide referrals if highly specialized types of aid are required.

Teachers and educators, too, often have special training and skill in providing objective, but sympathetic, help for many emotional problems, particularly those that involve a child's capacity to learn. It is especially helpful to consult with your child's teacher if your unsettled home conditions and your emotional reactions are causing learning difficulties—if for nothing else but to let the teacher know you are trying to get matters cleared up, and you appreciate her efforts, too. Often, feeling less beleaguered and alone because you have shared your situation, in part, with her, you may find some problems easier to handle.

Because he has long had to be an expert in many facets of human behavior, and because he probably has his expert understanding of certain facets of your reality situation that constitute significant pressures in your life, your lawyer is also helpful in providing counsel and emotional support.

Special groups often become organized to deal with a special common problem. Your local YMCA or Community Referral Service can help you locate groups that meet to discuss alcoholism, obesity, mental illness, or being a single parent. Many groups organized to discuss single parenthood have formed a single national organization, and its headquarters can be contacted for information and guidance in joining or organizing your own local group. Its address is:

Parents Without Partners, Inc.
80 Fifth Avenue
New York, New York

Most communities maintain numerous agencies that deal with the welfare of single mothers or their dependent children. Government-sponsored and private agencies can be located by inquiring of your local Community Chest or United Fund office. You can be sure of a sympathetic reception and a helpful orientation toward your problems in obtaining financial support, low-cost housing, housekeeping help, psychotherapy, or legal aid. In many cities, the easiest way to obtain excellent psychotherapy referrals is by initial contact with a welfare agency.

All in all, help for you with your problems is at hand; almost no community is so limited in its resources that it cannot provide help to you through one means or another. You need not feel alone. By using the assistance that your community provides, you can solve your reality and your personality problems. You can equip yourself to repay your community by giving to it the foundation stones on which the welfare of this democratic society exists: healthy, useful, mature citizens—you and your child.

# Your Child

Your Child

# CHAPTER EIGHT

# Childhood Development

PART Two is a brief review, not of ways to take care of a child, but of the underlying principles involved in childhood development that dictate certain methods. With a clear picture in mind of these basic concepts about childhood development, you can best understand the adjustments you must make in order to raise your child in a fatherless home.

Your child, just like you, needs to have freedom to develop, freedom to express and gain satisfaction for certain psychological and biological needs, or else, again like you, he must develop negative feelings of frustration and anxiety about himself and about the world and life in general.

Unlike you, however, he does not have a full complement of these needs; as a child, he only has some, not all, of the psychological and biological needs. They will develop as he develops; he does not begin life equipped with all of them.

The psychological needs that you were concerned with in your analysis of yourself through Part One of this book are all characteristic human needs. Inevitably, whatever you may do with your child, he grows and develops these same needs. His psychological and physical attributes emerge as he ripens inside, whether or not they have been stimulated, whether or not he has been protected from his mistakes while he practices a new personality factor, and whether or not he has been consoled for the pains he suffers as he learns. Willy-nilly, your child is going to grow up as a human being with certain psychological needs and certain physical capabilities because of the simple fact that he *is* a human being. Unless a child is a freak or a monster, and thereby not quite human, he is bound by his very nature to develop certain characteristic human traits.

Your expectations of your child and of yourself in relation to him must be geared to his development; and you can most confidently view his development if you pay attention, first of all, to what he is able to do physically, for your child grows and develops as a whole person, his mind and his body grow and develop together. As his body becomes capable of certain actions, the way he thinks and feels about himself and about the world—his mind or personality—reflects these same ways of approaching the world. There is a steady progression from his earliest infancy, when his body can do only a few things and when he has a highly limited attitude toward the world around him, to his adulthood, when his body has developed fully and when his personality reflects all the needs and attitudes that you or other adults have. By noting his physical growth, therefore, you learn something of great importance regarding your child's psychological growth. The course of development of the body and of psychological needs is called *psychobiological development*. Chapter Nine reviews the psychobiological development of a child in an ordinary complete family.

Since there are some body changes like crawling or walking that are dramatic and obvious, it is easy to classify body growth and development into a number of stages. And since these alterations in his physical capabilities usher in altered psychological attitudes and needs, the whole psychobiological development process can be referred to by terms that suggest these stages.

By seeing your child as a person who, through his increasing ability to get around and test things for himself, is able to learn about larger and larger bits of reality, you can figure out for yourself what he can think and feel, what his attitudes are, what he wants, needs, and fears. The psychological terms that label the stages of his development can be an easy shorthand for you, calling your attention to the one or two paramount needs that develop in association with your child's physical growth and maturation. (Additionally, they are terms used in many psychological works about children; thus broadening your reading is easier once these terms are understood and remembered.) In Chapter Nine, the terms used by psychologists for these stages are presented along with the discussion of the usual time in life when these changes take place.

As an alert parent, you are unlikely to have difficulty in recognizing most of the important physical changes that occur during the first few months of life and during the early part of adolescence. Other significant changes, however, not so gross or dramatic because they are mainly inner changes and maturation of nerves and muscles, must also be kept in mind, so that you may be alert to their emergence as well.

The idea that there is a totality of development and that it takes place through quite definite stages removes a great deal of the mystery from a child's development. In the light of this knowledge, your child can become an understandable person to you; and you can be confident at any time about what in him you must stimulate, what you must protect him from, what you must provide him freedom for, and what you can expect from him during his development.

Of course it would not be important to know how physical and psychological developments take place and influence each other if childhood had little lasting effect upon adulthood. In that case, a child might very well suffer throughout his childhood and still emerge as a healthy adult. But as you remember from the discussion about your own psychological needs, the way a person feels and thinks about the world and himself is based on the experiences he has already had in thinking and feeling.

Wherever a child grows up, he spends his few years between birth and adulthood learning certain attitudes:

First of all, he learns in characteristically human ways at different stages of his development about the *reality* within and about him. He learns that objects exist outside of him, he learns who he is and what he is like, and he learns about his parents and other people.

At the same time, he becomes aware of *responsibilities* connected to these realities. There is no set way for all people in all places—depending on where a child grows up, he learns various ways of assuming and discharging his responsibilities for himself, for his parents, or for society at large; but learn something during childhood about his effect on others he must.

At the same time, he learns in a characteristically human way what is *painful* and what is *pleasant* in his own experience of reality, especially the intimate reality of his own body. These pleasures and attitudes about pleasure can be construed either as nonsexual or as sexual, depending on the situation to which they are applied. Remember that in the context of a child's growth, they are not sexual in the adult sense; but in the context of final adulthood, they are the basis of regard for sexuality and love of other adults.

The ways in which he develops in relation to these realities result in his ability, as an adult, to work and to love in certain ways. For any individual, these are going to be unique because his experience is unique; but each adult has developed, during his childhood, some attitude about reality, about responsibility, and about sexuality. These are the universal results of childhood development.

Moreover, in *each* stage of childhood, successively, your child learns *different* attitudes about reality, about responsibility, and about sexuality. And since each stage is influenced by the preceding stages, what he learns and how he learns is a final product of all that he has learned and of all the ways used to learn. The material care you provide him with, the protection and stimulation you give, and the freedom you supply all shape his final sense of responsibility and his attitudes toward reality and sexuality.

Each parent plays a *role* in influencing the child. And whatever the culture or society may be, the fundamental biological differences between a man and a woman shape the roles each plays. While going through his various stages of physical and personality development, a child not only learns his inner feelings and attitudes about reality, responsibility, and sexuality, but also learns about the external ways of showing these feelings—he learns the roles played by men and women. You are important because you provide the first pattern for one role, that of the woman.

You have seen how there is a balance between the inner forces that push toward development of new skills in the body and personality and the outer forces of the environment that influence, shape, and limit the inner developments. The final balance achieved is the person's individuality. If only inner forces were supreme, each human would be in most respects like every other human; if only external forces were supreme, there could be no such thing as "human nature"—people in a similar external psychological climate would all be alike, but would differ totally from people in different climates.

Here, finally, is the bedrock of your importance as a parent. If inner forces alone were all that mattered, all that influenced the health of your child, you would not need to be a "good" parent. Parenthood would be nothing but a custodial function. You would merely be keeping alive a child whose ultimate personality would be immune to your influence. The only differences between your child and all other persons would be the differences caused, once and for all, by the blending and mixing of genes at the moment of his conception.

On the other hand, if external climate were all that mattered, you still would not need to be a "good" parent. You could, absolutely and omnipotently, create a person to fit your desires and change at will this creature made by you from the raw clay of your child. If you wanted to, you could make a child devoid of one or more of the human characteristics and needs. What you did with him in the past would not influence what you could do with him in the future, and there would be no limit to what you could do.

Obviously, these extremes are not valid. Your child's physical and personality characteristics develop from within him because of his inherited human nature and because of his special characteristics as the child of his parents' mixed genes. And his final nature is greatly determined by the ways he has learned to express himself—ways influenced by you and by the whole setting in which the two of you live. Thus, your importance lies in what you do with him.

Because human beings cannot be hurt and twisted without leaving after effects, you must be a good parent in order to prevent the development of such after effects. There is a limit to what you can do, either for good or for bad, but there is a minimum of what you must do as you help your child grow and develop healthily. You play a vital role in creating the unique individuality of your child, influencing him to later function as a useful member of his adult society, working productively, taking care of himself, and contributing to society by caring for his own family or other people.

Your functions as a parent are, first of all, to provide *care* and the *setting* in which your child learns how to satisfy safely his needs for relief of the body tensions concerned with hunger for food, water, and oxygen, with need to eliminate wastes, with sexuality and activity drives. You also permit him *freedom* to develop and practice the skills that are part of his physical and psychological development. This freedom includes allowing him privacy with regard to his physical needs.

You also provide *stimulation*. This does not mean pushing or forcing a particular skill, but rather, stimulating the little awarenesses and small coordinations that eventually blossom into a full, new skill that develops as his internal organization is ripe for it. Most of the time, you provide this form of stimulation by supplying toys and time and privacy to your child, for your child grows and develops as he plays. By playing, he exercises his newly developed skills, and he strengthens and coordinates all he has learned beforehand. Most of the time, you need not train or teach him how to use his time and privacy; such training only distorts the emerging activity. You merely get him going.

But when he has practiced a new activity thoroughly, and it has become well stabilized, you need to step in and provide the *guides* and *disciplines* that keep his freedom of activity from degenerating into license to act irresponsibly, run wild, and get himself into trouble. You can recognize the time to go ahead by watching to see when his play stops being concerned with a given activity. As long as he is still actively working to establish and integrate some skill, his play will center around it. As you stimulate your child to operate within certain limits, you are performing another function of a parent: assigning certain responsibilities to him. Usually, whenever he assumes a responsibility in this way, he also is assured additional authority for himself, so that his overall freedom is not seriously curtailed.

You also enlarge his freedom by performing the important task of *protecting* him and keeping him from hurting himself or from being hurt. This is especially true when you keep him from being hurt because he is childishly unrealistic and sees the world mainly in terms of his own needs. As you tell him the truth about life and stimulate him to take a steady look at reality, instead of only at his own fantasies about reality, you give him a bigger and less confusing world to live in. His unrealistic notions change as he changes—as the following chapter points out in detail—so by noticing his physical development, you can determine which unrealistic ideas he is likely to have at a given time. Accordingly, you can make sure that you correct his wrong impressions. You can also be sure that you do not, even in fun or games, substantiate his unrealistic fears that someone may suffocate or starve him, tie him up, shut him away from the noise and light of everyday life, tear him apart, eat him up, pound him to a pulp, or in any other way hurt him in the ways he childishly wishes he might hurt others when he is angry. By protecting him from games that involve these threats until his own spontaneous play indicates that he is well past a particular fear, you permit him to sort out his dream world from reality. His reality, therefore, enlarges.

In performing these important tasks, some of your spontaneity is interfered with. This is especially true whenever your inner motivations lead you occasionally to want to forget about stimulating his development, to stop protecting him from misconceptions or other harms, or to cease providing him necessary freedoms and privacies. But in return for governing your actions and making sure that you do not pass along to him your fears or other attitudes, you can enjoy watching him grow up free of the vulnerabilities and difficulties that you may suffer from yourself.

In the unique ways that you provide material care, protection, stimulation, and freedom to your child, you are enabling him to unfold his inherent individual characteristics. As his mother, you can thereby obtain the great joy of discovery, the fun of seeing how this new creature that was born with a unique constitution becomes a person.

Not only is your activity itself a great determinant of his personality, in the way that this activity influences matters of freedom, protection, and stimulation, but it also provides a model along which he can pattern himself. He learns most easily to do things by copying you, assuming that he has no inner conflict about what you are doing and assuming, also, that he actually can manage to copy you, given his immature body and lack of experience. So when he sees you as a person who is loving, responsible, active, and who enjoys life, he can easily follow this excellent example.

Thus, through your control over your actions, through your thoughtful attention to providing him the necessary guides and help he needs, you help your child grow up. As you see him playing zestfully and joyfully, you can relax and be certain that you have not dulled and deadened his individuality.

For specific details of good methods of providing material care, protection, stimulation, and freedom to your child, consult the following books:

*The Intelligent Parents' Guide to Raising Children,* Eve Jones, The Free Press of Glencoe, New York, 1959.

*Infant and Child in the Culture of Today,* Arnold Gesell and Frances L. Ilg, Harper and Brothers, New York, 1943.

*The Common Sense Book of Baby and Child Care,* Benjamin Spock, Pocket Books, Inc., New York, 1946.

These books also contain full discussions of what a child in a complete home typically learns about reality, responsibilities, sexuality, and adult roles as he develops physically and receives appropriate care.

Your expectations of the typical physical and personality development of a child in an ordinary complete family serve as background for you in your activities. With a clear idea of what he can do, what he is thinking and feeling, you can set about taking care of your child's needs and satisfying them so that he can continue to grow and develop healthily. To spare you the necessity of consulting other books for these expectations, the following chapter contains a review of the usual child's physical development and the concomitant development of reality, responsibility, sexuality, and adult roles.

# CHAPTER NINE

# Physical Development and Reality, Responsibility, and Sexuality

### Early Infancy—The First Few Months of Life

THE EARLIEST PHYSICAL CHANGES are usually taken so much for granted that they sometimes escape mention. These are the changes seen during the first few weeks of life, as the newborn infant gradually ceases to be a highly withdrawn, yet relatively irritable, unstable, and unpredictable baby and slowly becomes more relaxed, alert, and regular.

Essentially, his psychological attitude changes from being erratic, irritable, and withdrawn, to being passively receptive. The psychologist calls the withdrawn attitude *autistic,* and the passive, receptive attitude *oral-dependent.*

During the autistic stage, the infant has no sense of reality except as it is an intrusion on him; he is vulnerable to all stimuli; he needs protection from all unusual stimuli. The only thing he can do, in self-protection, is go back to sleep or thrash around and cry. He has no capacity for responsibility to himself or others except to withdraw in order to preserve himself from further pain. Pleasure is associated with the absence of any stimuli—he is happiest when sound asleep.

As the body rhythms become steadier, he relaxes in his dependency. Mainly, the reality he acknowledges is how he himself feels. Reality stops being something he must withdraw from; he begins to relax and accept it, staying awake and enjoying, apparently, the way he feels when he is full and warm and being rocked.

Gradually he begins to show a dim awareness of those around him who provide him with loving care, and he learns to trust them. As an oral-dependent infant, he regards his ever-enlarging world in the same way he regards himself—as good and satisfying. He develops emotions that adults identify as faith, hope, trust, and optimism.

Some fundamental accepting attitudes about responsibility and authority are developing, too, as he lets himself be cared for. In adulthood, this same attitude is reflected when a person trustfully and willingly lets experts take over their responsibilities, or when a person works cooperatively with a group. Without the attitudes about responsibility that develop during these first few months of life, the adult must attempt to do everything for himself and by himself; tense and unwilling to rely on anyone, he must strive, unrealistically, to be totally self-sufficient.

As the infant learns to relax, he responds selectively, accepting those things that bring him pleasure, paying little or no attention to minor discomforts or irritations. He is developing attitudes that the adult identifies with being relaxed, carefree, and spontaneously enjoying of the act of love-making.

During these earliest months of life, a father's relationship to his child is essentially the same as the mother's. He occasionally provides feedings and diaperings and cuddling, but his child shows little awareness, at first, of the father as distinguished from the mother. There is almost no emotional tie to the father. The father is mainly a help and an emotional support only to his wife. The close tie that existed before birth between the mother and her child is not abruptly severed with birth; instead, the mother immerses herself in her baby and his needs, and she is more mother than wife. The sharing that typifies marriages is concerned with the baby, so that the father is drawn into the mother-child relationship, rather than existing outside of it.

To the extent that the infant differentiates father from mother, he learns only that both people can be tender and loving; he extends trust to both. Later, as an adult, this development enables him to enjoy the tenderness of love and to extend it; he need not operate according to a mistaken concept that men are gruff, tough, and indifferent to pain or suffering. As an oral-dependent infant, therefore, he is learning how to express dependency as an adult by caring for others in need. He is developing an understanding of the succoring attitude.

## *Later Infancy—The First and Second Years of Life*

As his capacity to receive becomes stronger and more stable, another growth process results in a new kind of development: he begins to be able to exercise his muscles and senses in smooth coordination with each other, and he learns to move around. His increasing muscular strength and control combine with his increasing ability to perceive and sense, and the net result is that he becomes a coordinated and mobile person. Not only can he notice things and get to them, but he can recall them in their appropriate connections, thus he can remember a flavor, remember its connection with appearance, and, when some distasteful food is presented to him, he can refuse to take it.

He goes from sucking to biting and chewing; whenever possible, he puts all new things into his mouth to learn what they are like. He weans himself and impatiently tries to gulp huge swallows of liquid quickly so that he can get back to moving about again. Because so much of his physical activity centers around his mouth, he is still called oral by psychologists; but since his orality is expressed through so much aggressive muscular activity, it is called the *oral-aggressive* stage of development.

During this time, he is developing attitudes of independence, creativity, curiosity, persistence, and enthusiasm as he goes around his world and finds out how delightful it is. As each new stimulus from reality is discovered and investigated, he develops ideas about the safety and enjoyment of newness. He confidently trusts himself to explore this new and ever-expanding world. His over-all sense of reality expands; it now includes real people outside himself. He becomes, in many basic ways, a person—and a highly realistic person who judges things on the basis of whether or not they are directly pleasurable to him.

Combined with his attitude about reality around him, a new feeling about himself develops, a notion about himself that is much larger than the earlier engrossment in how his stomach or skin felt. Just as he formerly was stimulated and protected by his parents, he now feels stimulated and protected by himself. He becomes self-conscious, but in a pleasurable, approving way. His feelings of trust and optimism expand into feelings of general worthiness as he learns that those nice people who take good care of him, his parents, provide him with such an interesting world and seem to like it as much as he does.

He can tolerate some delays in gratification and even occasional unpleasantness if he is receiving plenty of loving attention at the same time. His tolerance for frustration mirrors his physical capacity to tolerate greater effort—both are accomplished as both bring more pleasures to him. He becomes more realistically responsive, and he also becomes eagerly responsible for himself. He feeds himself, grabs the washcloth to wash himself, plays by himself, and frequently delights himself. During his second year, he even tries to give to his parents some of the good things he cherishes, thereby showing that he has assumed a basic responsibility for caring for others. The adult attitudes of feeling kinship with others and affection for others have their roots in these loving attitudes developed during this oral-aggressive period. He feels good about being good, for he is praised and loved; seeking this feeling, he continues into adulthood to be good, to be courteous, to be considerate of others.

By the close of his second year, his curiosity is still strong, as is his enthusiasm, and his feeling of responsibility for himself and to others is reinforced.

His capacity to tolerate delay and to enjoy variety and change contributes to his enthusiasm and feeling of elation—feelings that later accompany adult sexuality and serve as the foundation of feeling refreshed by adult sexual experience. The concomitant feeling he develops as a child of being worthwhile and good when he provides stimulation to his parents or other adults is also later a part of sexualized desire to give pleasure to his loved one as he himself desires to obtain pleasure. As a child, he learns to identify with his beloved ones, and he truly, thereby, becomes able to join in the acts of love: generosity in childhood, sympathy in adulthood.

The father, when this rush of activity starts, begins to reclaim his wife for himself. She is no longer upset by the aftermath of giving birth; her sleep schedule is uninterrupted as her child sleeps through the night; her diet is not restricted because of lactation; she can participate safely in sexual intercourse. So she loosens her ties to her child and participates actively with her husband in a life less limited than the life primarily as a mother that she has led for the first several months after giving birth.

Thus the early indications shown by the child of increasing desire for independence are reflected, sustained, and supported by the parents.

The child, better able to distinguish people around him, regards his father as a person separate from the things his father does for him. Daddy no longer exists only as another person who feeds or diapers him. A "daddy-feeding" is recognized as different from a "mommy-feeding," and gradually, a daddy himself becomes a different person from a mommy. The same attitude of trust and acceptance is extended to him, because the same care and attention is received from him; so the final result is that the existence of at least two different people is recognized by the child, and each can be trusted and identified with. Father, with his special likes, dislikes, and ways of doing things, is a person who can be copied just as mother can. The child can appreciate more than just one way of doing things.

He develops ideas about women, ideas connected to sitting and waiting for things to get accomplished, as he watches his mother assemble all sorts of materials, put them together into a pan in the oven, and then remove a cake that in no way resembles the separate things she put into it. He develops ideas about men, ideas connected to making recognizable components into something useful, as he watches his father cut boards and nail them together to make a bookcase. But he also learns, as he sees his parents take turns helping each other, that maleness is more than just bookcase-making and femaleness is not just mysterious cooking. Simultaneously, he learns to respect different standards. He observes that his father expects different things from a steak than his mother expects, and he observes that his mother expects different things from a bookcase than does his father. The more he learns about such flexibility, about the steady give-and-take of family living, the more confidence he develops in himself. He imitates his parents in their separateness, and he almost begins to own them inside himself because he has copied them. So he can relax and permit them greater independence from him, for he is linked to them in his memory, even when they are absent. His inner reality is expanded; now he is almost three people at once, not just one.

He can rely on both of his parents and on himself as he seeks encouragement for daring independence or finds comfort in relaxed dependency. He need not rely on the old dependencies that are boring and stifling to his adventurer's spirit; he need not give up altogether his old refuges while eagerly approaching new challenges. He emerges from the oral-aggressive period, therefore, aware that things change, sure that he can learn to understand or know the new things, but also sure that he can count on some of the old tried-and-true relationships.

## *The Third, Fourth, and Fifth Years of Life*

At about the time of the child's second birthday, two extremely important inner changes occur that permit him forever to remove himself from the characteristic confines of his babyhood: the nerves that control all the tiny, complex muscles involved in talking mature, as do other nerves that control the muscles of his anal and bladder sphincters. Consequently, he can begin to talk intelligibly and let people know, not just what he wants, but how he feels. He can also deliberately release urine and feces and keep from soiling himself reflexively.

His size and strength increase, too, and so does muscular coordination. He can be vigorously active; he can run, he can climb, he can strike. He can put his body to use for release of tension and for gaining pleasure in release. He does not tire easily, he does not throw himself off balance when he moves quickly; combined, his increased strength and endurance and coordination enable him to use his body aggressively without hurting himself in the process.

His memory, too, increases because of inner maturation of nerve coordination. He can keep ideas in his mind for respectable periods of time, easily learning the names of things and developing notions of what to expect. He can even remember things that have no special meaning to him, so a part of his mind can auto-matically lay away for future use information about what is currently happening to him and around him.

This whole period of life is bound up in the physical acts of controlling forceful, aggressive activity. So psychologists have termed part of it the *anal-aggressive* period, also called the *anal-active* period, the *anal-destructive* period, or the *anal-expulsive* period. All these terms, used more or less synonymously, refer to the fact that the period starts with the physical capacity to expel feces voluntarily. But more than mere forceful expulsion is bound up in the anal function of defecating; the child also must be able to withstand some amount of distention in his bowel prior to the time he voluntarily releases bowel control. As he grows older, as he passes his third birthday, his capacity to withstand other tensions, as well, increases significantly—enough for psychologists to refer to this time of life as the *anal-conservative* period, also called the *anal-passive* period, the *anal-constructive* period, or the *anal-retentive* period.

There is no strict demarcation between one period and another, especially since first one muscle system and then another comes under deliberate, voluntary control. For example, the body control that is shown at one time by his being able to jump up and down without overbalancing himself—an expulsive function—develops into the kind of control that enables him to sit still when asked to—a conservative function. By the time he is a four-year-old, he gets so skilled in turning his activity on and off that he can even participate in games like grey goose or button-button, instantly responding to his cue to jump up, instantly calming himself down again.

The reality he lives in becomes a reality of strength, of control, of impediment, of tension. In the earlier stages of his development, he viewed reality first as disturbing or calming, then as good or bad, and then as old-simple or new-complex. Now he regards reality as either permissive and weak or restrictive and strong. Accordingly, he views himself with regard to the reality he finds around him. If he can be active with regard to it, if it cannot stop him in his tracks, then he sees himself as strong and good. By contrast, if his inner impulses are interfered with by the external reality, he sees himself as weak and vulnerable.

As he learns more about how people control him and control their own reactions, he learns about the reality connected with dominating and being an authority. He assumes authority over himself. He learns about abstract rules and regulations. He learns to give and take, to respect the rights of others as he himself wants his rights to be respected. He learns to keep others from hurting him by keeping himself from hurting them. He feels courage and self-confidence as he handles opposition and his own impulses. And as he gradually expands his self-control and bargains it for opportunities to release his tensions, he feels fair-minded, just, and law-abiding.

Almost all the concrete reality about him can be explored and understood; a large measure of the kind of sense of realism that is concrete and practical in nature emerges during this period and stays with him throughout life.

He can talk, so he can say how he feels instead of needing to express himself with his body. When tense and angry, he can shout and let everyone know he dislikes something; he does not need to thrash around and cry as he did when he was still a baby. He can try to destroy something that bothers him, and often succeed. He can run away from something that scares him.

Identified with his parents, he uses his strength to protect them, at times even curbing his own anger in order to promote their comfort, at other times putting his strength to work in performing chores for them. Out of his emerging sense of duty, his feeling that he owes something to the people he cares about lovingly, and because his self-control enables him to sustain tension within himself, he can even perform distasteful tasks.

Related to his adult capacity to enjoy mounting sexual excitement and release, confidently and without fear of loss of control, is the pleasure he feels when he is able to release tension vigorously and when he is able to sustain mounting tension, sure that he can release it suddenly when necessary. As an adult, relying on his identification with his loved one, fearlessly using his strength to protect while exciting himself and his partner, he can confidently make love.

Father, like mother, consistently disciplines or limits the child to protect him from harm or to keep him from harming his parents or others, and the child recognizes his father's authority in much the same way that he recognizes his mother's. But the father's role as an authority gradually becomes genuinely different from the mother's role, not because they are asking different things of the child, but because their ties to the child are different. The mother is with the child more of the time; she provides more of his care; she is easier for him to identify with. And so he can more easily temper his own impulses, because he trades some tension or discomfort within him for the pleasurable opportunity to please her, the person he is closely identified with.

His father, though, more separated from him, is seen more objectively and reacted to more abstractly. Following his rules still requires tempering impulses, but the child must derive pleasure mainly out of the knowledge that he can control himself. Less pleasure is available to him on the basis of pleasing the part of him that resembles his father, for less of him is identified with his father.

The father's authoritative role, therefore, is less connected to personalized needs in the child; but it is not less effective, for the very forces that tend to make the father more abstract also work to keep the child from feeling much need to rebel against the father's authority. The father is *not* around much of the day, limiting, reminding, almost nagging; so the child can more easily accept the few limits his father places on him. The father, too, typically provides greater opportunities for letting off steam in vigorous activity and for releasing tensions that might otherwise force the child to lose control over his impulses while he obeys an order.

There is less of this differentiation of authority roles now than formerly, because today's fathers spend more time in the family circle since the work day has become shorter, and because today's fathers so frequently provide the same kinds of care that once were only woman's work. Thus, the authority represented by the modern father is not the distant, stern authority that characterized the Victorian papa. Typically, it was the Victorian father who punished and the mother who bribed. But, because modern parents have wisely given up threats of punishment or promises of rewards in order to gain obedience, the child is saved from regarding the father's authority with fear and the mother's authority with opportunism.

Still, until both parents behave identically with the child, he must continue to view their roles as authorities with different emotions. Mother's authority is related to his feeling good and loving himself; father's authority is related to his feeling strong and respecting himself. In later life, these two ways of regarding authority persist and enable him to be different in his own assumption of authority and to respect each kind of authority and believe they are compatible with ordinary reality.

In the female way, he can be merciful, make allowances for good intentions, and be tactful and forgiving with people who are close, emotionally, to him. In the male way, he can be just and consistent, give credit where credit is due, and be straightforward and practical in his relationships with people who are not especially close to him. Most of the attitudes that mark the healthy school child and the responsible, civilized adult are developed during these crowded few years. Though still little, he changes during this time from a baby into very much a "real" person.

## The Fifth and Sixth Years

In contrast to all other stages of development, the physical changes that usher in the development usual during the last of the fifth and during the sixth years are not well distinguished; they have not been a focus of much scientific inquiry; consequently, little about the biological changes is known definitely.

The changes in the child's behavior and attitudes, however, are strikingly apparent and have been the object of much study. Psychologists have concluded that these altered psychological reactions indicate that there is some new or relatively increased tension and sensitivity in the area of the genitals. Whatever the basic cause of it may be, the new concentration of body sensation in the genital area is the major change; accordingly, this period is called the *phallic* period of development (phallus is an anatomical term for the penis and the clitoris, the only organs in the genitals that are biologically functional at this age).

Accompanying this heightened sensitivity is another new capacity, mainly of the brain: the capacity for creative thinking. The child can imagine. He can really think for himself, instead of merely remembering and collecting ideas and impressions from others, analyzing them, and arriving at conclusions. After spending all the previous years learning to recognize and understand reality, he is now able to leave reality, to play with reality, to dream up his own worlds that are not just child-sized replicas of the adult world he sees about him.

With his imagination now definitely taking the lead, he can go beyond merely responding to his body's needs; he can also stimulate desires, appetites, and wants within himself. Thus, he is able to control, in part, his own future reactions by taking care of probable needs in advance. For example, although he may not feel any genuine bladder tension, he can remember times in the past when he was uncomfortable during an automobile ride because he needed to urinate; in his thoughts he can represent the desire to urinate so intensely that, even though his bladder is not completely full, he can still urinate before leaving the house.

His imagination also permits him to extend his own feeling of control over himself by letting him escape from reality after the fact. After he has run into some limitation of his own and has had to take a back seat to reality, rather than striving to integrate his defeat by identifying with the reality forces, he instead removes himself from the defeat by dreaming it all over, but this time conquering the problem. He substitutes fiction for fact; usually, he substitutes activities he is confident he can carry out for the activities he will not be able to carry out until he is older and bigger. If he cannot ride a two-wheel bicycle, for example, he does not pretend he is a bike; he goes off in dreams of glory, instead.

As he combines his capacity to imagine the future with his capacity to imagine that he is like other people, particularly his parents, his fantasies frequently cause actual difficulties for him. His planning stimulates him to try to behave as if he were thoroughly capable of putting his borrowed, identified-with, imitated characteristics into real, productive action. And since he does not truly have all the skills that his parents have, he provokes defeat for himself. This brings back the necessity of saving face by substitutions and rationalizations. The net result is that he tends to become increasingly wrapped up in the world of his own imagination; his approach to reality becomes less concrete and more abstract.

This altered approach to reality stimulates him to feel great pride in himself when he dares and does. He assumes extra responsibilities for himself and for others. Not only is he capable of following rules and regulations in cooperation with others, but he is now independent enough to establish some of his own, as, for example, when in his play with friends, he proudly announces the rules of a game he has just created.

However, his major new stable attitudes, both with regard to reality and to responsibility, do not emerge at the beginning of this phallic period of development. Instead, they are the final results of experiences connected to increased tensions and sensitivity in his phallic area.

His capacity to imagine plays a great role in determining these experiences. Engrossed in phallic exploration and manipulation because of the heightened phallic tension and sensitivity, he automatically creates simultaneous fantasies and dreams up situations in which he and his penis are involved. These fantasies are populated with the authority figures who are most closely identified with his parents. Since his attitudes about phallic sexuality develop as his fantasies develop, these attitudes and the entire period of development are often called *Oedipal*, after the Greek tragic myth of a child-father-mother triangle. (Because one of the problems your child must endure owing to the absence of his father is connected to the Oedipal development, the following discussion is in great detail, clearly indicating the many ways in which a father is required at this time.)

Both the boy and girl, at the beginning of this period, show the same increase in phallic tension, the same attempt to reduce this tension by masturbation, and the same accompaniment to masturbation by fantasies. Both also dream at first of similar situations in which the mother is providing sexual stimulation and pleasure, just as she has always before provided the old caresses and cuddling. In both a boy and a girl, this initial kind of masturbatory fantasy evokes some inner, natural worry, because this dream puts the child back into the dependent position with the mother, although all the other current attitudes are ones that let the child feel independent and self-sufficient.

At this time, the child attempts to alter such unwanted, imaginary dependency by making, in real behavior, a variety of infantile attempts to assume the leadership in interaction with the mother. Complaints about aches and pains, almost deliberate accidents that will demand comforting and cuddling, and sometimes open exhibitionist commands that the mother inspect the phallus are some of the typical ways a child attempts to achieve the command position.

However, the child has another, easier way of coping with the anxieties provoked by the dependency relationship fantasied as an accompaniment to masturbation. This is the way that has already had such success in avoiding other difficulties: he can change the dreams so they are more comforting.

Accordingly, both a boy and a girl switch from the dependent role of being a baby in the fantasy, cared for by the stimulating, gratifying mother, into the active and independent role. In actuality, this role was already observed as being the father's role with the mother. Each, therefore, calls on all the accumulated memories of daddy, identifies with him as completely as possible, and then proceeds to behave, openly, the way the father has behaved. In a family where the father and mother have enjoyed a healthy, mutually rewarding relationship, each playing typical male and female roles, the child starts playing out the male role of being protective, aggressively seductive, and forthrightly provocative. The child, in short, seeks aggressively to win.

At this point in the Oedipal development, boys part company from girls. In the boy's mind, he is like his father and he wants his mother—his father, therefore, is a genuine rival, a possible obstacle to his success. Automatically, the boy dispenses with this obstacle by altering his fantasies, dreaming that his father will retreat. Action changes to suit the day dreams, and the boy becomes openly contemptuous of and competitive with his father. He devotes less energy to trying to succeed with his mother and more energy in attempting to show daddy how worthless a father or man he is.

As real life fails to confirm the child's expectations, as the father refuses to vanish in awesome respect for the child's greater

prowess, and as the mother fails to respond to her child's approaches (and good healthy reactions, common sense, and wisdom
keep the father and mother from behaving in any other way),
the boy becomes increasingly annoyed with his father. So his
fantasies start to be devoted mainly to the theme of annihilating
his rival or rendering him powerless. In his behavior, too, the boy
stops being competitive and becomes hostile toward his father.

But as both the fantasies and the behavior take this turn, the
very identification ties that were called upon in the first place
to save the child from being dependent are weakened. If he continues his fantasies, he will soon have no strong inner identification left. And also, of course, the hostility and rebellion, both
fantasied and real, make the boy feel guilty (just before this
period, remember, he learned to be a law-abiding person who felt
guilt when he failed to follow parental authority). Finally, real
fear is aroused in the boy as he thinks, in his childish, self-centered
way, that his father regards him the same way he regards his
father. Now daddy is not seen as a fair-minded rival; he becomes
a vengeful, threatening person.

And as the child's day dreams round this corner, his behavior
changes again; from being hostile, he becomes placating and ob-
sequious toward the father, trying by becoming passive to stop
his father from hurting him.

This is a final impasse. All the thought and effort that the
boy has spent in this development, usually spread over many
months of time, have accomplished no essential change at all. He
is now once again passive, not only with regard to his mother,
but now also with regard to his father.

During all this time, imagination has assumed increasing
leadership over impulse, just as in the example earlier in this section when imagination stimulated the desire to urinate even
though the bladder was not full. By the time a boy has arrived at
his final Oedipal impasse, he is no longer masturbating to reduce
the intense itch of phallic impulses while his fantasies follow the
impulsive action and let him feel in control of these phallic
impulses. Instead, the boy's fantasies take wing, stimulating
anxieties and other feelings that are then partially reduced by masturbating. The more the masturbatory fantasies unsettle the boy,
the more he needs to reassure himself by masturbating. Yet at

the same time that through masturbation he proves to himself that his penis has not been damaged by his father—as in his autism he would like to damage his father's penis—he increases his anxiety by the fantasies that automatically accompany masturbation.

By this time, there are no more roles to play in fantasy. The boy has been both passive and active with his mother and active and passive with his father. Every role has produced extra anxieties; the final accumulation is more trouble than masturbation is worth. Automatically, therefore, the boy's mind does what it did when he was a newborn infant and found that the world was more trouble than it was worth: the mind turns itself off. He no longer feels the primary phallic sensitivity or the secondary phallic stimulation produced by the fantasies; and he no longer day dreams of sex.

Thus, finally, the boy saves himself by setting sexuality aside. He rationalizes that some day, when he is a grown man, he will be able to win this particular battle; but meanwhile, he is only interested in being a boy who has lots of better things to be concerned about. He therefore reconfirms his identification with his father. With every realistic success experience he enjoys as he devotes himself to the objective affairs of being a boy, he has less need to console himself with a sour-grapes philosophy. He gains in realistic pride and makes his ties with his father ever stronger. Eventually, all the wounds are healed, and he can once again view his mother as his mother and his father as his father, while he feels genuinely comfortable and engrossed in being just a boy.

For the girl, the initial resort to identification with her father to escape the passive role of being dependent upon the mother for sexual stimulation is not so successful, even temporarily, as it is for the boy. In essence, her identification with her father is initially less strong because she simply is not like him. All the strong sense of realism that has developed during the pre-Oedipal periods forces her to acknowledge that she is not like her father. Even if she has had no experience of any sort to teach her that men have penises and women do not, she usually knows that women have babies and men do not, she can see that women have "bumpy" breasts and men do not. She knows, in short, that she, as a girl, is expected to become a woman, and women are somehow different from men.

So, although, like the boy, she starts to go through the phases of fantasying and acting out contemptuously and competitively toward her father, she does not get sufficiently involved in her own identification with her father to become hostile toward him. She is usually side-tracked by her realistic appreciation of her own sex and her difference from her father.

This realistic appreciation of her own sex poses only a temporary problem to her masturbatory fantasies, however, for she solves it by the happy expedient of dreaming that she is not really a girl, but is actually instead becoming a boy. Confident that the more she practices being a boy, the sooner the transformation will occur, she re-embarks on competing with her father for her mother, trying to show him up as less worthy. Temporarily, her fantasies allow her to masturbate without anxiety over dependency, because they reassure her that she is on her way toward winning her goal of becoming a boy.

But her relationship to her mother, with whom she is still most strongly identified, suffers. Seeing her mother as the person who gives her everything pleasurable, she cannot deal with the reality that her mother did not make her a boy in the first place. Gradually, she becomes intensely involved in disliking the mother who "cheated" her of her maleness.

The rebuffs she receives from her mother also increase her distance from her mother, decrease her desire for her, and increase her dislike of her. Even though she still rebuffs him, a mother naturally greets her son's seductive efforts with humorous, almost admiring tolerance; but she is likely to be totally lacking in humor about her daughter's seductive efforts, harshly or angrily rebuffing the girl and ridiculing her for trying to act like a boy.

The father, too, reacts less supportively to his daughter's boyishness than he does to his son's boyishness; he can be proud of his boy for acting like a man, but he is repelled by his daughter as she foregoes her femininity. And he does not humorously tolerate her competition and contempt for his masculinity; it nettles him a little, however mature he may be, to think that a girl—for that is how he sees his daughter—does not think him much of a man.

Thus, in her efforts to alter her fantasies while indulging her phallic impulses, the girl manages to put herself in a foolish and alienated position.

Since even in fantasy there is no point in trying to get someone she dislikes to like her, the girl's fantasies go through another change. They focus on defeating her mother, giving her her just deserts for having been so mean and withholding. This leads to openly hostile behavior toward the mother. This behavior then widens the gap between the girl and her father, for he is not hostile to the mother; and by showing his dislike for his daughter when she is hostile, he leaves her without a firm source of identification. She is exposed additionally to the threat of having to acknowledge that she is not yet becoming the boy she wants to be. Finally, her guilts are awakened by her hostilities.

To save herself from all these difficulties, her fantasies now lead her to strive to regain her identification with her mother, if only so she will not be guilty and alone, and she strives to regain her father's favor—at least until the time comes when she becomes a boy, and her father can really appreciate her. So the fantasies now become ones in which the girl, by being even a better woman than her mother is, wins her father.

In behavior, the girl now becomes a feminine competitor with her mother for her father. At first, she seeks to take care of him in the ways she sees her mother using; then, as her identification with her mother leads her to dream that she is a woman, she becomes dependent upon her father whom she now sees as the person to give her a baby so she can be a mother, too.

But such competitive feminine identification, first of all, does not result in her winning her father. And secondly, it has the effect of increasing the strain on her ties with her mother.

By the time the girl has reached this point in her Oedipal development, she has tried everything, yet nothing has worked. Her anxieties are not so great as the boy's by the time she has reached the end of her repertoire of roles, because no one is threatening her with annihilation in her fantasies, but her depression is extreme. She feels hopeless. She is only sure, because this impossibility has never been put to the test, that if somehow she became a boy, she could win success; but she cannot imagine any way of succeeding in becoming a boy, aside from convincing her mother to make her one. Since competition with her mother leads to further estrangement and less likelihood of convincing her mother to make her a boy, she must stop the competitive strivings. And so the girl goes back to being passive with regard to her mother.

At this impasse, the girl's mind, too, just like the boy's, turns off the whole drama. Sexuality is dissociated; the fantasies stop having a great deal of sexual content to them; masturbation stops. The girl continues to practice her feminine role because it at least lets her get close to her mother again; but she puts aside the thought that it might, just might, actually result in being rewarded by the hoped-for granting of masculinity from her mother or, at the very least, receiving a baby from her father.

At the end of the Oedipal development, the boy is fairly sure of himself and of his sexual role, confident that when he is older and bigger, just like his father, he will be able to defeat the old man and win his mother. Since there is little point in troubling himself about sexuality until it is time for this certain victory, the boy turns away from all considerations of sexual roles, and spends his remaining childhood years playing action games like cops and robbers, games that only symbolically represent the pursuing aspects of the adult male sexual role, and that directly represent no other aspects. Sure in his male identification, the boy gives up most of his earlier feminine identification, retaining only enough to be able to appreciate the way his woman feels when, as a later adult, he seeks to win her in repeated marital intercourse.

At the end of the Oedipal development, the girl is, however, still unsure of and dissatisfied with her fundamental identity or self. She feels hopeless about winning anything, when she grows up and plays the adult female sexual role, but a chance at a new start on the whole perplexing business she has just lived through. She is forced to wonder if she will be loved at all for doing this. She cannot permit herself to arrive at any conclusions about who will give her sexualized affection, the father or the mother, because making a choice could close out the possibility that she might still have a chance to retain her original love object, the mother, yet gain the malelike and active position that would enable her to be realistically active in pursuing the mother.

The only clear aspect of any sexual role that she can forthrightly assume, without provoking the whole Oedipal struggle all over again, to the same generalized defeat, is the mothering role. So, fundamentally unsure of herself in all other aspects, the girl ends the Oedipal period by going back to the games which characterized her pre-Oedipal play and which resemble the adult mothering role—games like playing with dolls, keeping house, and dressing up. The retention of ambiguous identifications with both parents permits the girl, when later an adult, to understand her children, both male and female. Too, it enables her to adjust to her likely marital role in which much of her behavior is conditioned by her husband.

Thus, the Oedipal period leaves the boy equipped to play a set and stable sexual role, adjusting his occupational role to his immediate circumstances; it leaves the girl equipped to play a sexual role determined by the immediate circumstances of her husband's behavior, fulfilling an occupational role as a mother and housewife that is stabilized by many years of playful practice.

Throughout all this development, both parents play a similar role in maintaining their ordinary relationship with each other and in correcting their child's autism when it shows up in sexual or hostile aggression toward either or both of them. The parents provide the child the safe arena in which to act out all the masturbatory fantasies, with no success, yet with no retaliative punishment from them. Their behavior remains essentially all that it has ever been—it is only the child and the child's fantasy that alter. So it is in the child's mind, but only in the child's mind, that the father or mother becomes a love object, a buddy, a competitor, or an ideal.

All through this period, both parents recognize the roles they are consigned to by the child's fantasies and steadfastly make sure they are not pushed into playing them. The parents do nothing to encourage the various Oedipal fantasies—these develop because the child develops and must make sense out of his world for himself, even if he occasionally needs to get involved in nonsense. Unlike all the preceding stages, the Oedipal period requires no new attitude in the parents; this is a time when the good father and the good mother are characterized by *not* responding to the child's apparent needs; instead, they respond to the apparent reality—that this child who presents complicated wishes to them for actualization is but a child. They continue, therefore, to represent genuine reality to their child.

The colossal egotism of the Oedipal child, the extreme immersion in self-perpetuated fantasies that bear little relation to the objective world, all give way, finally, to the child's development of a new appreciation of reality. Since Oedipal development is different for the boy as compared to the girl, the kind of realism and sense of reality that emerges is also different.

The boy's realism includes an appreciation of abstract qualities and aspects of objective reality; he can imaginatively derive comparisons between things (like the ones he has drawn between himself and his father) and between things and ideals (like the ones he draws between himself as a child and himself as he will be when he becomes a man). He can feel confident that such logical and rational exercises are sensible and productive. The girl, however, who has never really been sure of how she differs from either her mother or her father, who has never really been able to prove to herself that her romanticism about what would happen if she became a boy is sheer nonsense, but who is always steadfastly rooted to her knowledge that she is a girl and not a man, is less confident that logic and observation make sense. She can go through the exercises in comparisons and abstraction that the boy completes, but she maintains a belief in the existence of another reality, somewhere, that can be approached and understood intuitively.

The boy, in becoming a man, continues to express his logical view of reality in what is called the masculine way of thinking. The girl, in becoming a woman, expresses her view of reality by a mixture of steadfast pragmatic concreteness and romantic idealism, both heavily influenced by intuition—a mixture that is referred to as the feminine way of looking at the world.

Each learns how little effect wishes have on reality unless they are put into action by a person skilled enough to realize them. The child no longer assumes that surface similarities of action are enough to gain similar ends.

Connected to this newly acquired view of the difference between fantasy and fact, the child learns that a proved and established expert must be observed if expert ways are to be learned and practiced. In the complete home, the child learns to take a good square look at the father, to see the contained, self-assured, responsive and responsible, affectionate, intimate maleness appreciated by his mother. It is not possible just to decide what is likely to be characteristic of the expert and then act on unconfirmed opinion. Ideas of what maleness is or the empty and artificial patterns provided by storybooks are not enough to let the child convincingly act like a man.

Later on, in adolescence, the child has a chance to re-examine and reconfirm all these new appreciations of reality, but they remain stable for the remaining childhood years.

His own feeling about himself alters with regard to responsibility and authority, too. Now he can admit that his parents were really humoring him and being very nice to him when they let him think he was boss in some respects; he certainly could not push them around even when he most earnestly and intensely desired to do so. By the end of the Oedipal period, the child feels less arrogant, righteous, and self-satisfied, and more humble, realistically appreciative, and grateful. The girl, of course, retains some feelings that force her to be less appreciative of authority.

The combination of respect for the expert and respect for authority enables the child to appreciate the abstraction, *truth*, as well as tangible reality. Ultimately, this leads to his consideration of other people. They stop being puppets as he stops assigning roles and feelings to them, and as he begins, instead, to seek to learn what they want and how they feel. The self-centeredness of the early Oedipal stage is transmuted into genuine regard for them.

All in all, though during most of the Oedipal period the child is wrapped up in his sexuality and its accompanying fantasies, so that he is not sure of himself, realistic, responsible, or responsive, the final result of his development through this period is that he becomes a much fuller person in each of these aspects. His relationship with his parents, previously so extremely dependent and, during the Oedipal struggle, so extremely fantastic, finally emerges as highly independent, yet warm and close and friendly.

## Grade School Age

Just about the time that his sexuality is firmly submerged, another inner alteration offers up another new world to him. In about his sixth year of life, a part of his brain becomes dominant over other parts, and the newly coordinated brain becomes able to receive, understand, and reproduce real symbols.

With the acquisition of this ability to use symbolic language, he becomes more objective about the world, better able to regard it without immediately seeing it only as good or bad for him. He reaffirms his allegiance to the standards and rules he has learned in all his preceding years, but these become more abstract and more complex. His tolerance for others and his respect for authority increase. But since all these attitudes have been present previously, nothing new, psychologically, is actually forthcoming during this period. Thus, this period is called by psychologists the *latency period*.

With increased coordination and understanding come increased learning, not only of abstract information, but also of attitudes about symbols. Thus, the child can learn and demonstrate reactions to people determined by their symbolic status, not their actuality. A teacher is not a woman, she is representative of authority; and the child reacts to her with the attitudes he has learned about an authority symbol.

Because of inner maturation of the activity of the brain, leading to complex patterns of subordination of various brain functions, the child becomes able to sustain his attention span, and he becomes less fidgety and needful of a chance to run around between periods of concentration. Patterns of how-to-learn get established, so that his mind automatically studies material, collects information from it, and thinks about it.

He learns much during this time about the ways of the society about him; and he practices and stabilizes his allegiance to social custom at the same time that he develops social poise and becomes accustomed to conforming to most of the important rules and regulations.

His new skill in reading and writing enables him to take care of many of his own needs; for example, he takes major responsibility for his own amusement, he can learn to get to appointments independently, he can handle money, and he can leave written messages. All this gives him both freedom to develop his likes and dislikes and freedom to increase his pride and self-confidence.

As his control over emotional reactions strengthens, his attitudes toward many skills change. For example, he stops priding himself on doing chores; these become matter-of-fact and routine, part of the normal contribution made naturally as a member of the family. In later life, this tolerance for routine plays an important part in successfully carrying out most occupations. He can make long-range plans and follow them without needing to alter them in order to get immediate gratification. In short, he is capable of plain, hard drudgery.

His foremost responsibility during latency is that of learning the methods and the information presented in school.

Just as a large-framed, very energetic person is likely to do better at playing tackle football than a small-boned, lightweight, sluggish person, a highly intelligent person is likely to be more successful with the intellectual task of learning than is a less intelligent person. So, a child's success in school is governed to some extent by his basic intelligence, which, like size, body frame, eye color, and energy level, is an inherited characteristic. But grade school and high school present ideas that can be grasped, and grasped completely, by the child with average intelligence. The smarter child just learns this material more easily, more quickly. A high intelligence level is not required to guarantee ordinary school success.

The spirit of inquiry is the most striking characteristic of a healthy person; he is always eager to know, to learn, to investigate, to analyze, to evaluate. Thus, when given a chance to learn at school, to learn even more than he has been exposed to at home, the basically healthy child leaps eagerly upon this opportunity and uses it to the best of his ability. He is well motivated to learn.

His successful learning of methods and information at school equips him to handle his later adult responsibilities more easily. The economic advantages of education are obvious, of course; but it must also be remembered that education enables the adult to have and to find things to think about when he is not occupied in his work or with natural activities like sleeping, eating, and making love. So the child, in learning his school subjects, is equipping himself to increase his own pleasure in living when he later becomes an adult.

During the latency period, parents tend to take a back seat in the development of their child. Any activities with the parents are instigated by the child. Most of the time, aside from participation in meals and attendance at religious ceremonies and family visiting, the child spends his time by himself or with friends, not with family.

The contrast between parental roles is very slight during this time. The important parental relationship during these years, provided without any definite, obvious moves on the part of the parents, is the continuously safe and protected environment of the home. Home is the place where the child can relax and not have to work constantly or prove himself constantly. Home is the place where he can try things, confident that failure will not result in trouble or ridicule. Home is the place that is orderly and predictable, that need not be studied and re-evaluated all the time. Home may even be the place where the occasionally over-taxed youngster can just stop coping with things and lean on the parents for help or blow up over trivia without punishment.

Father provides an important part of this continuity as he reacts stably and reliably with his constant-as-the-northern-star, masculine temperament. Both parents represent different points of view as well as united outlooks, so the child can usually obtain support for new ideas from at least one parent. The child's activity patterns and identifications are strengthened by these many years of constancy with his parents.

By and large, leadership passes to friends and to the teacher in the school. The parents have already taught most of what they can teach in preparing their child to become a constructive part of the school-room group.

All in all, though the latency period is a time in which the child learns a great deal of new information and learns many new methods of exploring the world, nothing new goes on within him except for the abstraction and symbolization of what has happened before. The patterns established in the pre-Oedipal periods, tempered with the humility and the proud enthusiasm gained during the Oedipal period, become extended and strengthened by being abstracted; but basically, the school child leads a reasonably stable inner existence.

## Puberty and Adolescence

Then adolescence brings about a further upset, this time as puberty calls forth a totally new set of sensations and capacities. With the ripening of the sex glands, the body changes both inwardly and outwardly.

The oldest parts of the nervous system become influenced by strong new chemicals manufactured in the body, some for the first time; and these alterations cause reorganizations of many functions of the brain, with consequent moodiness and great emotionality. Hunger increases as the body grows rapidly. And there are changes that make the child no longer at all familiar to himself. The boy's voice deepens as his voicebox enlarges; his beard grows; the texture of his skin alters. The girl's muscles soften; her breasts enlarge and develop. The skeletal system enlarges and alters the body's contours, with consequent temporary awkwardness and weakness of muscles. As the sex glands themselves mature completely, the emerging young man and woman become biologically complete. Short of some minor additional growth before the bony structure stops changing, their physical maturation is done. Until senescence begins and marks the end of the "biologically ripe" period, no other physical changes of import occur except the temporary ones of pregnancies in the woman, undramatic amounts of wear or tear, or the changes caused by more or less controllable diseases and accidents.

As adolescence brings its many definitely new physical aspects, considerable alterations in attitudes toward the world and self develop. Activity patterns change. The boy's drives become more intense, more sustained, and more thrust into the world about him; his attention span and quickness in learning new coordination patterns are higher than they have ever been. The girl shows these same changes, too, but for only a part of her menstrual cycle, because the glandular changes accompanying the cycle impose physical alterations on her body as a whole, and her activity patterns reveal this cyclicity. Thus, following ovulation, she becomes less energetic, more passive and vegetative, until the changes that cause menstruation cause some short-lived and uneven disturbances in both body and personality; once these changes pass, the girl demonstrates forceful, boyish energy and attitudes until ovulation recurs, and the cycle starts over again.

The egotism that characterizes adolescent behavior is another reflection of the involvement of the self with the body. All the changes taking place over so many months after the onset of puberty need continual re-evaluation; the youngster, except during short periods of quiet and absence of physical change, has no energy left to devote to outside reality. Everything must take second place to the first problem, getting reacquainted with himself.

Most of the sense of responsibility developed during earlier school years remains essentially unchanged, but until body rhythms have evened out, the adolescent is occasionally lazy or thoughtless, because he is so wrapped up in himself or so exhausted in his efforts to understand himself that he cannot pay attention to rules and regulations any more.

A new dimension of responsibility and self-control is opened up by the adolescent's necessity to prepare for an adult occupational role; usually, the adolescent can hire himself out for pay, too, and this leads to additional responsibilities. He is helped to be realistic in his choices and in his conduct by the accumulated attitudes developed back in early childhood; thus, though his role and reality differ, the sound ideas and attitudes about authority and autonomy learned before he even entered school still apply and are helpful.

The most important change in adolescence is directly related to the new capacity and urge to engage in sexual intimacy. The sexuality of adolescence gives rise to new attitudes about reality and responsibility, as well as presenting a new reality and a new impulse over which to develop self-control.

Once any child enters puberty, sexuality becomes a completely real force. No longer is it merely a sensation without overt external accompaniments, an emotion unconnected to definite bodily changes.

Now the attitudes developed about sexuality are not derived

from general attitudes about bodily sensations, nor are these attitudes only a minor part of the over-all adult sexual attitude. Now they are connected to real genital sensations, the most important, overwhelming sensations in the body at this time. And how a child regards his phallic sexuality during adolescence is likely to be the mainstay of his attitudes throughout his adult life.

Real though the sexual feelings and sensations are, at first the major changes concern the child's fantasy activity. Fantasy activity about sexuality is renewed. At first the old Oedipal fantasies are dredged up, but these are soon dismissed as silly. Thus, for example, a child who was able to dream, with quite a little thrill, about being naughty, being spanked by his mother, and then making everything all right again by cuddling, is no longer able to derive much more than a feeling of being shamefully silly from such a dream. In his new maturity, he mentally shrugs his shoulders in surprise that he once thought it was exciting to be placed in such a ridiculous position. Adult fantasies replace the Oedipal dreams as soon as these can be replayed and discarded.

The healthy child who has resolved the Oedipal problem has already discarded most of the earlier Oedipal fantasies anyhow. There remain only the last-formed notions about himself which he can now appropriately think through and test out. You remember that he ended up with the idea that he would someday be a grown man who would act toward women the way he saw his father act toward his mother. In his adolescence, therefore, he tests these ways, then discards a lot of them because they no longer are sensible ways for the new generation with its new conditions of life. He takes the dreams he had when younger and puts them into practice, but with the differences that his experience and his times produce. So, for example, a girl who dreamed of wearing a tight-waisted tweed suit and ankle straps—the fashion when she was six—now blossoms out in the current version of the basic suit. The style is different, but the content, that she will dress becomingly as a woman, is the same.

As a person capable of making many decisions and implementing them, the teen-ager deserves and requires the same respect accorded to an adult. But as a person who still lacks sufficient experience in life to be able to see the far-reaching effects of certain actions, the teen-ager still requires guidance given in the form of interpretations of reality to which his attention is drawn.

The autism of this time of life is to believe that everyone is competing, trying to gain the limelight of individuality and newness, anxious and unsure about which limits can be safely and comfortably approached and which cannot.

The limits of many of the nonsexual concerns are tied in with the approach to reality developed by the attitudes and practice of sexualized activity.

At first, some of the attitudes about reality that were formed during the Oedipal period emerge; but these are altered as the child re-evaluates them in the light of his newer learning, the objectivity developed during latency and the trust, optimism, courage, self-control, and pride that are now amply substantiated by his maturation.

He learns about his sexuality and what it makes him feel. He understands its effects upon his judgment and attitude about reality and responsibilities, and he eventually controls his sexuality— all gradually, through the six or seven years between puberty and young adulthood. From the initial position of being overwhelmed and confused by his sexuality, he goes eventually to integrate his sexuality, so that it blends with his pre-existing personality and does not dominate him completely. (This sexuality, still primarily concerned with the pleasure that can be obtained for the self through stimulation of the phallic organs, is still called phallic sexuality by psychologists.) The period of adolescence is sometimes referred to as the *phallic-competitive* period.

He accomplishes these integrative steps by expressing some of his sexuality symbolically, while restraining his phallic impulses through the use of judgment and self-awareness. An optimal amount of freedom to explore and release some of this impulse is used in order to get acquainted with it without feeling overwhelmed by it. He needs protection from being ensnared into intercourse, because intercourse is an overwhelming and disturbing experience to the adolescent. To the extent that the environment continues to support his self-preservative readiness to control his sexual impulses, the adolescent can feel assurance and confidence while exploring sexuality.

Usually the healthy adolescent first expresses sexuality symbolically by competitive strivings with friends of the same sex; sexuality is only symbolic in this form of competition, not directly represented.

A second stage of symbolic expression of sexuality occurs as competitive strivings lessen, while exhibitionism toward friends of the opposite sex looms large. During this time, the healthy teen-ager is showing off to his girl, and she is showing off to him. He may demonstrate his prowess at bowling; she, at baking cookies. In no way does the healthy middle adolescent get involved in frank and open exhibitionism of the phallic organs: holding hands, dancing, and kissing are sufficiently stimulating to arouse anxiety along with pleasure; and sexual exploration, accordingly, halts at these overtures.

Eventually, an older adolescent's sexual impulses become controllable and less erratically and crucially intense. The body evens out, the experience in picking dates has resulted in some refinement of judgment and taste. Partners in explorative adventures are discarded—the girl who was so wonderful last week is now seen by the boy to be completely at odds with his whole appreciation and understanding of himself, and he finds another girl who seems more like what he has always dreamed of. Necking and petting release his sexuality, but he is less urged to date a girl by the desire to neck and pet with her than the reverse. His judgment is put to work, first, to decide whether or not she is the kind of girl he likes—then whether or not she is easy to neck with and whether or not he wants to. As his judgment becomes more accurate because he is swayed less by the forces of desire, his feelings of tenderness and concern for the girl emerge as paramount.

In essence, the adolescent goes through a series of boy-girl ties that first permits him to discover what a little sex is like, without any concern for the girl he is kissing; then lets him see what sex is like with a girl he likes a lot because she is a nice person; then teaches him what sex is like as an expression of mutual concern and affection. Sex is still expressed only in a limited way.

During all the adolescent stages, whether competitive, exhibitionist, or idealistic, the parents play exceedingly important roles in providing the reality limits the teen-ager needs. Like the Oedipal period, adolescence involves the assignment of images to each parent within the teen-ager's mind in accordance with his problems. The adolescent certainly cannot see his parents as people who are genuine and real and who have various characteristics— autistically, he creates an image of them as he needs them to be in order to solve his inner problems. Thus, from the adolescent's point of view, the father and mother may be pals, rivals, dominators, slaves, or nothings.

Both parents, in wisely resisting their child's efforts to inveigle them into behaving in accordance with his autism, continue to represent protective limits to him.

These limits concern reality and responsibility as much as sexuality. So, for example, the parents remind the teen-ager that he must continue to demonstrate the same courtesy and friendliness that they have always expected, that he must complete his chores and take care of his school responsibilities, that he must maintain the same basic, sensible diet and rest habits. They insist that he understand the limits they set for him and that he discuss his reactions and listen to their viewpoints; they do not let him act out without remonstrance from them. In short, they keep him from forgetting that the world is still going on in the same old way, even though he is so shiny and new a person.

They provide valuable information about their child's new reality. For example, a daughter is helped by information about menstruation, underarm deodorants, use of face powder and lipstick, walking on high heels, and getting her stocking seams straight when she wears seamed hosiery. In the same way, a son is helped by information on the use and care of his razor, the selection of shaving lotions and deodorants, or the meaning of his nocturnal emissions. The details of deportment at dances or dinner parties, how much to tip, and other social information is also necessary to the adolescent in his new reality, and parents can easily and supportively provide this information.

The wise parents also frankly discuss sex, indicating the absence within them of either a licentious or a censurious attitude, and stating the limits they find appropriate. As a mother wisely indicates to her daughter that she may neck at home—when an adult is elsewhere in the house—but not in a car, on the beach, at a party, or in the woods, the mother is acknowledging that she respects her daughter's new maturity, but is not abdicating a mother's responsibility to keep her daughter safe. In the same way, a father helpfully indicates to his son that it is not permissible to drink alcoholic beverages on a date, nor is it permissible to coerce a date into more sexual intimacy than necking in her own living room.

Phallic sexuality is turned into what psychologists call *genital sexuality* by this tempering and moderating process. Genital sexuality expresses tenderness and concern for a person who is seen realistically and accurately as having desired characteristics and as reciprocating the loving feelings. (Genital, like the related word "generative," is used to indicate that sexuality is not merely being spent to produce pleasure for the person spending it, but rather, generates additional pleasure in both persons concerned, and generates happy feelings that result in its own perpetuation and repetition.)

Genital sexuality emerges as the teen-ager passes into young adulthood. By the time it is well established, it permits him to use his young-adult powers of evaluation, appreciation, and control in order to find a partner with whom he can live and be in love. He can then work to fashion a relationship with her that is likely to be stable, to be socially acceptable, to be gratifying and challenging, as it is fun, safe, secure, and fulfilling of his realistic standards.

Mainly, each parent separately and the two together serve as backdrops for the melodrama their child is performing during adolescence. The teen-ager likes to brag about his parents; he feels uncomfortable when his parents are unusual and different from those of his friends, but he is not especially interested in his parents as people. Only when his phallic sexuality is altered to genital sexuality is he able to regard his parents objectively again. By the end of adolescence, their healthy and now mature child regards them primarily as real equals, persons in their own right, although still people better known in a few ways and less known in others than his contemporaries. They no longer play roles, as such; in the good family, parents and child alike are at ease with themselves and with each other in mutual respect and love.

# PART THREE

# You and Your Child

# CHAPTER TEN

# Your Role as a Single Mother

THE FOLLOWING CHAPTERS discuss how to raise your child in his fatherless home, how to make up for the absence of his father. They also discuss what frequently happens to disturb the mother-child relations as a consequence of the absence of the father.

With the preceding review of healthy childhood development in mind, you have a clear picture of what you can expect to observe in your child as you successfully raise him. And the review of healthy parental roles gives you a clear picture of what you can expect to have to compensate for and substitute because your home is fatherless.

Father is not essential as a person, but what a father does and means is. It is your task to carry out the planning and hard work necessary in order to provide the same kinds of interaction—as in most instances, you can from within your own personal resources —or to provide your child with other figures, other people who interact with him in a fatherly way. As your child grows and develops, you must keep up with the altering father needs. As you have seen, the role of the father is different, both in regard to his relation with his child and his relationship with his wife, in the different stages of the child's growth.

The following chapters are but a guide to you in your analysis of your role as a single mother. You must fashion your own individual prescription for your activities with your child to fit your unique circumstances.

As you read through the following chapters, keep in mind that the ways suggested of resolving most of the problem situations discussed are limited to ways a healthy single mother can find from within herself.

In the following chapters, problem situations that might occur even in a complete family because of a mother's own neurosis are only occasionally discussed.

But before continuing to analyze your situation to see what is missing or upset and how it can be supplied or corrected, it is helpful for you to have in mind a clear, over-all view of the problems and negative reactions that may occur in a complete family, so that you can judge and analyze the ones that occur in your home. The books previously recommended contain ample descriptions of problem behavior and negative reactions; so this is but a short review of some of the generalizations about negative parent-child interactions.

Previously, the ideal parental role was analyzed as consisting of a few general functions: giving material care for the physical needs of the child; giving him freedom to develop his newly emerging physical and personality capacities; protecting him, yourself, and society from pain and damage; and stimulating him in further development, in the assumption of responsibility, and in helping him to acknowledge as much objective reality as his still immature personality permits. There is little likelihood that parents playing this role well are causing many negative feelings or any neurosis in their child.

In most respects, the reverse of these activities constitutes the completedly "bad" parental role, and this is usually associated with neurosis in both parent and child. Keep in mind that, although good parents can completely fulfill their parental roles, bad parents, fortunately, can usually fail only within limits. Thus parents are limited in the extent to which, ordinarily, they can fail to satisfy the physical needs of their children and to protect them from physical harm. Society itself steps in when the children start to sicken from lack of food, rest, shelter, or clothing, and also when the children are hurt by cruelty or other failures in protection. And though parents are not so constrained by law to provide stimulation and freedom as to provide protection, and so can narrow areas of freedom drastically and inattentively or deliberately fail to stimulate the sense of responsibility or the sense of reality in their children, the child's own nature limits the total effect of such inhibitions. One way or another, even if only in dreams or by bizarre, symbolic, neurotic behavior, the child's growth continues to be expressed. If his irresponsibility or unreality finally threaten to hurt others, society intervenes to take the child away from the neglectful parents.

Whenever any kind of failure occurs, any kind of lack or incompleteness in the good parental role, the child necessarily develops negative feelings; some of these were listed at the close of Chapter Three. Although many kinds of faulty parent-child interactions can cause different negative feelings, the negative feelings have one feature in common: they all include a basic primary anxiety that may often cause additional disturbances.

Different negative feelings are developed in reaction to such factors as when in his life the child is hurt, whether he is hurt through neglect, rejection, and prohibition or through precocious or overly intense stimulation, and what relationship there is between previous hurts and the current ones. Either by failing to satisfy a need or by overstimulating a need, you can produce essentially similar negative feelings in your child.

More complicated negative feelings arise when you stimulate a need before it has developed naturally into an important one. In essence, by doing this, you are foisting a need upon an organism very immature in relation to the particular need, and thus provoking your child to learn to do something that does not provide any intense pleasure. Because all people learn best and most easily to do those things that bring immediate pleasure to them, your child must thereby learn less efficiently. Usually he learns in a way different from the way he would if allowed to wait to learn naturally later on. In the absence of the organized and developed portion of the nervous system appropriate to a given need, he learns precociously only by calling into play brain centers like those involved in rote or conditioned learning; and these centers can be used only if you continually reinforce precocious training either by lavish praise for proper performance or else by punishment when a lapse occurs. So, both your child's brain and nervous system and you are working harder than would be necessary if things were allowed to develop naturally. It is like using a race horse to pull a plow; the higher brain centers could otherwise be engaged in understanding the world, not policing the child's body and getting it to respond to tensions which are not arising naturally out of its own needs. Premature urging to walk, to talk, to be toilet trained, to be constrained, to be graceful, to be sexy, or to be nonemotional—to name just a few aspects of training that are often stimulated precociously—all involve the same wasteful distribution of effort, the same artificially stimulated anxiety, and the same wasteful inner rigmarole developed and executed to relieve part of the anxiety. Because the anxiety, once artificially aroused, is kept going by the primitive brain that responds to very slight body sensations, it is not allayed by notices from the higher centers that the trained behavior already has been accomplished and the anxiety is no longer appropriate. So your child is never quite free of the negative feelings of anxiety and tension.

You can create exceedingly complicated negative feelings in your child by simultaneously failing to satisfy a currently developing need, stimulating precociously another need, and overstimulating a need that has been well stabilized.

Another way of producing negative feelings, ones that are exceedingly disturbing, is to stimulate a need precociously but rigidly inhibit all expression of this need past certain limits. This kind of teasing usually leads the child to shun associated activities as much as possible; and thus teasing eventually keeps him from ever learning to enjoy and integrate the need and its satisfaction.

All these many ways of producing negative feelings can be carried out by any neurotic mother, single or with her husband, who is behaving according to the pressures of her neurosis. Keep in mind, too, that the negative feelings and problem behavior characteristic of a child's reaction to his neurotic mother—be she complemented by her husband or not, living with her husband or not—cannot easily be distinguished from the negative feelings and problem behavior characteristic of a child living with his healthy single mother who is reacting nonconstructively to her pressures and letting these reactions of her own promote problems for her child.

Therefore, it is useful for you to consult the books previously recommended to get a fuller view of usual childhood problems, and it is useful for you to be alert to signs of these problems in your child. Remember that you cannot automatically assume that the presence of negative feelings in your child is an indicator that you and he are operating neurotically. For the interaction between the two of you, just as you have seen in Part One with regard to yourself alone, it is still necessary to distinguish whether or not neurotic problems are operating.

Remember that neuroses are not easily and simply changed by common-sense corrective methods (like the ones suggested in the following chapters) although temporary reactions to stress situations can be. The difference is like the difference between feeling hot and uncomfortable due to a fever or due to being out in the sun exercising—the simple, common-sense corrective measure of a cool drink can cool down and "cure" the temporary reaction to exercise and sun, but cannot change the fever, because it cannot cure the disease that causes the fever.

So, when you notice troubled interaction and consequent negative feelings in your child, you must distinguish between: (1) situational reactions caused by the way you react because you are troubled by some aspect of being single, and (2) those that are not situational in nature, but are neurotic. The way you can best determine which is which is to try the common-sense corrective measures suggested in following chapters to discover if they work. If they do, you automatically have proved that the problem they have solved was not a neurotic problem.

Most of what you do with your child is intangible in nature and not directly connected to his body needs. You can confidently expect to be able, without requiring professional help, to alter intangible interaction patterns and promote positive feelings within him as you restore good relationships between the two of you.

The more fully you understand what happened to the two of you, how things have gone up to now, and what has been missing because the father has been gone, the more confidently you can expect to be able to make up for almost all the difficulties your child faces. Except for some features of the Oedipal development that you can only keep from becoming distorted, pointed out in

Chapter Fourteen, you can satisfactorily help your child develop fully and healthily in all ways.

As you read the following chapters, you may find yourself recognizing that some of the problems have already occurred; you may find yourself needing to grant that your reactions or your child's reactions have led to the development of negative feelings. It is in order to provoke such insights that examples of problems are provided, for your insight into problems is the first step toward eliminating the unfortunate results. Most of the time, by taking immediate and constructive approaches in the future, you can gradually eliminate the problem and the negative feelings.

If the problem has come about because you have omitted some necessary function, restoring it usually has a reasonably prompt remedial effect. For example, if you have been making a mistake by not requesting that your child pick up his clothes, just about the only corrective measure you need take is to start requesting that he assume responsibility for his things. No formal announcements and explanations are necessary; he can gradually, if belatedly, learn to respond to your requests in the natural course of events.

However, if the problem has come about because you have been actively committing an error, you may find it additionally helpful to explain to your child what was wrong about what you have been doing and to indicate to him what you plan to do in the future. For example, if you have been hitting your child when you have been angry, and you recognize that this has been wrong, you need to explain to him that you now realize your behavior was wrong because it scared him and made him rebellious and angry. You also probably need to announce to him that, from now on, you plan to keep your hands to yourself, just as you have always told him not to hit people when he is angry.

Explaining past mistakes and declaring new ways to your child —especially if you are able to apologize simply for your mistakes —provides your child with the opportunity to discuss his reactions. This usually leads to a much improved and more free relationship between the two of you. Your child is able to sort out some of his confusions about why you have been telling him to do what you said, rather than what you did. He can now, without confusion, feel free to follow your example—remember that copying you and identifying with you is the most natural thing for him to do and is the easiest way for him to develop additional new skills.

Even if you are unable to alter your behavior completely, this kind of talk between you and your child helps him to understand why he is expected to be different from you. You are, at least, still giving him a part of yourself, an ideal you have presented to him to pattern himself after. So, if you are unable to control your temper thoroughly enough to keep from hitting him occasionally, help your child to develop a realistic understanding of his mother and of what you want for him by explaining that you did not have a mother who taught you well to habitually keep your temper under control, but you want him to do better. As you explain why you think he will be happier being more controlled than you are, he can better identify with your ideal for him; and he can also more easily forgive you your occasional lapses in self-control.

In Part One, it was pointed out that professional psychological treatment is the best help to seek if you believe your negative reactions are based on a neurosis and not just on your situational pressures. If your child's negative feelings seem to be part of a neurosis and not merely easily-remedied, temporary reactions to unusual reality circumstances, seek similar professional help for your child's problems. If neurotic mother-child interactions have been the cause of your child's neurosis—as they often are—both you and your child may need diagnostic and therapeutic procedures.

Because many behavioral changes may be caused by physical difficulties like infection or disease, poor eye sight, loss of hearing, malnourishment, or faulty rest and exercise habits, and may not be caused by emotional difficulties, your pediatrician or family physician ought to be the first person you consult.

The resources discussed in Chapter Seven can be used by you in your efforts to understand and remedy the cause of your child's troubles. The grade-school years, particularly, because they do not involve any new personality or physical developments, are excellent years during which to evaluate and remedy the results of early childhood experiences. You must remember that your child is much more limited than you are in the ways he can express his reactions. Ordinarily, because his approach to reality is made through the content of his latest, most stable, well-established body need, he expresses his negative feelings about being left alone—or being hurt by you unwittingly because you have been left alone—through altering his behavior concerning this body need. For example, when he is in the oral-aggressive stage, he shows how unhappy he is by changing his behavior about the needs concerned with the just established and well-practiced oral-dependent stage: he may stop eating, sleep poorly, and refuse to be cuddled; or he may express his unhappiness by eating too much, refusing to explore, and clinging—all related to oral-dependent ways, but reversed in type.

The importance of recognizing his reactions lies in the fact that you must do something to interrupt them lest he arrive at the point where he gives himself severe negative feelings. When he refuses to eat because his daddy has left him, he is doing to himself the equivalent of your neglecting to feed him because your husband has left. There are some internal psychological differences, of course, but the same frustration of his body needs is occurring. In his unhappiness he may not feel much appetite, but his body is still quite healthy and hungry; in not eating, he is hurting himself. And as this self-imposed pain accentuates his feelings of unhappiness, the whole reaction setup becomes self-defeating.

Though such a reaction need not cause lasting neurosis, it does not help your child. You must help him regain a constructive outlook on life by interfering with his self-defeating reaction once you observe that it is prolonging itself more than a few days.

Remember, however, that this kind of corrective interference is totally different from any interference that disturbs a natural, healthy need or its expression. You are correct in keeping him from hurting himself by coaxing him to eat after you have permitted him a reasonable mourning period of a few days. On the other hand, you are but hurting him if you coax him to eat when he is otherwise happy and healthy and has already finished half of his meal.

You can expect your child to react in self-defeating ways to all major stresses, not just to the departure of his father. So at all times of severe stress, like moving to a new home, getting a new full-time baby-sitter, or remarrying, observe your child's reactions and step in to correct them if they appear to be self-punishing.

In the following chapters, some examples of when professional help is needed are provided as guides to you in making this decision.

You must remember that the effect upon you and upon your child of being left in a fatherless home is related to the time at which this happened. In a sense, you and your child are both different people at different times of your child's development; so the event of being left alone causes different reactions in each of you, hurts different needs at different times, and usually results in different behavior.

If you have more than one child, the situation remains essentially unchanged; you must understand your role with each child as you would with one child alone. But keep in mind that differences in their past experiences as part of a complete family make for profound and radical differences among your children in their separate interactions with you and with each other. For example, a child of six reacts quite differently to the death of his father than does his brother of thirteen, not only because of the psychological differences between them, but also because the six-year-old still has an older "man" in the family. At times, differences in sex also cause different kinds of interactions. A six-year-old girl with an older brother is quite different from a six-year-old boy. So, in understanding your children, you must continually keep in mind this additional factor of age and sex.

In short, by taking the same thoughtful analytic approach to understanding what you must do for your child in his fatherless home that you have already taken in understanding what you must do for yourself as a single woman, you can be confident of coping with your enlarged task.

Your own reactions to being alone were discussed in Part One as they related to your being a woman. In the following chapters, these reactions are related to the way you mother your child.

So that the following chapters may more easily serve as reference guides to you later on, each concerns a particular function of your role and is organized around the progressive stages of a child's development, to present the ways your function may be disturbed by singleness at each stage. Because a given function is usually most important to your child at a particular stage of development, the functional problems connected to this stage are emphasized in each chapter. For example, in providing material care to your child, your role is most complicated and most meaningful during early infancy; during later infancy, you must concentrate on protecting him as he begins to explore the world. Chapter Eleven, on material care and protection, therefore emphasizes the problems connected to being single during early infancy. Thereafter, although material problems still arise and although you must continue to provide your child with care and protection, the deep significance of this function lessens, and such care becomes mainly mechanical in nature. A succeeding chapter, Chapter Twelve, on freedom and stimulation, emphasizes your role during the oral- and anal-aggressive stages, that is, the time from about your child's first efforts to crawl, to about his third birthday when he is a very accomplished runner, jumper, and climber. After this period, since you are most concerned with stimulating your child to assume a sense of responsibility and to broaden and perfect his sense of realism, you provide fewer freedoms and more restrictions. Chapter Thirteen emphasizes the restrictions and responsibilities learned during the anal-conservative period, the fourth and fifth years of life, and during his school years. Chapter Fourteen emphasizes your role in promoting a sense of reality and an understanding of sexuality in your child during his Oedipal and adolescent periods.

In order to analyze your role as a single mother as completely as possible, you need to read the following chapters through. What you may suspect as a disturbance in a particular function of your role with your child may be described in a section concerning a developmental stage behind or ahead of his present stage. Some single mothers encounter certain problems concerning a particular function which are unrelated to any specific developmental stage; these are discussed in a separate section of each chapter. It is hoped that this explanation of the chapter organization facilitates your use of the following chapters as reference guides.

# CHAPTER ELEVEN

# Providing Material Care and Protection

OF THE MANY ROLES you carry out as a single mother, the one most crucially meaningful to your child and least disturbed, actually, by the absence of his father is your role in providing material care and protection.

If you believe that your reactions to being alone may be overwhelming, keeping you from being able to do all that a good, constructive, helpful mother must do to insure her child's health, be sure to neglect one of your other functions, *not* this one. Your child easily can be helped to recover from the bad effects of poor practices in stimulating his development and sense of responsibility and reality; it is only with greater difficulty that the psychological wounds and distorting scars of hunger, cold, and injury can be healed.

Fortunately, however, even with a limited budget, you can usually count on being able to provide the elements of good material care and protection; where your own income fails to cover the basic, real needs, social welfare agencies can supplement your resources.

Are fathers still necessary? No, not in this connection, for you live in a modern, civilized society where a man's strength and swiftness are not necessary to provide material care and protection.

Thus, as you keep emotional reactions to the absence of father from interfering with your good care in satisfying the child's need for food, clothing, shelter, playthings, and protection, you can confidently expect to be able to keep him from suffering the anxieties that disturb his personality greatly and that automatically follow whenever genuine physical pain and deprivation is borne for a sustained length of time.

The only injuries that you cannot prevent are the ones that no mother can prevent: a few almost negligible childhood diseases, a few minor bumps and falls, and the occasional rough adjustments in getting along with people. As you stay alert and interested in protecting your child, you can keep him from suffering greatly from major injuries caused by carelessness, from fights caused by inadequate controls, and from embarrassments caused by ignorance.

## General Problems

Even though your child need not suffer from want of minimum essentials, you can easily feel unhappy about minor problems, like what and how much you can provide for him, and more significant problems, like how to protect him if other people over whom you have little control have direct and intimate contacts that can be injurious to your child. In a home made fatherless by divorce or separation, the grandparents and especially the father can create difficulties of both sorts.

### GIFTS AND POSSESSIONS

Conscious that in the harsh, concrete, materialistic world of a young child, no compensating points are given for reasons, motives, or efforts, but just for actualities, you are sensible to be concerned about your child's natural reactions to gifts from other people.

Since you are the one mainly responsible for helping him to develop helpful attitudes about material care and possessions, you must set limits and propose them to the people concerned, indicating that you intend to maintain them.

If your former husband is causing the trouble, one easy solution to arrive at is to have his presents of clothing and toys be limited to holiday times or else to a budgeted, low price. If the two of you cannot agree, you can still insist that his presents be kept at his home for your child to use there. Do not let this stop you from providing a reasonable supply of playthings for your child at your home, of course. Remember that your child needs toys as part of his ordinary equipment for daily living.

As for special treats like going to the circus or a movie, try to aim for a reasonable compromise in view of the frequency with which your child visits his father. If your child sees his father one day of every week, take turns. One week you can take your child to something special, and he can visit quietly with his father during that week; then the following week, your husband can treat your child to something terrific, while your time with your child is spent in a more subdued, routine way. If your husband refuses to agree to compromise, you must still take your child to exciting places, of course, for he needs the pleasure of such outings with you, too. You can, however, reduce the number of times you do this, for your child is already receiving a lot of stimulation of this sort from his father.

If he begins to compare you and his father, call attention to reality, so that your child is helped to keep clear the distinction between getting everything he wants and everything he needs; keep him from losing sight of the fact that love is not based only on gifts. As you keep yourself from foolishly overindulging him in an effort to compete with your former husband, you save your child the confusing trouble involved in believing that his pleasure is something with which to control others, rather than something he enjoys himself. Remind him, for example, "Of course, you enjoy going to the circus with your father more than you enjoy going to the grocery store with me. I expect you to, just as I'd like to go to the circus more than I like to buy food. And of course you like the new big bike at your father's more than you like your old one here, just as I like my new dress more than my old one. But if you were living with your father, you'd still have to live an everyday existence that wouldn't have circuses and new bicycles all the time, even though your father loves you. I love you too. I'm sure you have the things you need, don't you?"

People other than your former husband are much more easily dealt with in this regard. You can easily forestall presents from most relatives, for they are unlikely to have independent visiting rights with your child and will, instead, send him gifts through mail or store deliveries. If reasonable requests that they not shower your child with expensive gifts do not lead to their observance of sensible limits, inform them that you will return unopened all presents from them except at holidays when gifts are ordinarily presented. If, however, your own limited financial resources prohibit your being able to provide any luxuries for your child, permit your child to receive a reasonable amount of presents from others. Indicate to him that you will provide similar presents as soon as your finances permit, and that you are happy that meanwhile he is able to receive them from others. Even if you feel convinced that the presents are given as acts of meanness to show you up, compassion for your child's desire and need for sufficient playthings dictates that you smother your reaction and present these gifts to him in good grace. Remember that if your pride leads you to make your child wait for a special holiday to get something like a ten-cent box of crayons or a bag of marbles, you are causing him an inordinate amount of frustration that may eventually cause him to decide it is not worthwhile to want anything. Both of you are better off if you swallow your pride.

This kind of problem is not unique to the fatherless home; any mother in poor financial circumstances faces a similar conflict between the desire to maintain her pride and the desire to give things to her child. But your problem *is* unique because you have few resources to back up your pride in yourself; in fact, as you remember from Part One, your pride may have taken a terrible beating, especially if you are single because of a divorce, separation, or desertion. But rather than help yourself by resorting to practices that tend to hurt your child, reassert your pride through the methods discussed in the first part of this book.

Hand-me-downs can sometimes cause a problem. You may find yourself feeling unhappy about accepting from friends or relatives clothes in good condition for your child. Your child probably has no innate feelings, positive or negative, about wearing used clothing, as long as it is in style and suits his taste. So take a cue from his reaction: do not encourage him to feel bad about being a poor half-orphan who needs to wear used clothing; do not encourage him to feel indignant that others might think he needs such used clothing; do not encourage him to feel contemptuously triumphant because people pity him so much they have given him good used clothing that hardly looks used and cost nothing. Just explain in a matter-of-fact way that the wardrobe additions can be used—and be sure to buy him a few items that are brand new. In the same way, deal with used playthings.

### EXPENSES

Your role in providing material care for your child also includes footing occasional bills for his expenses—not the ones connected with his care, of course, but rather the ones connected with his need to be generous, his need to conform to usual neighborhood practices, and his need to be occasionally wasteful.

You may find yourslf resenting something like your child's desire to give a gift to his father or your former in-laws. Whether or not you like the people your child wants to send presents to, it is important for him to be able to play his role as a giver at such times as Christmas or birthdays. So pay for the materials he uses to make gifts for special people.

In a similar way, though you may feel that your neighbors are not particularly generous toward you in their understanding of or sympathy for your position, you must not let your child become involved in your reactions. Provide him with the wherewithal to hold his own with the neighborhood children, even the children of those neighbors who are not kind toward you.

Be sure, too, to let him spill and break things occasionally without berating him. Even if your budget is tight, you must remember he is a child and cannot be held responsible for all waste and accidents.

### MOURNING

If you recently have been widowed, you may be wondering what to do about having your child participate in mourning practices. Your religion probably determines much of your decision about this; but if your religious practices do not dictate strict rules about children, your decision about whether or not to let your child attend entertainments, wear ordinary clothes, celebrate special days like Halloween, or otherwise participate fully in usual childhood activities needs to be influenced by your consideration of your child's needs.

Most psychologists agree that a young child ought to be protected from and ought not to participate in elaborate mourning practices that go on past the immediate funeral time. The loss of his father is not likely to be quickly forgotten, whatever his outer actions are like; and his feelings about death are only complicated by practices that lead him to feel he is somehow being punished for enjoying life.

As you remember from Part One, it is natural for you to feel a moderate amount of desire to blame someone, somehow, and to resent signs of liveliness in others who have not been so terribly hurt by your loss. But as a mother, you are responsible for keeping this reaction from adding further hurt to your child's pain; start limiting yourself by refusing to involve your child in whatever open mourning you feel appropriate for yourself. Indeed, as pointed out in Part One, because you set the tone of your household, you must seriously question your own need to engage in open mourning practices. You may find you need to analyze your reactions with professional help so you can work through your reactions before you create a damaging impression upon your child.

If you have already let your reactions interfere with your child's behavior, stop hurting him further. Begin right away to make up for past actions which he has probably viewed as your failure to remember how much he needed you and needed reassurance from the ordinary events of life. A warmhearted and sincere apology and an honest explanation of what you have been feeling lets you make amends; and though it may seem a dramatic and somewhat embarrassing switch, a shopping trip to buy him some bright, new clothes and a trip to the movies easily put you back on the right path together. As you show your child that you are determined he not be hurt further by an artificial absence of fun and games, your joint faith in each other and in living is restored.

REJECTIONS

As is more thoroughly discussed in the following chapter, your child's identification with his father—whenever this is not overly painful to him—is an added source of personality strength. However, it is difficult for a child to develop a positive attitude toward his father if the father can only be viewed through the artificialities of usual prison visiting conditions or under the constrained conditions of chronic-disease hospital environments. Fears and dislikes are easily stimulated by the conditions themselves and then associated with the idea of his father, so that your child's over-all attitude is often confused. If he is old enough to have picked up the usual societal attitudes towards criminals or people with chronic diseases, he may also feel shame and guilt, even anger, and be reluctant to associate himself with his father.

It is wise to obtain additional professional advice about whether or not to let your child visit his father; the social workers and physicians in attendance at either a prison or hospital can offer you good advice about your particular situation, because they are close enough to the special circumstances to understand them fully. Ask for their help.

If the decision is that it is unwise for him to visit his father, you must protect your child from the feeling that he has been cut off from his father and from the feeling that he, somehow, is responsible for having rejected his ties to his father. Reassure your child that a child his age is expected to be scared by the strange sights and noises of a prison or of an extended-treatment-care hospital, that it is also difficult for you to feel at all easy about your visits. Explain that when he is older, he will not be so troubled, and then he will visit his father.

The only conditions that force you to shield your child from his father are ones that the courts recognize as the basis for enjoining his father from visiting him—alcoholism, promiscuity, cruelty, or gross dereliction of care. Should a court order already be binding, or should you need to obtain one because of the evidence of your former husband's behavior with your child, you must help your child understand why his father has hurt him. Explain to him that his father is very unhappy about other things that happened to him long ago when he was a child, and that he wrongly tries to take his unhappiness out on other people, even when they have had nothing to do with causing his unhappiness and even though they may love him very much and want to make him happier. Be sure to remind your child that he has had no part in producing his father's misery. Encourage him to think that some day his father may be able to straighten out his problems and then will be both eager and able to visit enjoyably.

It is almost always preferable to continue visits than to discontinue them, and it is almost always possible to work out arrangements that are neither confusing nor provocative of argument and therefore frightening. However, you must live with the reality that confronts you, and you must keep your child from being continually hurt by it.

A similar type of problem is presented by the father who flatly refuses to visit his child. Usually the refusal is explained as his way of protecting his child from the confusion of knowing a part-time father or the horrors of observing flare-ups of the old arguments that separated the parents.

If your child's father has this reaction, you need to protect the child from the pain of concluding that his father does not love him—true or not. Your child is ill-equipped to believe this, and even less well equipped to live comfortably with you if he believes that you are the sole reason his father does not visit.

You are not likely to be very convincing if, by insisting that his father does care for him, you try to correct or prevent your child's conclusion that he has been rejected. However, you do relieve this pain somewhat by explaining that his father wants to see him very much, but does not believe he is able to. You also comfort him by reminding him that, when he is grown up, he can go to visit his father and get to know him.

Do not make the mistake of buying presents for your child and pretending they are presents from his father. Things are not substitutes for a father's presence and love. Present gifts as coming from you or the sandman or Jack Frost or the elves; your child is much more likely to be comforted by thinking that someone magical and unseeable cares for him, than by thinking that his father has bought him some roller skates but will not come to see them used.

Generally, if you do not recall the existence of his father to your child, his interest in seeing him again will gradually lessen.

You also must protect your child from the implied rejection of having his father show up late or inconsistently for visits. Explain that you are sorry you do not know when his father is coming and reassure your child that he will have a pleasant time with his father, sooner or later. Remind him of the previous visits when he had pleasant times. If you make certain you do not attempt to sway your child and make the visits tense times that lead to great emotional upset afterward, your child is likely only to respond to what he experiences. And if his visits with his father are genuinely pleasant, they can be enjoyed thoroughly.

Essentially, the major problem caused by various kinds of rejections is the strain it puts on your child's identification with you —leaving aside all consideration of his ties to his father and the pains and losses directly involved. Remember that you must protect your child against pain in order for him to think that you are unshakable and strong. There will be plenty of time when he is an adult for him to realize that you are, like everyone, fallible and weak. But during his childhood, it is necessary for you to help him regard you as strong, so that he can regard himself as strong; and his identification with you is the bridge through which this conviction is established. If you are unable to protect him, if you are weak, then he, in turn, is also made additionally vulnerable, is also threatened. Because he already has an increased need to count on you as the primary source of his strength through identification, due to the absence of his father, you must ensure that his identification with you is kept free and clear of impediments.

Thus, when you absolutely cannot cope with some difficulty, you must help your child regard the difficulty realistically. Point out to him that no one can cope with everything. You keep him from feeling guilty about his human condition as you help him identify in a wider sense with the whole of humanity. Emphasize the generalities; do not emphasize your individual weakness.

### SPECIAL CHILDREN

Your role is complicated if your child is special and different from the average child.

If you must provide extensive medical care for a sick child, or special instruction and treatment for a crippled child, you must be certain to work with the professional counselors associated with the medical or treatment center he attends. Help in handling the increased financial demands, help in controlling the role played by your child's father, and help in analyzing your own and your child's emotional reactions can often be found through consultation with an appropriate professional worker. Be sure to call for such help. Let neither mistaken pride nor mistaken fears force you into wasteful self-sufficiency.

Do not struggle against almost fantastic difficulties in caring for your special child alone, because of fears that any admission of relative weakness may lead to a decision by social authorities to remove your child from your care.

Remember, the same laws that protect your child against cruelty and dependency and delinquency also specify what can be construed as any lawful reasons for separating a child from his parent. Consult your lawyer or a lawyer at your nearest Legal Aid office for specific advice about your particular situation; but keep in mind that your need for help from a social agency is no reasonable basis by itself for being separated from your child. Earlier in this chapter it was pointed out that because American society is not a jungle or primitive world, a man's strength and swiftness are not necessary in order to obtain food, shelter, and protection against the natural foe. Law has been substituted for force; and today what you lack because you lack a husband can usually be obtained either through your own efforts or through the help of lawful agencies like welfare bureaus. These agencies are obviously not designed to punish you for needing them. Consequently, protect your child from possible additional difficulties by seeking the aid available to you. Do not be bamboozled by your own pride or shame, and do not submit to threats from your former husband, your parents, or his. Protect and take care of your child, first, through every appropriate help; and be confident that, just because you need help, you will not be considered an unfit mother by any agency empowered to make this decision or to act on it and take your child from you.

Your job is less concrete, but more difficult, if your child is special because of what you believe to be an outstanding superior characteristic. Although many welfare agencies can take care of the needs of children who lack the usual characteristics of health, there are few agencies available for help for those children who have extraordinary talents—particularly if these have not yet developed into virtuosity of one sort or another.

Consult the authorities connected with education and development of talented children for help and suggestions about how to obtain the special instruction your child needs. For example, if you believe your child is musically well-endowed and you seek help in obtaining lessons, the principal of a music conservatory can often direct you to a suitable benefactor who may be interested in being a patron of your child in his development. The swimming coach of a winning team, the editor of a children's magazine, or other similar authorities are sure, at least, to take an interest in other problems and can provide constructive suggestions and help.

Of course, any mother with a child who is special faces similar difficulties if financial or other resources are inadequate to provide the care needed. But a married woman need not sort out the emotional complications of, in a sense, admitting weakness twice over. For her, the admission of need is made less disturbing; since she and her husband, united, cannot cope with the need, she can conclude it would be unreasonable to expect that it can be met by any resource except a special agency. Your problem, however, is made intensely personal, despite the greater objective rationality of the facts in your case, because you may find it hard to request help. Remember, though, that your child's needs are also increased by the absence of his father. He may find it difficult to love and respect you if he later realizes that his failure to develop a special talent is associated with your unwillingness to ask for help because of your personal problems. Avoid such complications by seeking help.

## The Working Mother

As a single mother who is working, you must make certain that your child is cared for in a manner as much like your own as

possible. Agency resources are usually available to help you with
the problems associated in finding care for your child. Remember
that about one out of four American families with children under
thirteen are without a father, and about one out of six women
who work are the sole support of their children. So the problems
you face are by no means rare.

Be sure to consult the books referred to in Part Two for additional suggestions about baby-sitters. Keep in mind that your
forced circumstances as a worker must not keep you from discharging a baby-sitter who causes negative reactions and acting-
out behavior in your child. Although your own need for occupational stability is extreme and usually greater than that of a
mother in a complete home, it is wiser for you to forfeit your
salary or take your vacation early, during the time necessary to
find a replacement for a neurotic baby-sitter, than to try to cope
alone with the huge problems made by the combination of your
working, your child's father being absent, and your baby-sitter's
failing to care properly for your child. Should you be forced to
seek new employment because of a work interruption caused by
your firing an inadequate baby-sitter, remember to consult your
local state unemployment office or state employment service for
legal advice about severance pay and unemployment compensation, as well as re-employment rights.

Be sure, too, to consult an agency for advice about temporary
placement of your child in a foster home. It is generally agreed
that a child is less likely to be hurt by staying with his mother,
even under adverse material circumstances, than he is if placed
anyway but permanently in a foster home. So before you place
your child temporarily in a foster home, seek all available social
and legal aids. If you are sincerely interested in keeping your
child and taking care of him yourself, you can usually find a
source of help that makes this possible.

If the tie between you and your child has already been strained
by former foster home placement, follow the appropriate suggestions about cementing identifications given in the following chapters, and work with professional advice to consider the special
circumstances of your particular problem.

In short, as you analyze the special problems concerned with
protection and with material care born of your singleness, you

will discover that your freedom to protect your child against pain and anxiety is almost unlimited. You can either take direct action to reduce the problems, or you can console your child as he puts up with certain ramifications of the problem.

## *Problems Connected with Childhood Development*

Because there is no vital and necessary father's role concerned directly with providing material care and protection for a child, the general problems that arise in the course of your child's development arise only because you let yourself be overaffected by your singleness. Natural though your reaction may be, normal and frequent though similar reactions may be, they are still, strictly speaking, unnecessary ones. With thought and determination, you can avoid and eliminate them.

Your child's reactions to becoming fatherless, however, are *not* unnatural or unnecessary. Because he is a child, he is forced to regard whatever happens to him, including being left by his father, as something connected with dangers he worries about because of the autism emerging out of his physical and psychological development at his time of life. This autism leads him to fear different fantasied threats. When something bad happens to him, it confirms the existence of these fears; so, instead of developing a sense of reality that eventually permits him to discard these fears as foolish fancies, he becomes partially convinced that he is right to be afraid.

As you are alert to signs that he is expressing inner difficulties in behavior connected with material comforts and fears, behavior that is not especially good for him, you can help your child alter his reactions so that they become both more comforting and less disturbing.

### EARLY INFANCY

Every mother, during the immediate time after giving birth, is naturally tired; her body, in the course of a few months, must change from being a body that carries and nourishes a rather sig-

nificant drain upon its resources, to being a body that alters its
skeleton, weight distribution, inner fluid distribution, energy
stores, and emotional approach to life so it becomes again the kind
of body that can procure insemination for the seed of the new life
it once again manufactures. The best arrangement for the mother
of a newborn infant is one that lets her continue her closeness to
her baby without needing to care for other concerns at all.

However, if you are alone at this time, you alone must keep
up with the demands of a day with your baby, even though your
natural resources are low, and you lack the mechanical help a
husband can provide.

If you try to do everything that a mother in a complete home
can usually accomplish with help, you are likely to push yourself to the extreme limits of your strength. And since your irritation increases as your exhaustion increases, and you are unable
to lull or play with your child when you are irritated, you tend
to promote a situation that affords relief and satisfaction neither
to yourself nor to your child. Disorganized or stagnant, your
child naturally increases his discontented complaints and his demands upon you. And as you continue this uncomfortable setup,
until exhaustion intervenes to let you both retreat into sleep
long enough to be partially refreshed, your despair and guilt increase and promote additional frenzy in your infant.

Remember you must protect your new infant absolutely from
your troubled reactions. So rather than attempt to meet all your
everyday chores—the many hours spent just in feeding and cuddling your infant, plus the laundry, shopping, cleaning, and cooking—let most of your chores go; make sure, before anything else,
that you are able to soothe and satisfy your child without hurry.
You need to feed yourself, of course, but you are wise to spend
a little extra money to eat well-balanced canned or frozen entire
meals and thus save energy and time from meal preparation
to spend instead for your child. Learn to take catnaps while
your baby is sleeping and to do necessary laundry or shopping
while he is contentedly awake. Though you may not be able
to relieve your unhappiness about being alone during this time,
you can, by these means, at least keep from increasing your own
and your child's tensions.

Deliberately cultivating an attitude of distinterest to chores must also be matched by realistic attention to cultivating a similar attitude of disinterest about many of the natural, but usually pointless, concerns of any new mother. Because you are alone, you must do without the reassurances a husband provides in keeping his wife from going overboard about these natural concerns. For example, most new mothers require occasional reassurance about a new baby's erratic breathing. In a complete home, a new mother can frantically clutch her husband's arm for reassurance and restraint when she becomes afraid that her child is not breathing; as a single mother, you can only sternly discipline yourself to keep from waking up your child to gain the relief of knowing that he is alive and breathing. If you are a woman who has been widowed during pregnancy, be especially alert to your sensitivity about death, and work hard to keep it from leading you to interrupt your child's sleep or wide-awake contentment to check on his health.

The birth of a child is a crucial stress to a marriage that is close to breaking up; while still married, a mother whose husband objected strenuously to her having a child may have tried to keep the new baby from troubling her husband. She may have tried to keep the baby awake when she was alone with him, in the hopes that exhaustion would force him to sleep when her unreasonable husband was home. As the baby responded uncooperatively, her guilts over her treatment of her child increased, and her hostility toward her husband increased because of the irritability caused by the guilt. The resulting tension and exhaustion could have easily pushed the marital conflicts to the point where the husband departed, leaving her alone with an upset baby.

If some ill-planned considerations like these have led to current problems, to the exhausted inability of your child to relax, remedy the situation and restore peace in your fatherless household by making a strict return to giving your infant his needed privacy. First of all, do not awaken your child; if he sleeps, he must be allowed to sleep without any interruptions, even for feedings or other care. He can demand such care himself when

he needs it. Because he has become extraordinarily irritable due
to his past experience, you must guard his sleep by methods that
are unnecessary for a child who has not been upset in this way.
Be deliberate and attentive about keeping almost all noise away
from him, lowering the lights, and keeping the warmth and
humidity of his room consistently high. When he wakes himself,
be as subdued as possible, so as to give him a chance to experience
being awake without being over-stimulated. Refrain from playing with him and laughing a great deal with him, and once he
has been fed and had his diapers changed, just sit quietly with
him, rocking him gently, crooning to him softly.

In short, treat him with velvet gloves. After a week or so of
this kind of return-to-the-womb existence, your child can become
self-regulating again, no longer irritable, and the two of you can
go back to where you started, only a little, if any, the worse for
the misunderstanding.

If, as a newly single woman, you are unable to remedy this
situation, be sure to consult your physician for help. He may
prescribe tranquilizing or narcotizing drugs for your child or
for you. Under no circumstances, of course, use drugs indis-
criminately and without medical advice. Though the effect of
prolonged drugging on a newborn human is almost indetermi-
nate, studies on other animals have indicated that it produces
a lasting inhibition of some body reactions that are extremely
important in later life. Should you have engaged in *any* un-
authorized drugging of your child, consult your physician for
advice on further steps to take. Be certain to seek this advice
even *before* discontinuing the drugs, for some disastrous reactions—even death—can be caused if use of some drugs is stopped
abruptly.

Of course it is usually easier to avoid problems than to correct
them, so you must seek to make up for the absence of the counter-
balancing force of a husband by severely challenging yourself
whenever you are tempted to experiment with extraordinary
ways of child rearing. Do not let being free and unopposed lead
you to being uncritical. Consult the books previously recommended to see what is said about a particular method. One excellent way of checking up on a child-rearing method is to connect it with the time and place in which it has originated. If, for

example, you are considering swaddling your child, examine the times and places it has usually been practiced; you can see that it has mainly been used when a mother has had to work away from home with her hands free for labor, and where the living conditions have not provided good protection for the baby against rain, snow, insects, and birds. Whatever else can be said for or against swaddling, it is unlikely to be necessary in the circumstances of your daily life. Consequently, you may reasonably determine not to use swaddling.

Remember that your job as a single mother is sufficiently difficult even when you carry out all your necessary tasks; so be doubly resistant to any methods that are unnecessary in your situation.

Although the most common reaction to depression is apathy which leads to cursory and perfunctory treatment of your child, your reaction may be to attempt to give your child as much as you can in the effort to make up for the father you cannot give him. Combined with your natural apprehension about your child's welfare, this reaction can easily lead you to worry about whether or not he is eating enough. You may end up giving him food at every sign of discomfort, trying mistakenly to feed him out of the irritations he may actually feel because of such other things as cold or noise or your own muscular tension when holding him.

Neither of these two reactions, indifference to the feeding or overfeeding, is helpful to your child, for neither one succeeds in taking care of all his needs and protecting him from painful stimuli. As difficult as it may be for you to restrain your anxieties, take time to see whether your child needs something other than food to make him contented before you bring on the food. Overfeeding cannot magically erase his discomfort from other irritations. Discipline yourself to keep from trying to substitute for a father by milk. Your child is thereby saved from getting fat and from being frustrated in his other needs.

As difficult as it certainly is for anyone suffering fom major grief, you must exert yourself to give your child at least the trappings of a leisurely feeding, holding him closely during the feeding, and letting him have plenty of time to complete his meal. (Although many a child can empty a breast in about five minutes, most like to suck longer when the state of the mother's nipple allows; and if your child is not nursing, but using a bottle, the feeding may often be twenty or thirty minutes long.)

Even if your child has plenty of time to suck during his feedings, in very wholesome, warm, cuddly circumstances, he may want additional sucking pleasure from his thumb or a pacifier. You may find yourself resenting his show of dependency, because your feelings about your own dependency hinder you from seeing your child's needs clearly. Remember that your child has every legitimate right to be dependent; you may envy him, but not thwart him. Like any mother, you need to provide him with the one plaything he really needs during this stage of life: a pacifier. Especially if you recognize that you do get tense during the enforced passivity of the feeding, or if you realize you have cut short the feeding time in the past, you need to try to restore peace and contentment by compensating for the sucking deprivation. Offer the pacifier and let your child suck it to his heart's content; although it is nonnutritive, it is still pleasurable.

During the first few months, very little is needed for your child's happiness: cuddling, food when he wants it, protection from cold or other irritants, and an occasional bit of extra sucking. Everything else that you can provide is an extra. He cannot notice an expensive bed, matched china containers for his bath needs, a silver spoon and porringer, or print diapers.

But if these contribute to your happiness during this time, you must view them as necessities. So long as you do not let them intrude on your child—leaving him cold and wet, for instance, while you go for the bath towel that matches the washcloth you used for his bath—and so long as they do not take crucial funds away from present or likely future needs, they can give a vital lift to your spirits when you are low. It is almost fundamental to a woman's nature to decorate and embellish the purely practical; as you combine this drive with your proper care of your infant, you can create additional happiness for yourself. So, as a single mother who wants to make things pretty for yourself, you are being, in a sense, more realistic than another mother who bitterly keeps herself from making these efforts because there is no one to praise her for them. Especially if there are no people close to you with whom to share your pleasure during these first few months, you must remember that the pleasure of your own eye is often pleasure enough. So, by all means, put forth the small amount of effort spent in prettying things up; it yields rich returns in your own sense of contentment and self-pride.

But be careful to recognize that these efforts are concerned with bolstering *your* own pleasure—do not project other, deeper feelings on your child and thereby increase his discomfort.

Keep fears and anxieties separate from the considerations leading you to adopt certain practices like overdressing or underdressing. Although you undoubtedly feel unprotected against the world, in some respects, and although you undoubtedly feel defensively self-sufficient, your child's need for clothing to keep him warm and safe from drafts has absolutely no connection with your feelings. Do not symbolize your worries by putting too many clothes on him, and thereby immobilizing him, irritating him, and causing the loss of valuable body fluids by excessive perspiration. In this kind of defensive reaction, you are really hurting your vulnerable child. Clothe him just enough to keep his limbs comfortably warm to the touch without being moist from perspiration. Be sure, too, to stop yourself if, instead, you have been underdressing him in an expression of your need to prove that neither one of you is overwhelmed by anything that has happened to you. Your child, remember, does not know that he is supposed to be worried about whether or not he can manage to get along without a father. He has no need to strip for action, combatting the world singly. In fact, he is irritated by being cold, and the net result of these tactics on your part is to make your child additionally demanding and additionally restricting to your freedom. All is easier for both of you when you stiffen your feeling of I-can-do-it-alone in less concrete ways that do not involve your child.

If your own past has contained little that you feel successful about—especially if the conception of your child was accompanied by strong feelings of defeat and disappointment—it is natural for you to regard this baby of yours with fierce defensiveness, perhaps as the only success you have ever achieved, as the only person you have ever felt secure about being close to. With this kind of reaction, you may try to make your child the perfect image of all the illustrations and photographs of babies you have ever seen. Like dressing up his crib, this reaction is not unhelpful by itself; your child *can* be dressed in fussy and fragile clothes and still be comfortable and untroubled. But you must be careful to avoid letting this kind of reaction lead you into cleaning your child too often and so irritating him by frequent re-dressing or wasting your limited energies. Save yourself and your child a minor amount of trouble by limiting yourself to occasional dressing up when you take your baby for an outing; do not try to make your baby look perfect every minute—the next step is trying to make him *be* perfect, and that, as you will see in the next chapter, can lead to serious difficulties.

During the earliest months of your child's life, your protective efforts are mainly concerned with keeping yourself from hurting him through neglect, misunderstanding, or accident. He cannot get himself into trouble during this time; in order for him to be hurt, *you* must make the mistake.

The absence of your child's father during this time can be considered either a hindrance or a help. The fewer people that come into contact with a newborn or very young infant, the less chance of passing along to him some communicable disease against which he cannot be immunized. So if you are a single mother during this time of your child's life, you probably do not have to contend with numerous head colds or upper respiratory infections in him. On the other hand, you do not have the additional eyes and mind to regard both the physical setup of your home and your methods of handling your child, to criticize and make valuable suggestions about changes that promote greater safety.

Compensate for this by making a special point of requesting your doctor's suggestions about safety; it is likely that he has pamphlets and checklists which he can provide to you. Use them to check on your habits. Do not let living alone and being the only adult around lull you into a false sense of security about your safety measures. Although you may be accustomed to walking carefully across a loose rug, for example, a baby-sitter may not know it is likely to slip under her. Get busy and anchor loose rugs, and look around for other sources of trouble. Be especially careful to guard against the kind of mistakes that are called "accidents" by kind people who hesitate to blame a careless mother who is already suffering, either with an injured child or with her own injuries. Remember that because you live alone, you are more vulnerable; if you alone are to take good care of your child, you must prevent such freak happenings as making yourself unconscious because you take the wrong medicine.

Do not let being weak and helpless in typical feminine style serve as the excuse for sloppy habits that may lead to trouble later on. Although you may not be able to do as good a job as a man can do, be sure you repair furniture that is subject to occasional folding up or breakdowns. For less cost than it takes to care for an injury, you can hire a professional carpenter to do the repairs you cannot manage by yourself; so take care of these chores.

Though it is a great deal of trouble to ask someone to stay with him for short periods of time and, certainly, a great deal of trouble to pack him up to go with you, do not leave your child alone in the house or apartment for longer than the few seconds it may take to get a buggy outside or inside—even a few minutes to take a letter to the mailbox on the corner has sufficed for an infant to hurt himself seriously. Discipline yourself to concentrate minor errands for scheduled times when your child is with you or with another adult.

Do not overestimate your strength. For example, a mother in a complete family can occasionally permit her husband to take the buggy down steps with their baby in it or can let him juggle both heavy packages and the baby, because a man's shoulders are strong enough and constructed so that they can take this kind of strain; but you cannot safely do anything similar with your female body. Take buggy and baby separately. Carry baby securely in one arm and stay free to drop a package from your other, if necessary.

Do not let the fact that you are a single woman prevent you from asking for advice from your physician when you notice your child acting irritably. Your physician can be trusted to respect your confidence and to honor your position. He is very unlikely to develop negative reactions to you or to treat your child less well because he finds out during a house visit that you are without a husband.

Your young infant is unlikely to develop any definite reactions to the absence of his father. He can only be troubled by you. So if you notice disturbances of sleep or eating, particularly, be sure to consult your physician and be sure to give careful thought to what you may have been doing with your child as a consequence of your emotional reactions.

Remember, too, to remind yourself from time to time of how strong you are and of how much you are able to do for your child because you care for him. This is probably the worst time to be without a husband as far as you are concerned; keep in mind, though, that your child suffers less directly now than at any other time of his life.

### THE FIRST AND SECOND YEARS

Just as you can be confident about protecting your child and taking care of his material needs during the first few weeks and months of life, you can be equally sure of success during the next period of his life, even though he is growing and is better able to get himself into trouble, as well as becoming better able to provoke negative reactions from you.

As a woman left single at this time of your child's life, your reactions are more likely to be less extreme than if the aloneness had started before or at your child's birth. Even the few month that pass between your child's being a newborn or very young infant and his becoming a crawler and toddler are enough for your body and basic emotions to have readjusted completely to the usual female menstrual rhythm. And though your child's demands upon you are more varied, actual time needed to take care of him has probably decreased. His feedings go faster, particularly, and he can spend long hours playing by himself.

Though your stamina is increased relative to the immediate post birth period, your reactions to being alone are of the same kind. You are still naturally depressed, worried, and resentful; you can still, in caring for your child, let your emotional reactions to being alone distort the quality of care and protection that you give and that your child needs. Your child's demands upon you are no different from those of any child; it is only your own emotional resources, differing so much from the mother in a complete family, that make the significant difference. Alone, needing to tolerate all the assaults of noise and movement, needing to meet all the demands for removals and reminders and cuddles and play, you may easily conclude that too much is expected of you. Your emotional reserves are likely to be bound up in your own problems connected to being left alone at this time (life is simpler if you have been alone during the earlier childhood, and are already over your first intense depression and anger), and you may find it exceedingly difficult to pull yourself out of your own thoughts long enough to pay attention to your child.

Mainly, your reactions are likely to be those that overemphasize his dependence upon you or those that overemphasize his independence from you. Since both qualities are necessary, but not to extremes, either reaction is likely to cause trouble for him.

In order to have a clear picture of why he needs a just-right mixture of independence and dependence, remember that he learns to identify with you as he practices doing the things which he *can* do that are like the things you are doing. Thus, he is unable to identify with you if he is forced back into being dependent, only blindly trusting you to take care of him, but not really sure of anything other than his feelings as he is cared for. And he is also unable to identify if he gets hurt in any way by trying to copy what you are doing—if he gets himself into trouble, if he is too weak or immature to handle the task he has tackled, or if you punish him for doing what he is trying to do. The reason he cannot identify when he has been hurt is that he has learned to regard himself in accordance with the sensations he feels. Unlike when he was just born, anxiety is not now the automatic response to pain. Instead, before feeling the anxiety that eventually is felt when pain goes on and on, he feels bad about himself. Just as he loves himself when he is feeling well takencare-of and all his sensations are pleasant, he hates himself when he is feeling pain. He wants to forget about himself; pain causes him to alienate himself from himself.

In short, if he is to learn to identify with you, he must be encouraged to emerge from the stage of just identifying with the feelings of pleasure or pain within him. He must be able to come out of himself and stretch, psychologically, to you.

Of course, this is true for every child; the important difference for you and every single mother is that your child's identification with you is his only major source of strength during most of his childhood. You must do everything within your power to keep this identification from being strained or estranged in any way.

Remember, he cannot learn a thing except how he feels inside himself if you push him back into dependency with regard to something he is beginning to be able to take care of for himself. And, if you force him into premature independence, you are both subject to the same troubles mentioned in Chapter Ten when precocious stimulation was discussed: he will develop wasteful inner patterns, and you will exhaust yourself in having to remind him and reinforce his wasteful "conditioned" premature learning. This occurs particularly if you have chosen, incorrectly, to teach him to take care of himself by letting him hurt himself or else by hurting him yourself through slapping or other forms of physical punishment.

Though the automatic response of forgetting about himself helps him bear pain caused by illness or injury, he might just as well get away from the pain since the pain does not do him any good, such a response has obvious drawbacks if the pain is supposed to make him keep something in mind, if the pain is supposed to teach him something. Slapping him when he gets into the ashtrays, for example, does not easily remind him not to do this again, because you run into the possibility of his merely withdrawing from his pain. The conscious, wide-awake, beginning-to-think child cannot keep his pain in mind if he is just trying to escape from the whole confusing and disturbing situation. He can learn, of course, to associate certain signals with the possibility of the pain he has felt, so that he can be trained, just as a puppy can be trained, to avoid certain parts of the house. But his mind is just not yet able, with the tiny background of remembered experiences he has accumulated so far, to distinguish between objects and the feelings they call to mind. This kind of training is wasteful. It depends on his using the "best" part of his brain to watch out for ashtrays or other signals, instead of having it free to watch what you are doing, observe the big

world, copy you in your strengths and skills, and thus learn to
be constructively independent.

If you want him to learn to take care of himself as soon as
his inner development permits, make it easy for him to associate
and remember and learn. You must constantly insure that you are
able to do what is really necessary so that the whole job of taking care of your child and protecting him is carried out fully.
Throughout his childhood, you must constantly be seeking to
make the job you must do as easy and simple as possible—and
one of the best ways to accomplish that is to help your child to
learn to take over more and more of the job of his care.

In order to help him learn what he is supposed to do, encourage him to do what he is supposed to do. Do not let him do what
he is not supposed to do; keep him away from dangers; stop him
from dangerous behavior; remove temptations out of his reach
and his line of vision; remind him of previous instructions and
prohibitions, *but do not punish him physically*.

If you cannot muster the will to stay with him and help
him learn how to play enjoyably with the big world of your
home and its objects, take the safer, though still not good, alternative of limiting the variety, the space, the freedom he can
enjoy. If necessary, put him in his crib when he becomes too
much for you—even though you recognize that you are at fault,
not he—and let him cry for the time it takes you to call a friend
and get some of your feelings expressed. Better yet, establish a
relationship with a professional psychotherapist and pour out
your misery on the phone. Then, relieved, get back to taking
care of your child appropriately.

Remember: the thing your child must do, more than the
child who has two parents around, is identify firmly and positively with you.

The worst possible reaction, therefore, for you to act out in
response to your negative feelings as a mother left alone at this
time of your child's life is to fail to notice your child's needs
for new kinds of protection from you. It will certainly cause him
pain. From your child's point of view, painful experiences met
in the course of unsupervised, undirected, unwatched activity
are as disastrous as painful experiences met in the course of your
mistaken ways of instructing him, or even met if you were to

take out on him your anger against the circumstances of your life. He does not care about motivations and reasons; he is a very concrete and materialistic person who only knows what he can feel or perceive objectively.

Although you may retain enough control over yourself to avoid these kinds of reactions, you may greet the first signs of beginning independence in your child with exaggerated relief. And you may then fail to let transitions be sufficiently gradual. Weaning, for example, which occurs naturally over a period of weeks, may be made a very abrupt learning experience. You may insist that your child, inside of a day or a week, either learn to drink from a cup or go dry; you may not continue for weeks or months to give him a cup first, followed by the bottle or breast. Or you may abruptly stop the cuddling that has accompanied feeding him his solids, so that he is suddenly forced into being by himself in his high chair, sometimes with the full responsibility of feeding himself as well. You may put him into replicas of the kinds of clothing worn by school children and actually end up by increasing his dependency, not his independence, because he must be immobilized so much longer to have his diapers changed if his pants are not infant ones with snaps at the crotch, and because crawling and moving is so much hampered by stiff pants or skirts as compared to overalls or leggings that follow the contours of the body.

Divorcing your child from the good and the familiar increases his irritability and disrupts his feelings of trust in himself and in you. So—particularly since you cannot realistically hope to be free of responsibility for your child for another eighteen years— remember not to rush his independence. Keep his trust in you well supported.

If you waited to return to work until your child weaned himself, and you noticed that he was extremely upset and cranky after your return to work, you may have miscalculated the source of his disturbance. It may not have been that he missed the continuity with you; it may have been merely that you were subtly pressuring him to make a very fast transition in weaning himself.

To remedy such overemphasis upon independence, you cannot, of course, try to start nursing him again or push him back into using the bottle. But you can regain your child's good graces and make him happy again, better identified with you, by spending extra time with him, cuddling him, and serving his favorite foods.

Watch your reactions connecting mobility and independence with masculinity. It is a natural connection to make, but you must be sure it does not lead you to push independence in your toddler son because you want him to be "manly." For example, do not let him get his legs chapped crawling around without overalls during cold weather on bare floors, because you think he is more "tough and masculine" with short pants and his sturdy legs bare. He has a long lifetime ahead of him in which to become a man and learn to suffer hardships; he is not helped toward that goal by having to learn that being active and inquisitive involves putting up with sore legs.

Like any mother, you can look to your child for guidance and direction as to how much newness he wants and can tolerate. If he still wants you to hold him on your lap, for example, he probably only eats and drinks happily when he is finally seated there; if he wants to sit by himself, he probably squirms enough so that he manages to free himself from your lap. If he is still mouthing his toes and feet, you need to leave them free of covering. If he is still using the sides of his playpen as supports for walking, you need to keep the pen up although he may no longer play inside of it, and so on.

Your reaction may not be to rush independence, however; instead you may seek to forestall your child's independence. One way this may be accomplished is by failing to exercise ordinary precautions to keep within reason the demands upon you of this period of your child's life. This may not cause immediate trouble for your child, but it can cause immediate trouble for *you*—and later on, for him, too. For example, after your pediatrician has advised you to introduce solid foods to your child, you may insist on preparing these cereals, fruit, vegetables, and meat from "scratch," because you regard a certain amount of labor as necessary to prove to yourself that you really do love your child. This conviction can easily spring from the guilts that always follow even the most temporary of angers and resentments, emotions easy for you to feel because you are alone, your child is a burden, and he is a symbol of a marriage that now is nonexistent. Of course, your child could not care less about whether you have scraped a freshly seared lamb chop by hand to make his meat course or have instead purchased it in a jar. Your reaction actually does not hurt him directly. But remember that behind that chop you are hiding negative reactions you ought better to face and solve, and you are also trying to express your feelings through a medium that will rapidly lose its trade value for love as your child grows. It is true, of course, that food will always be a pleasure to him if these earliest experiences of his with food are pleasant, but he is unlikely to mature with so little discrimination that he will continue to equate food with love. Even at a few months of age, he can have intensely positive happy feelings at times that are unconnected with feeding and cuddling at all. So by equating food with love, you are already insisting on an outworn means of proving to him your concern for him.

Before you find yourself, later on, unable easily to communicate your positive feelings for him, make deliberate efforts now to lessen your emphasis on food preparation; increase your attention to the other forms of stimulation (described in the following chapter) that tell him more effectively that you love him. Once you have thrown away the screen produced by your emphasis on food, you are also likely to find it easier to have more candor about your negative feelings related to being alone.

Another way in which you can try to work out a penance for feelings that you have every right to feel, but no right to release in such poor ways, is dressing your child in fussy or fragile clothing. This may not bother your child, but it does require extra laundry work or expense for you. Even in the way you provide safe play space for your child and his playthings, you can subtly be making trouble for yourself, while in no way either bothering or helping your child. For example, your young toddler is no more likely to be happy getting into your pots and pans and books than he is with his own toys, and no more likely to be happy crawling around all over your home than if limited to a single room or even, for suitable periods, to a playpen. So keep in mind that his play is instructive and fun for him even when it does not wear you out. Remember to keep unnecessary chores to a minimum; take back your things, and give your child the simple and inexpensive toys that are perfectly adequate substitutes for your kitchen equipment.

Other dependency-encouraging reactions that have direct affect on your child, however, are serious; they must be analyzed and removed. Whether you have only recently been left alone or have been alone for some time, you must be sure to guard against a few ordinary, yet dangerous, reactions.

For example, since there is no husband around clamoring for your attention, you may wonder why you need to cooperate at all with your child in letting him assume greater independence. You may reason that it is more bother to you to clean him up after he had smeared vegetables all over himself and his high chair than to feed him yourself. But the reason you must encourage and support his growing independence has nothing to do with other claims on your time; it is connected only to what he needs to experience. He needs to experience independence. Food, the stuff he has trusted all his life, is the safest substance to experience independence with. So every time you insist he let you feed him, or insist he put down the cup he is spilling all over and take his liquids from a bottle again, you are taking away from him, rather than giving him care.

If you recognize that you have been struggling with your child to keep your hold on his spoon, or that you have put the cup away you first used a while back when your pediatrician suggested it, stop yourself right now and go to work permitting your child to have his independence. Provide foods he can pick up easily, yet still gum and swallow; praise him for taking sips from the covered, spouted cup. Sit on your hands, if necessary, to keep from interfering with his chance to learn to feed himself. As you will see in the next chapter, by letting him participate in feeding himself, you are stimulating an important factor of personality growth.

Another unhelpful reaction you are likely to show that increases dependency is not connected with *how* your child eats or explores; rather, it is confined to the simple matter of *what* and *how much* your child eats.

In your depression, or in your guilt over your anger and resentment, or, indeed, in any possible emotional response to being left alone, you may seek to prove that you are acceptable in every way to your child, or you may seek to prove to yourself that you can control him and make him be what you want him to be, even down to details of taste and opinion, by forcing him to eat everything put before him.

Your very young child, like all children, needs to be able to eat what he wants of the foods you serve him at a meal; he needs to be free to reject a food he dislikes at a particular meal; and he needs to be free to decide to eat it when next it is served. There is time enough when he is older to insist that he sample every food served.

Remember that with any child younger than a two-year-old it makes little sense to try to force any taste, especially tastes in food. (The only time such action could be reasonable is in time of great famine and deprivation. Certainly in most modern American homes, this kind of argument—that he will starve if he does not eat everything at a given meal—is not a valid excuse for the mother's forcing her tastes upon her child.) However tender you may be because of the rejections you have faced, you must not behave as if your crawler in rejecting his carrots were identical to your former husband when he rejected you. You must not be afraid to try to change your child's mind. If your child dislikes carrots at one time, bring them back in a few weeks. Do not make the easy mistake of viewing a refusal of the moment as a refusal for all time.

If you let apathy and depression dominate your attitude toward life, you may shy away from anything that differs from the repetitious routine that characterized your child's earlier infancy and thus fail to offer him needed variety. In this kind of rejection of change, be sure you are not hiding a desire to punish yourself and your child because his father is not there to notice his growth along with you. Do not limit yourself to a narrow selection of foods that your child reliably accepts to eat; continue to experiment, and to let him experiment, with the foods your pediatrician recommends you try. If nothing else, arrange an artificial system that ensures variety for your child. For example, arrange a half dozen different baby cereals in line on a shelf, so that, by taking one from the right for a meal and putting it back on the left end of the line, you can avoid serving one sort, time after time; do the same with other foods, too.

If your apathetic reaction lasts longer than a few weeks, at most, stop relying on such artificial props; instead, seek a professional psychotherapist's aid in regaining your own natural desire for variation and your own natural willingness to extend this to your child.

When extreme, dependency-promoting reactions are severely disturbing to a child; so you must be alert not to act out this way.

One such reaction is a refusal to let your child grow because he is growing away from you. It is true that your life is realistically altered because of your child; and it is true that his tiny being, with so much power to alter your life, quickly grows away from intimate, tangible closeness with you. After only about six months, usually, he no longer wants your breast; in another few months he can feed himself almost the same variety of foods and in the same way—give or take a few messy slips with his spoon—as any adult. But you must remember that, in giving your child new taste sensations, you are not necessarily permitting distance to grow between the two of you. You are, equally, forging new links between the old, familiar closeness with you and all the new taste sensations.

Occasionally, this feeling of worry about your child's leaving you merges with confusion about what is and what is not rejection of dependency needs themselves. If you feel strong guilt about separating your child from his father, for example, you may not be sure that the child is not likely to connect his growing independence to your possible rejection. You may mistakenly decide that you had better force your child to keep on sucking past the time when he indicates his impatience with this slow way of drinking; you may insist that he nurse so that, as you see it, he can be positive that you are *not* trying to take everything away from him, pushing him away.

All of these wrongful ways of enforcing dependency often can be changed just by letting your child do what he wanted to do when you failed to recognize his growing urge to independence. Encourage him to use a cup, let him demonstrate his food likes and dislikes, let him have plenty of opportunity to feed himself—particularly the foods that he can very successfully handle, like crackers and bananas. After a few weeks of such encouragement, your child is likely to perk up and lose the list-lessness that ordinarily accompanies overdependency. A short while later, he is likely to be as independent as he ought to be in view of his age.

Although you may not have any of these relatively complex reactions to your child's growing independence, you may still find yourself naturally regarding meals with a lack of enthusiasm. You have probably, like most adult women, associated cooking varied meals with an act of love and care performed for a man. Single, feeling many different negative emotions about the man with whom you have shared the conception of your child, you may neglect to cook, and you may instead grow accustomed to a dreary sameness of diet. Since you and your child are likely to be sharing mealtimes for many years to come, this masochistic kind of reaction is not beneficial. Take steps to jolt yourself out of it. Making a minimum of work for yourself in meal preparation during the immediate postbirth period may have let you regain your strength, but now such a reaction is no longer useful.

Make an effort to redevelop your appetite; baby yourself by making your favorite dishes for several meals in a row. You may find it too hard to make an intricate dish for yourself and your child alone, because you somehow do not consider yourself worth all the effort, and you know your child does not really appreciate the difference. Or, like many women, you may find you cannot cook well unless you cook for an adult audience. So make an excuse for enjoying your own talents by inviting other people to share a meal with you. Your baby may be too young to be comfortable being fed at the same time that you and your company eat, but let him share the fun; have him nearby (feed him first), so he can notice that mealtimes need not be mainly silent times. He needs the stimulation of seeing convivial people.

Your child, in his reaction to being left fatherless at this time of life, may show similar reactions to yours; he may refuse to loosen his dependency ties and may even revert to infant ways that had been given up; or he may become fiercely independent and isolated, refusing to accept any cuddling, sometimes even refusing to eat or to sleep.

Although if he had a great deal of interaction with his father, he probably does have a vague feeling of loss, remember that most of his reactions are due to your reactions, and not to the actual absence of his father. Your child is absolutely unequipped to be isolated in his emotional response; so if you see him developing rejecting reactions, you have an obligation to provide him with babying and comforting. Without letting your anxiety turn into anger at him because he is worrying you, insist that he let his food remain in front of him throughout the mealtime, that he stay in his bed after bedtime, that he permit you to stay near him for short periods each day. Do not force him to eat or to sit on your lap; do not grab him or touch him whenever he comes near; but do insist that he let himself be exposed to some of the comforts he is rejecting in his pain and shock. Should he refuse to eat at all— even especially tempting foods like lollipops and ice cream—and maintain this hunger strike for more than a few days, you must be sure to consult your physician. Close cooperation between the two of you is essential at a time of crisis like this.

If your child has reacted by reverting to a former dependency, you are more easily able to provide him the consolation he is basically seeking. However, give him all the care he is seeking only at first; then after a week or so, without seeming punishing or heartless, be sure to perform for him only the tasks you have recently been carrying out, leaving the others that he was previously able to accomplish for your child to do. For example, if he refuses to drink from his cup by himself, but did formerly, after a week of holding the cup for him, place it before him, and leave it there.

Let him know you find his behavior understandable. Give him plenty of extra cuddling. His reaction, called a *regression* by psychologists, is his form of mourning a loss of someone familiar to him. Helping him bring the mourning out in tears helps him give up the unconstructive regression to inappropriate dependency. Since he can be sure of receiving extra loving tenderness from you, he usually need not continue for long to deprive himself of the opportunity to be independent in other areas. After a few meals without his milk, for example, but with plenty of patient and quiet consoling from you, he is usually able to pick up his cup and drink by himself again.

Without the male, who typically resents seeing anyone, even

a baby, being coddled and overly shielded from a few bumps, and who, accordingly, tones down the mother, you may make too much fuss in comforting your child.

Living alone with your child, you may encourage an exaggerated response in him to ordinary bumps and falls. If you have been recently widowed, your natural reactions to pain and illness and death tend to make you especially overprotective. If this kind of reaction happens to coincide with some of the other reactions already described—if, for example, you are paying little attention to your child until he has hurt himself, and then, remorsefully, you devote too much to him in the effort to undo your guilt—your child can develop complicating reactions to any and all kinds of pain. You may succeed in erroneously convincing him that he cannot tolerate any pain at all; and he may shrink from exploration and expansion, because it involves possible terror through pain.

Your own identification with your child, never helpful to any mother when carried to excess, is heightened by your aloneness with him; and this identification, too, leads you to want to save him as much pain as possible, even from minor bumps, so that vicariously you may keep yourself from being hurt.

You may also cause your child to decide that the only way he can get attention is to hurt himself, and this leads to his becoming accident-prone.

Your only safeguard in this connection is your deliberate self-discipline. Restrain yourself from rushing to your child. Keep in mind the harshly practical reality that he is seldom terribly hurt if still conscious enough to scream; if he is not terribly hurt, he can usually come to you for cuddling. Keep control over yourself, and make a deliberate point of handling your child's demonstrations of unhappiness over minor bumps by calling his attention to how minor they really are and how he is really mainly angry. Because your child is naturally so full of bounce at this time of life, you can easily re-stimulate his enthusiasm and confidence.

Remember that safety is often connected to how something is used. For example, hammering a nail is safe when done properly. Although you may not know how to hammer a nail safely and may not be able to instruct your child in the use of a hammer, most men certainly can. This is an additional reason for your being careful not to project your own views, standards, and tastes rigidly upon your child; they may be just the result of your feminine point of view or your special experience. So you must be sure to let your child have opportunities to form his own opinions. (The following chapter discusses more fully your role in replacing a father at this time. Basically, a father provides his child with helpful variation and relief from the experience the child has with the mother, and though the father is not absolutely necessary, his difference from the mother is.)

As you provide your child the care and protection he needs in the way he needs, his feelings of power and optimism sustain him in his efforts to move around and find out what the world is like. He is not afraid, because he has not been badly hurt; and he is convinced that he can succeed, because he has always succeeded in what he has done in the past. In addition, since he has identified with you, and you can do the things he is trying to copy, it is as if he had already succeeded. Nothing buoys up a struggling person better than the conviction that success is inevitable; so by your example and support, you can help your child use his experiences as stepping stones to greater maturity.

### THIRD AND FOURTH YEARS

Once your child is into his third year of life, his pace of obvious growth and development slows down somewhat. He needs little food during his third year, when growth is very slow; he increases his needs when his physical activity takes a spurt during the fourth year.

Most of his development, as pointed out in Chapter Nine, concerns the processes of muscular control bound up in vigorous activity, in talking, and in sphincter activity. As the following two chapters discuss in greater detail, his use of freedom and his development of a sense of responsibility are the major psychological tasks of this time. His material needs, which served as the arena for playing out his development during the earlier periods of his life, now begin to subside in importance.

You still need, of course, to be sure to maintain good nutrition without sacrificing variety and interest; but you can now begin to require that your child taste and swallow a bite or two of everything in front of him, rather than let him be totally free to decide for himself whether or not he intends to eat something that does not look appetizing to him. As he obliges you, he learns that things are not always what they look like. All through this time, he gains in his appreciation of inner realities, ones different from the surface characteristics that he was learning about previously. And he also learns that he can give up some of his independence without getting hurt. So, as you provide him with enjoyable foods but still insist that he give every one a try, you are making it easy for him to reassure himself with food while he is learning to cope with an entirely different continuum of reality, the one made up of abstract relationships like authority and responsibility.

Clothes, too, assume part of this function. As you provide him with tough clothing to run around in and with special clothes for special occasions, you help him reconfirm the awareness of differences he has been learning about. Responsibilities are tied to his clothes, too, so that you can now require that he come in to change from his good clothes before engaging in hard play. In encouraging him to take care of his own possessions, you are cementing much of the learning about responsibilities he is so actively engaged with during this time.

By and large, your reactions to being left alone at this time of your child's life are not likely to influence how you provide material care.

If you note that your reactions about food and clothing are like those more appropriate to earlier childhood developmental stages—the ones discussed in the preceding sections—you can eliminate a great deal of later discomfort for yourself and your child by consulting a professional psychotherapist. By now you have had too much experience in raising your child to let your singleness influence such things as the emphasis you place on clothes or eating. Only if this has deep meaning for you, therefore—a meaning that probably can be understood only after several visits with your therapist—is this erroneous connection likely to be made.

But if you are newly single, far more than is likely for the mother left single when her child is younger, you are very prone to develop reactions that influence how you now protect your child. In both phases of the protection that he now needs—protection from his own impulses and from those of others—you are likely to face a dual set of difficulties: first, forces that are the natural result of your feminine nature acting without opposition or support from a man; and secondly, ones that are the result of your particular reactions toward being left single.

In order to have a clear picture of how these forces operate, remember that your child is spending most of his energy during this time either in vigorous play with his own play things or else in vigorous play with other children who are close to him in age. His play things need to be mainly ones that he can put his whole body into, so that he can work out his muscular tensions and, from this hard play, derive the important feelings of being strong and courageous. His playmates, too, have the same needs and drives. Less interested in group play and games than they will be when they reach kindergarten age, right now they are mainly interested in running around and hollering and hanging on the jungle gym and bumping into each other. Only when your child is thoroughly tired out is he likely to be interested in the lotto games, puzzles, and picture books that he can share with you. Mainly, he wants things to play with that he can attack. Boy and girl, alike, are roughnecks during this time.

Once he is playing with other children, of course, he needs to know that he is protected from their belligerence. Although he knows how to respect others' rights and privileges, and so is unlikely to provoke trouble for himself, he still needs reassurance that you or some other authority can be counted upon to help him when some playmate tries to hurt him or dominate or bully him. Life is not so simple that the only requirements for a feeling of safety are self-respect and respect for others. Your child feels safe only to the extent that he can feel backed up within himself by his identification with your strength and courage.

It causes him a great deal of trouble if, in your reaction to being alone, you overemphasize your child's forcefulness, if you project your own belligerent desires because you regret you have not been more forceful and less inhibited with regard to aggressions against you. If these are your reactions, you may even feel threatened by your child's healthy lack of hostility and seek to make him feel angry. Even though you have been doing a fine job of letting him have sufficient freedom and equipment to work out his aggressive drives, so that he does not feel hostile and pent-up, you may still think he is lacking in courage if he seeks help and protection from you, or if he does not fight for his rights, but merely insists, lawfully through authorities, that he be given them.

You can come more freely to the aid of your child once you remember that there is a far cry between an adult woman seeking to avoid the consequences of her mistakes and a three-year-old or four-year-old seeking to avoid the consequences of the angers of others. You must not make your child suffer because some other mother has failed to instruct her child in how to play without bullying and hurting. You must not make your child suffer by encouraging him to forego his healthier urges that are noncombative. He needs to feel that he has a right to return to you, not just for protection, but also for dependency gratifications through cuddling and quiet games. If he is forced to conclude that he must always either be on the move or else solitary, he tends to form incorrect conclusions about the importance of brute strength compared to quiet activity. Without the daily opportunity to observe a father and thus see that men are neither always fighting nor always active, your child can end up feeling guilt about his natural, passive inclinations. Though this, presumably, is what you mistakenly seek, you must control yourself; instead, learn to accept his passive needs, too.

So be sure to provide him with quiet-time equipment. If you realize you may have placed too much emphasis upon very active kinds of play, remedy matters by gradually introducing the playthings that are fun only when played with quietly, the coloring books, the puzzles, the board games, and the books. Cut down drastically on television and its constant diet of vicarious activity. Even if the programs he watches offer no violence, they are almost always filled with action; combined with the imposed passivity of watching, this complicates his already mixed-up feelings about activity and aggression.

Overprotection causes other problems, ones that are equally

troublesome. Your child needs to know that you feel confident that he, like you, can handle small amounts of aggression turned his way. Though he needs help when others hit or bully, he must learn to handle arguments that are nonviolent. If you step in, he thinks you do not trust him. If you insist that he avoid all openly angry remarks, he thinks you are weak. He is not old enough to understand that your kind of courage in refusing to argue is an inner strength. He concludes, instead, that if courage does not show on the surface, it does not exist. When this mistaken conclusion is further supported by your definite acts preventing him from being vigorously argumentative, he can only come to one combined, incorrect conclusion: you are afraid for him; you do not think him strong enough to be courageous; you are just as afraid of anything forceful as he must be because he cannot possibly even tell people to stop bothering him; he cannot count on you for help or to give him courage; he had better go away from everybody or else learn to suffer being picked on.

The tendency toward overprotectiveness is one you must be alert to, for as a woman you have probably lost completely the quality of forceful aggression that marks all boys and girls during their third and fourth years. You may not even remember that you once used to act the same way; you may not have any capacity intuitively to see your child's need to be forceful. From your present-day, feminine vantage point, brute strength forcefully applied is shocking. Your womanly nature tends to spend its energies in more sustained, more controlled ways. This reaction against force is separate from your rightful concern about the results of force wrongfully applied, as in the destruction of his toys or damage to other things and to people. You are simply demonstrating a female characteristic of repugnance to force, a reaction that is basic and universal.

But your child does not share your adult, womanly reaction. Without a man around to counteract this natural tendency, to reassure you that your child is not going to hurt himself by throwing himself so intensely into his play, you may become unnecessarily alarmed. If you stop him, he knows only that he is stopped from being what his nature insists he be: active.

This tendency may be supplemented by additional forces

springing from the circumstances causing you to be single. If you are widowed, your experience with death makes you additionally sensitive to the effects of injury, and you can easily worry lest your husband's life stream not even be able to continue through his child. If you are divorced, your hostilities may be sufficiently high to increase your anxieties about force; this is especially likely if physical violence marked your former marriage. If you are an illegitimate mother who has gone through the first hard years of rearing your child alone, you may be additionally worried lest some accident during rough play take away the child you have struggled so hard to keep.

Still, you must manage to govern yourself so that you do not interfere with your child's natural spontaneity and vigor during this period. Realistically and objectively, your child, like any child, needs to express his new strength, and he must learn to do this by aggressive, but nondestructive, nonhostile forcefulness.

Put a rein on your tendency to stop him or try to tone him down. If you find yourself too troubled by watching him play brutally, pounding a lump of clay or driving his tricycle around the playground, send him to nursery school where the teachers are accustomed to such vigorous activities. Or else, once you have made sure he is playing where he cannot hurt anyone or anything —including himself—leave him strictly alone; get your fright and shock under control before you return to watch him.

Do not try to make it impossible for him to be vigorous by keeping away from him all the toys that let him pound and pummel and charge and ride about. This play equipment is a much safer way for him to work out his great stores of energy than ways he will still invent, like just running around or throwing his puzzles on the floor or flooding the bathroom with water. Unless you are prepared to make a thoroughgoing neurotic out of your child and to work at this horrid task from one end of the day to the other, you cannot expect to be able to keep your child quiet. So give him the things he can enjoy and use for noisiness and racing around.

Instill confidence in your child by studiously avoiding all actions that might detract from his happy-go-lucky self-confidence. Show him you approve of him; show him you are afraid neither of him nor of noise and hullabaloo. Secure that you are confident about him, your child can then take the steps necessary to develop genuine control over the situations he is likely to meet in play with his friends. He has no inner store of anger against you that he has just been waiting to release on the first person who opposes him, so physical fighting is not resorted to; instead, he can tell a friend to stop hurting him, ask an authority to stop the friend if this request has not worked, or leave and go off to play by himself.

By restraining yourself from interfering with your child as he works off most of his aggressions through hard play, you make it possible for him to develop the self-confidence and self-control that make relaxed and carefree play with others possible.

If you recognize that you may have cut into your child's courage by too many cautions and too much protection, introduce more active and vigorous play. You may even find it helpful to obtain professional advice to get additional insights into your child's reactions. During this time, as hard as it is for you, you must be sure to keep your reactions to being single from being obvious to your child; for if he knows that you can be hurt by others, particularly his father, he feels less sure of how strong you can be when he needs you.

This kind of insecurity can complicate his own natural reactions to being left alone if this occurs now. By this time of his life, he has developed a genuine tie to his father, so that he is quite conscious of the father's absence. Because his current preoccupations are with his own feelings of power and weakness, he is not sure that his new strength is unconnected to his father's absence. He may even conclude, mistakenly, that his father has left because of terror over all the new strength and power.

Guilt is caused by this mistaken conclusion, and most of his reactive behavior is his way of making a token sacrifice to expiate the guilt. Occasionally, his behavior is likely to reflect his desire to control his strength to bring back the father. So he may be lethargic and uninterested in activities he previously enjoyed; even eating and quiet play may be given up along with more forceful activity. Or he may be sullen, isolated, resentful, and restless to the point of behaving in a frantic and intensely belligerent way. If the magical use of his power to bring back the father is his major concern, he may even start behaving in a ritualistic way, doing things he never did before that bear some resemblance to ways his father behaved.

Whatever his reaction, you must try to lessen its duration and intensity, bringing the emotional meaning out into the open where it can be understood and expressed, and reducing the unconstructive, self-defeating emphasis. Your goal is to help him express his feelings through words or directly mournful actions like crying, and to stop him hurting himself by starving himself or refusing to eat anything but perhaps a few trusted foods. Draw his attention to the connection between what he is doing and what he is feeling by comments like, "Chocolate tastes good, even if you're unhappy about Daddy being gone," or, "I guess starving ourselves isn't going to make your father come back home to live, so let's have something special for supper; let's have ice cream, okay?"

Though this is the time of his life when he is having particular trouble in reconciling himself to his own weakness, he must not be permitted to act out vain ideas that he can do the impossible. Explain to him that you understand how much he would like to bring the whole family together, but remind him that acting like his father is not going to bring him home; point out that since, after all, he was not the cause of his father's leaving, he cannot very well be powerful enough to bring him back.

If you are divorced or separated, he needs reassurance that you were not weak and powerless with regard to the breakup of your marriage. You must help him to understand that a divorce is two-sided and takes place between two adults, it is not something that you just suffer and have had no part in creating. It is helpful if you link this to his own preoccupation with controls, if you point out to him that one of the main reasons why you want him to learn to be able to get angry without hurting other people is that you and his father never learned that too well, and that is one of the reasons why you ended up deciding you did not want to be married to each other any more.

He needs reassurance that death is not a way of punishing people—in his mixed-up way, he may have decided that this kind of link exists, and part of his inactivity may be due to fears that a similar punishment is waiting to overtake him soon.

You must also reassure him that his father has not gone because of your child's hatred for him. Remind him that wishes and thoughts are not actions.

Your child may direct hostility toward you during this time, accusing you angrily of keeping him from having a father. A direct counter-statement is useless; point out to him, instead, that you have not let others hurt him and that he knows he is often happy, as are you.

If his reactions take a destructive turn, so that he breaks his toys, throws food around, tries to hurt you or others, or cuts and tears his clothing, you must be careful not to react with anger. Without any suggestion that a part of you may be vicariously joining him in his attack on the world, explain to him firmly that this behavior is pointless and must not occur again. Remind him that it cannot succeed in solving his loneliness. If he is angry, he can shout and cry but not try to hurt anyone, including himself, or destroy things, no matter whose they are.

If there is a repetition of a destructive outburst, be sure to consult your physician so that you can rule out any developing sickness that might be undermining your child's controls. Be sure to follow through if he suggests you consult a psychotherapist.

During these years of a child's life, the father exists as a definite person with whom the child has a definite relationship, one that is usually less protected than he has with his mother. As you refrain from curbing your child's aggressiveness in your efforts to protect him from injury, you are replicating the typical father's role.

### Fifth and Sixth Years, the Oedipal Time

Most of your role during this Oedipal period is connected with your child's sexual development and is discussed in detail in Chapter Fourteen. As you remember from Chapter Nine, this is the time of his life when he tries to live out various fantasies in which he is a grownup; so your role throughout the period is to resist in any way the temptation to substantiate his fantasies.

You must be particularly aware of his efforts to manipulate you into this position—very often, the comfortable and secure activities that deal with eating, clothing, playthings, protection from accidents, and comforting for minor injuries, are the ways in which he most obviously shows what it is he is trying to do.

These manipulative efforts are not limited only to a child who, like your child, is fatherless at this time or has just been left fatherless. The universal Oedipal fantasies create similar problems for every mother. But without a husband to champion you, you must often carry out tasks that are uncharacteristic of a mother in a family; and you must always take the responsibility for being constantly cagey, alert, and analytic. As was true of the immediate postbirth period, when the single mother must take over the entire responsibility for all material care and protection of her child without a husband to share these concrete burdens, you must, during the Oedipal period, take over all the responsibility for keeping proper care and protection from becoming like Oedipal versions of what this care and protection mean. In many ways, you have a twenty-four-hour, everyday job of being a home-style psychologist.

Your own reactions to the loss of your husband at this time must be screened from your child and kept from causing distortions of caretaking and protection, else your child is likely to distort the meaning of these reactions. If you pull away from your child, giving him only perfunctory care, he sees this as rejection or repulsion of his sexualized and seductive efforts toward you; if you react by getting overinvolved in your child, he sees this as a beginning success to his seductive efforts.

Differentiate between your child's reactions and distortions and yours. If you yourself take the lead in causing alterations and distortions, your reaction is not realistic, and you must seek outside help in order to restore a sensible perspective. It is difficult enough, if, because you do not have the support of your husband, you merely let yourself get inveigled into your child's fantasies and so get caught up in something unrealistic concerning food and clothing. Your reaction is an expected one to being alone at this time; you must, however, be on guard against it.

The various "ploys" that your child can use during this time are legion. The only guide to recognizing them an excellent sense of realism.

For example, your child may seek to flatter you by eating

enormous quantities of food, particularly if there has been a previous tendency on your part to equate food with love and obedience. To resist these efforts to distort, call his attention to the amount he is eating. Comment that you hope the reason he is eating so much is not because he thinks you believe it a good way to prove he loves you. Tell him you would go right on cooking food for him even if he started to hate you, because he is your child and you love him and want to take care of him. If you see that he is actually making himself uncomfortable by constant overeating, put a stop to it. Remind him that just as he cannot become a little baby again by doing nothing but eat and sleep the way a little baby does, he also cannot grow up instantly into an adult just by eating a lot. Explain reality to him, time and time again; remind him that it takes years for children to become grown-up, and though they need to eat in order to grow, they cannot rush growing up by getting fat. If you know of a child who is overweight, call your child's attention to this example: "Look at Janet, she's awfully fat, and I bet she ate lots and lots in order to get that fat, but she still isn't any taller or more grown-up than you are, is she?"

He may use clothes as a vehicle for the same routine. Objecting to wearing little-boy clothes, for example, he may insist that you let him wear a necktie every day. Of course, unlike overeating, this actually does not hurt him, so you may be additionally tempted to yield to his eagerness to look like an adult. But remember that almost all the important psychological development taking place during this time is unreal, fantastic, and intangible. So stick to your usual routine; tell him that ties are for special days when you want him to look particularly good, but a child wears tieless polo shirts and sports shirts for every day.

A daughter, of course, can also show these responses or, perhaps more typically, demonstrate almost opposite reactions. She may become finicky about her food, criticizing you or it; she may insist on wearing overalls all the time for a while and then become insistent that she wear her party dresses all the time. Handle these reactions by reminding her of what is usual and sensible. It is difficult to avoid feeling as if you were bragging or refusing to take criticism when you resist her comments about your cooking, especially if she phrases the criticism by referring to the mother of another child. But even though you do not have a husband with you to tell your child that your chocolate cake is as good as any he has ever eaten, you must avoid getting caught up in competing with another mother because your child has egged you on. Do not tear down the neighbor—particularly by indicating that she has a husband and so has more time for fancy baking—and do not change your style of cooking in the futile hope that this is really what your child is after. If you start making better chocolate cakes, for example, even if your child finally grants that they are the best, you are making yourself vulnerable to chronic teasing. As soon as she figures out that she can tease by saying she does not really care much for chocolate cake, she can say that the mother down the block made a spice cake that she liked very much—and so the process begins again.

Do not let your feelings about being powerless to control your own life and previous marriage get involved in your objective regard of your child's efforts to wrest control of your home away from you. Calmly remind her, if necessary, that even though you may not have been able to keep her father with you, you most certainly are big enough to go right on making the decisions as to what gets cooked and eaten in your home. The same reminders are needed for a boy, too.

Although you must stoutly resist your child's efforts to manipulate you so that he does not end by concluding that he is the big cheese, you must be careful to differentiate these efforts from the reasonable and healthy ones related to his showing you off to his friends. If, for example, he asks you to make a chocolate cake for his friends because you make the best cake, you need to support both his generosity and his pride in you.

This aspect of his behavior with his friends—not only with you—in which he tries sharing and giving can sometimes be distorted by you as you react to your own past. Your natural feelings of resentment toward your former friends who have deserted you now that you are single must not be allowed to color your child's experience in making friends. You need to remind him that friends are not purchased; but remember to remind yourself that generosity *is* an appropriate part of friendship. Your child may well be luckier than you have been, so you must not let your disillusionment keep him from learning practical generosity and a dignified expectation of fairness from others. Protect him from the possible psychologically crippling effects of your past sad experience.

Because your child, like any child, helps himself out of the Oedipal dilemmas by creating minor rituals that reassure him he will become an adult in time, you can, without encouraging in him a distorted appreciation of himself, indulge him when it comes to deciding special facets of life at special times. So long as you keep him from thinking that he is going to decide what is for dessert every day, you can permit him to make the decisions on Sunday or at Thanksgiving or Christmas, for example, letting him choose from the list of traditional desserts. On such holidays, he can be helped to feel less deprived due to his father's absence if he is permitted to play part of the father role, sitting at the head of the table, tasting the seasonings during the cooking, and so on.

In providing playthings, be sure to include toys that encourage the assumption of the appropriate role your child finally settles upon at the termination of this period: provide toys like embroidery kits and doll sets for a daughter; tool kits, erector sets, and model vehicles for a son.

Should you note your son reacting to being left alone at this time of his life by radically altering his choice of playthings, or of clothing, to those appropriate for girls, you must pay additional attention to reassuring him about the inevitability of becoming an adult after a few years. Reassure your son that he will become a very good man when he grows up, remind him that now he is a very good boy. If this does not result, after a few weeks, in his once again preferring boy's clothes and playthings, be sure to consult your physician and a psychotherapist; the unnecessary conflicts that usually underlie this kind of behavior can more quickly be eradicated with professional help. Tom-boy behavior in a girl is less likely to be indicative of serious inner problems, but if extreme, take the same steps to remedy it.

By now, most protective efforts are focused, not on keeping your child out of trouble, but on keeping him from troubling others, particularly you; these efforts are discussed in Chapter Thirteen. You must be sure, however, as explained in greater detail in the following chapters, that you protect your child against being sexually molested. Although a criminal pervert can, of course, select a child of any age to molest, usually only a child in the Oedipal period is subject to the blandishments typically offered—a younger child gets scared and runs away, and an older child knows enough to run for protection.

Because there is always an undertone of sexuality and seductiveness to most parental discussions of sexuality with a child, you are likely to find yourself partially inviting additional tensions by calling attention to these topics; so your role at this time, already difficult because of the absence of your child's father, is further complicated. By keeping the discussion on a level of concern about injury and pain, however, you can minimize the tension-provoking aspect. Tell your child that some very unhappy adults and even some very unhappy children sometimes try to hurt other people, particularly happy ones like him. Remind him that he is not supposed to let anyone buy him candy or other presents, that he is not supposed to let anyone offer to take him for a treat elsewhere. Remind him that only when you have given him permission may he accept invitations from another person. You must emphasize that it is your direct instruction to him that is required, not familiarity with the other person—unfortunately, many sex crimes are committed not by strangers, but by people well known to the victims.

Many of the same precautions that protect your child from molestation by an adult or disturbed older child also protect him from the injuries and infections that frequently follow "let's play doctor" games with other children his own age.

The likelihood of phallic infections is diminished as you instruct your child that he may not open or pull down his pants to play with other children. Remind him that when he wants to masturbate, he should go to his own room and must make sure he has washed his hands first. Should your daughter develop an infection, your physician can also help remind her that she is not supposed to put things in her vagina.

Of course, as Chapter Nine has pointed out, the importance of having two parents during this time cannot be overestimated. Your role at this point cannot be a replacement for a father's role. Your child's basic need is not even a simple matter of needing to observe a male role and a female role; your child, like any child, actually needs to observe and interact with two parents who like each other and relate to each other as male and female. You can and must protect him against the development of lasting distortions of his understanding of his own sexuality and of differences between people. This role, protective, yet instructive and imposing definite responsibilities on him, is discussed more meaningfully in the following chapters.

Of the nonsexualized aspects of a father's role during this time, probably the most important are connected to use of different playthings. A man, for example, gives his daughter a great thrill by playing dolls with her and gives his son deep pleasure by working on a model airplane with him. You cannot, of course, duplicate the maleness of his participation in games and housekeeping with your daughter (although you can provide help by greater ties through identification with you). You must not fail, though, to exert yourself to provide the necessary help to your child—boy or girl—in figuring out how to use some of the equipment, like an erector set, that you may not yourself be very familiar with. If you cannot learn from the instruction sheets provided with the outfits, you must ask a friend to teach you and your child.

Do not let your feeling that you are already taking care of enough responsibilities interfere with providing your child a most valuable addition to the household at this time, a live pet. Having a pet reassures him that he is not just a baby, but is really becoming grown-up enough to be able to take care of other things. Even a drugstore aquarium that costs a quarter and contains a single goldfish can be used by your child at this time for his own pleasure and reassurance.

During this period, your job primarily consists of keeping your child and yourself from symbolizing incorrect conclusions about the Oedipal problem. Once he has passed through this period, the added alertness required of you is no longer necessary. Not until adolescence, in fact, is there much ordinary, nonneurotic use of material care and protection as symbolic equivalents of inner emotional problems, except for the ones immediately following extreme emotional stress.

### GRADE SCHOOL YEARS

Once your child is in grade school, although either of you may react negatively to becoming newly single and alone, and may symbolize these reactions at mealtimes, through other material concerns, or through those connected to protection, the reactions are likely to be short-lived and easily remedied by the ways suggested in the foregoing sections.

Occasionally, other minor problems crop up, though, connected to the fact that you are without a husband to share the responsibility or blame. For example, because of the natural development of your child's tastes and interests, he may need some relatively expensive equipment for sports, music lessons, or other hobbies. If, once you have purchased the equipment he needs, he loses interest in the activity, you are "stuck" with only yourself to berate for having been foolishly optimistic in thinking that your child's interest would continue. You may then feel less than willing to provide equipment for his next new interest. Rather than take the mistaken approaches of either insisting that your child continue to do something that is no fun for him at all or insisting that not develop new interests—thereby showing him that you do not trust his judgment—you do well to consult experts who can advise you. The band teacher at school, for example, can help you to decide whether or not to purchase a musical instrument once a rental period has passed, and the gym teacher can offer advice on things ranging from baseball mitts to dancing classes.

In large part, the kind of protection he needs from you is connected with his development of a sense of responsibility and reality about authority, topics discussed in following chapters. But should you live in a community where either school teachers or the neighborhood children often engage in injurious practices, you must help your child maintain his sense of security by protecting him from harm.

Misuse of school authority by school personnel probably poses a unique problem to you, because you cannot ask your husband to argue with a teacher who has been unfair to your child. You also cannot gain the added assurance that many mothers in a community can gain from deliberately emphasizing their husbands' community positions, drawing upon the prestige and status of their husbands to increase inner confidence. You may even fear that an open argument between you and a teacher might lead to remarks about your single status, remarks that are hard to confront and dismiss, like, "Of course, we've found that only the unmarried mothers of our school children object to our usual disciplinary measures."

But, as with everything else, you must make a decision between substantiating unnecessary inner shame and guilt or repudiating it. Stop letting either yourself or your child suffer needlessly because you are single. You need, even more than a woman whose husband is present, to let your child know you will stick up for his rights.

Consciously determined to refuse to back down from any activity or any argument just because you are single, you can easily figure out the appropriate approach needed for a particular situation. Just as you encourage your child to be realistic, you must remind yourself to be realistic. If a teacher has unjustly punished your child or utilized a disciplinary method that infringes on your parental rights and transgresses her lawful rights, stick to discussing only these misuses of school authority. Do not let red herrings lead you away from the realism of your objections. Even if it is true, for example, that only single mothers object to a school's punishment by fining a child money or by corporal punishment, your realistic objection still stands, firmly rooted in traditional concepts of family privacy and school authority.

Should protecting your child from harm caused by neighbor children finally turn out to hinge on the absence of his father—a highly unlikely happening—you ought to give serious consideration to moving to a new neighborhood. Most of the time, a social agency can help you obtain an apartment even though you cannot provide references to a husband's place of employment.

Before arriving at the conclusion that your child is having special difficulties because of the absence of his father, though, be sure to meet with a few of the other families in the neighborhood and investigate what, if anything, the fathers may be contributing. Also be careful to be utterly realistic about your child; if he is provocative, either because he seeks to bully or else is inordinately timid, his inner emotional problem needs care before anything else claims your remedial efforts.

Keep in mind that there is a significant difference between not having many close friends and being picked on, beaten up, or otherwise harmed. Even though your child may not have interests in common with most of the neighboring children, and so may have few friends, actual protective efforts on your part must be confined only to occasions where his personal privacy and integrity are threatened or violated.

The same kind of strict attention by you to reality is demanded whenever you are required to protect your child. As is more thoroughly discussed in the following chapters, you must not let yourself feel that your child ought to have special social privileges because he lacks a father. Just as he must learn to hold his own against reasonable aggression (remember, though, no person, big or little, ought to seek to handle physical fights by anything other than recourse to lawful authorities), he must measure up to his usual social requirements.

Though without a husband, take special care not to add to your child's occasional social discomfort by refusing to participate in activities that ordinarily involve both a husband and wife. You are likely to find that you are not the only mother attending a family meeting alone, and your special status as a single mother is also unlikely to be unique. Remember, almost one of three marriages is broken by divorce or separation, and many of these broken marriages involve school-age children. Join the church groups and other community affairs; they provide both you and your child added gratification.

Protect your child from embarrassment, when an event calls for the attendance of a father, by arranging that he attend either along with his favorite adult male relative or friend or with another father-son combination. Encourage him to put his feelings of constraint to the test; insist that he attend, even when he does not want to, and thereby actually experience how much or how little he feels out of place. If it turns out that he was disturbed because he could not participate in a part of the ceremonies, however, shift your protective emphasis to helping him evaluate the experience as realistically as possible.

Since most of a father's role during the latency period is connected to matters other than care and protection, you can be confident that you can supplant his minor role completely in these matters during this time.

With the exception of the problems just described that are realistic and directly connected to the actual absence of your child's father, problems at this time are an indication that something requires the careful attention a professional psychotherapist provides. Because the school years are the latency years, the years during which no new physical developments take place in your child, the years during which he demonstrates by his behavior much that will be characteristic of his behavior when he becomes an adult, these years provide an excellent time for remedial efforts worked out with trained professional help.

Some of the signs you must be alert to, therefore, are severely limited food tastes, with consequent overweight or underweight; overemphasis upon clothes or peculiar dress habits; and contempt for or a destructive attitude toward or an overemphasized possessiveness about playthings. Usually, one or another of these attitudes accompanies the isolation, dependency, hostility, or withdrawal that are emotional consequences of problems in the past. Should you recognize the existence of problems like these, be sure to consult your physician and ask for his help in selecting a psychotherapist.

## ADOLESCENCE

At your child's puberty, the many body changes cause some direct and real differences in his needs for material care and protection. During this time when he faces an almost completely different person as he looks at himself, he requires a great deal of tactful help from you, even as you provide him with these familiar cares, so that his emerging feeling of independence is not injured.

Although your role as a mother by now is sufficiently stabilized so that you ought not to react to being left single at this time by altering your handling of material care and protection, the significant differences in your child may tend to provoke this kind of reaction from you. You have been familiar with a little child; now, confronted by a mature person, you may find yourself uncertain of what to do.

However you may react to being left alone and to finding that your child is, in many respects, a stranger, you must not permit yourself to be relegated to the position of a second-rate citizen in your home. Although a certain amount of playing up to a teenager's new sense of adulthood is helpful in sustaining his confidence, temper this with quiet reminders that you will continue to rely on your own experience, primarily, as a guide to your decisions. The heady wine of authority over others is too strong for a teen-ager to have except in small, spaced doses.

His needs are simple: he needs enough good food to keep his altering body growing well; he needs clothes that are sufficiently varied and sufficiently stylish so that he need not face ridicule because of them; he needs an expanded allowance (or the freedom to take part-time jobs that will supplement his old allowance); and he needs protection from all the sexualized and nonsexualized threats of this time. Chapter Fourteen discusses in detail the conflicts about sexuality; Chapter Thirteen discusses in detail the problems connected with part-time jobs, including the protection you must provide against his being exploited.

As Chapter Nine pointed out, an adolescent typically engages in a great deal of substitution and rationalization. It is your teenager's capacity to rationalize and substitute, in fact, that most often causes the moral quandaries you may experience when you mistakenly get seduced into viewing things from his point of view.

As a cook and feeder, your role during this period is difficult because you must insist that your child eat appropriately at mealtimes, yet his social independence leads to frequent between-meal snacks that may seriously interfere with his appetite at mealtimes and also may involve his participation in activities that conflict with usual mealtimes. In a home with a complete family, mealtimes tend to be oriented around the return of the father from work; usually the family meets together at mealtimes so that the father may see his children. In the complete family, too, when an adolescent has guests, they are still merged with the family, subordinate, in a sense, to the father and mother. In your home, though, it may be difficult for you to see clearly any good reason for insisting on having mealtimes together or at a specific time. Eventually, led by your misguided sense of rationality and flexibility, you may face the situation of having been transformed into a short-order cook. Your willingness to support your child's generosity and sociability—rationally so desirable—may lead to your being a waitress for him and his friends, almost required to be grateful that you need not delay your own meal for the "second table"—an end state obviously undesirable.

Abandoning your own dignity is no help to your child at this time. So, though this kind of consideration may seem trivial, it still is important for you. Your adolescent is now, in many ways, just an Oedipal child—bigger and now able to put his fantasies into practice if he wishes and is foolishly permitted to—but still not sufficiently experienced or responsible to be allowed to manipulate or boss you.

So stiffen your resolve and once again assume responsibility for protecting him. Now you are not just protecting him from the actual physical malfunctions that can result from poor nutritional habits; more importantly, you are keeping him from the emotional consequences of his self-centered dismissal of you.

Keep in mind that your adolescent must have a sufficient bond to you to be able to communicate with you in order to obtain information and emotional support when he seeks it. If he is permitted to estrange himself from you early in adolescence, just because you submit to the apparent rationality of his claims that other interests are more significant to him at the time, he is forced to resort to friends, books, or other authorities when he needs help—or else, even worse, forced to be totally self-sufficient.

So, though you are not viewing mealtimes, clothes, or other material cares with a distorted eye, take steps to insure that these material considerations are not being used by your child for symbolic, acting-out operations. Such acting out leads to his cutting himself off from you, if only to avoid his guilts. In essence, you must make sure that you are not being used, that the care you provide is not being used. You must not substantiate your child's adolescent, autistic belief that he is the only important person on earth.

Whether you are newly a single mother or have been one for years, avoid one of the trivial difficulties of adolescence by insisting that your child and you sit down together to discuss the fair apportioning of his clothes budget. Do not let him convince you that he needs everything. As your child is helped to see that his extra sweater is only possible if he gives up special bowling shoes, he can more easily accept necessary limitations. Because he can not borrow his dad's things, a son probably has more difficulties of this sort than a daughter who can borrow yours.

In all matters save one, you need not expect any problems about equipment. One tennis racquet, one pair of ice skates, or one of whatever else is needed is sufficient, can be budgeted for, and can last.

But one piece of equipment purchased by parents and loaned under strict conditions to the teen-ager, can cause trouble, especially in your fatherless household—the automobile.

Knowing that prestige is often vested in car ownership, forgetting that this is pure-and-simple substitution, a mass hysteria of teen-agers, you may be tempted to permit your teen-ager to purchase his own car, or you may yield to his supplication to get one for him, one he can use most of the time, and occasionally let you drive.

Every recent scientific study of poor scholarship has indicated a close relationship between car ownership and poor grades and poor attendance at school. Even when the ownership papers are not in the child's name because of insurance technicalities, constant car use is found to be connected with poor grades. And significantly for your situation: single mothers most frequently are the ones who let their youngsters own or use a car each day.

Some of this association may be explained by the occurrence of mistaken, displaced, neurotic behavior in single mothers who believe they must try to make up for the absence of their children's fathers by substituting cars. But a healthy mother, for other reasons, may also make the mistake of giving her child a car. You may well recognize that these reasons can easily arise from your child's appearance of rationality, just another illustration of the old appeal by your teen-ager to your sense of fairness or your practical common sense. As such, it is an appeal you must be alert to and must be ready to turn down on strictly realistic, rational grounds.

If, for example, your child points out that it is silly for him to take the bus to school or walk eight blocks when he can just as easily take the car and do your shopping for you, especially since you never use the car for anything else, you must carefully sort through his argument. Though logical, it is unrealistic; it ignores your emotions. You must remember that your freedom of action and decision is a right you have won by assuming all the other responsibilities of an adult. You must keep in mind that whether you do or whether you do not usually use your car before late afternoon when you go to do the shopping, you are the only one who ought to be limiting your freedom of choice and action—and you must carefully refrain from giving up this right of self-determination. Remember, too, that your contacts with the store-keeper are a source of pleasure and gratification to you, one that you also must not lightly give up. Thus, do not let your teen-ager do you favors, especially ones that require the sacrifice of your independence.

As you analyze why you want a car, you may find that you actually do not need it. In that case, sell it. For, no matter how much you try, if the conditions that *you* live under do not require a car, you are unlikely to find any good reasons for your child's needing it. If your town is so small that you or your teen-ager can walk to do your shopping and visiting, it is also small enough for him to walk or take public transportation to school. And if you do, indeed, need your car, but only a few times a month when you do such things as going to the cemetery or doing charity work at the hospital outside the town limits, decide, realistically and objectively, if the car is worth its cost to you, or if you would not be better off and could not manage more inexpensively with taxi service.

In short, resist letting your child's desires influence you. Keep in mind that cost alone is not the major consideration. If your child argues that he will pay for the car, remind him that he can also put this money to use in paying for part of his advanced training, either in college or in a trade school.

If he argues that no one will date him unless he has a car available, point out that you are willing to let him use a car for occasional dates, under the conditions described in the following chapters (mainly conditions governing his responsibilities while on dates), but that you are no more prepared to *keep* a car so he can have a means of going on dates than you are prepared to go out and *purchase* one for this purpose.

When he finally gets around to pleading that he needs a car to run around in with the gang in the afternoon, you have him cornered. For it is exactly this kind of operation that you must seek to protect him from.

Remember that during adolescence he has many tasks of personality integration to accomplish. Some of these can be sidestepped by substitutions, with consequent loss of opportunity for maturing. One usual example of substitution is the substitution of clanning together for personal competition. As a member of a gang, one that is mobile, especially, your adolescent child does not need to learn a thing about really coming to grips with what he has to offer and what he expects from a friendship, with either a boy or a girl. The tacit avoidance of genuine competition and self-expression that accompanies going in a gang is a force that your child often has difficulty withstanding. His way of looking at things is that he would be a fool to let his friends know what he does or does not approve of in them while they spend all their time together. And when they become mobile, with a simple goal before them—cruising in a car—even this problem vanishes. As people who genuinely are only casual acquaintances, they can spend time in a car together and never be bothered by questions of closeness. Instead of friends, they are a car team, similar to a basketball team. Intimacy is not required, so it is not earned. Unlike the ball team, however, car riding offers no real competition or even a workout to more than the driver.

Since they can pick up girls easily, without taking individual responsibility for "pitching" the girl for a date, since they present to the girls only the obvious information that a car is available, there is no direct boy-to-boy competition and no need to get to know the girls as people. Everyone becomes a symbol or image—reality is forgotten.

Your child's personal growth and development, all in all, are not enhanced by having a car to ride around in at will—no matter how much he does in the way of errands for you in token payment. He ought to know how to drive, of course, for this is a good way of learning about additional responsibilities and controls. But as a plaything serving to increase his personality development constructively, a car is useless and must be refused.

Buy a car if you need it; keep your car if you use it; sell your car if you do not need it. But always make your decisions because of your own rights and needs, never out of primary consideration of what your adolescent child might desire. Take the same attitude you would if your child were only a year old: own a car only because it is a tool for your use, even though you occasionally put your child in it.

Because your adolescent child is so new to you, you may find yourself occasionally symbolizing your feelings about him through expressions concerning material cares—not altering the quality of care, of course, but merely your reaction to it. For example, you may find yourself "complaining" that your child can now eat five hamburgers and a quart of milk in one sitting, or needed new brassieres three times last year to keep up with size changes. Unless you are careful to analyze the meaning behind such boasting—for that is what your complaints really are—you may gradually begin, yourself, to close off communication bridges with your child. Your teen-ager certainly wants to be recognized by you, but not for size or eating capacity; congratulations are healthily sought for strength and maturity. So be forthright and direct about the content of your bragging. Once you have tried it, you are likely to find it very simple to brag to your friends about how handsome your son is or how graceful and pretty your daughter is. It is very easy to compliment your child directly, as well. Do not let superstitious beliefs about expressing your joy keep you from showing your pride in your child or from showing your pride in yourself for having brought up so fine a child.

Although you may successfully have resisted any temptation to provide too many things to your child all during his earlier childhood, you may find this urge a very strong one at this time. It is part of your normal reaction to recognizing that real dependency is getting less and less, your way of trying to be still necessary. But it is difficult for your child to assert his independence and self-control if you change the rules of the game. In a complete family, the father might well oppose unnecessary and extra purchases; in your family, you must remember that you two have already agreed upon a fair allowance. If you see that your child cannot quite stretch his funds to get everything he wants, if you see him practicing economies, do not interfere—remember, this is his way of proving maturity to himself. He cannot fight your competition, your help; all he can do, if you mistakenly proffer aid, is to hate himself for not having enough strength of character to resist. So, respect his right to suffer minor inconveniences.

As discussed further in following chapters, protect him from exploitation by others who may recognize his fervor to make money. You need to be careful, too, that you do not let him attempt to exploit himself in a job, even if this is in order to provide money to the household. Although he may be permitted to earn reasonable sums of money for his own current and future needs, he must not be allowed to become a money-mad drudge. You must, of course, protect him from the dangerous burden of assuming responsibility for your care; the social agencies can help you much less dangerously.

If you recognize that you have been making some of these errors and letting your adolescent rule the roost, remember that a responsible father during this time of a child's life is unlikely to let his child take over, show implicit disrespect to his wife, estrange himself from major considerations of family, and use the household only as a parking place at night and a quick lunch counter at other times. So play the role that you can easily imagine an outraged father would play. Explain to your child that you have been foolish, that you will now stop being foolish, and he will once again remember what is what. Remind him that you have enjoyed him up to now, but that you cannot enjoy living with a person who is developing into an arrogant and selfish person. More importantly, explain that you really do not like to have to regard yourself as a sucker who falls for his line.

There is no need for anger from you unless he fails to respect the halt you eventually call to his complaints and tirades. Although relations are likely to be strained for a short while, your child's natural need of you must soon reassert itself. As the following chapters indicate, this need is likely to become extreme during late adolescence; so you are protecting him against future pain as you refuse to let him hurt you now.

Your child's reaction to separation from his father at this time is likely to be highly influenced by the cause for the separation. If it is due to divorce or legal separation, his reaction will probably be a basic confusion at being confronted with the idea that his parents have such extreme emotions; and the behavior he is most likely to demonstrate is an embarrassed avoidance of the entire topic. Remember that he views the entire world and all people according to whether or not they are noticing him, making him look ridiculous, or making him feel emotionally upset.

If the separation is due to death of his father, he is likely to show a typical mourning reaction and to feel the loss deeply, too. But like all intense emotions, this one also must be put aside, for the adolescent rejects open shows of emotion. He is likely to emerge from his mournfulness only with some added resolve to be self-sufficient and to try to take care of you. Reactions involving his needs for material care and protection are not extreme. Should they occur, be sure to consult individual professional advice.

As he emerges from adolescence into adulthood, your youngster, like all children, ceases to be completely and necessarily dependent upon you for his material care and protection. You may continue to provide this care while he is attending college, but generally he is at least supplementing your care of him by part-time or summer jobs. By the time he is well settled in a job, you no longer have any true responsibility of this sort for him.

Finally, therefore, you can throw away all the formerly necessary scruples about using material necessities as the basis for demonstrating love to him. You can buy an occasional present for him to remind him that you still think about him. He can take you to dinner; he can also love you especially when you cook his favorite foods for him. Aside from possible indigestion or a tightly stretched budget, no harm comes to either of you from this kind of indulgence.

All these ways of showing love may be used because now, at last, there is no compulsion about them. You do not need to give him anything, he does not need to accept material care from you in order to get anything else.

Without confusion about the close tie between you, both of you can accept each other and can accept and extend the material tokens of your friendship.

# CHAPTER TWELVE

# Providing Stimulation and Freedom for Your Child's Activity

ONCE THE IMMEDIATE POSTBIRTH PERIOD is over, the most influential part of your role is not protecting your child against immediate pain by providing material care, but rather guarding him against future pains by making sure he develops and grows naturally and freely. As you provide him with stimulation, freedom, and privacy, and so create opportunities for him to try out the new abilities that naturally arise when his development is not interfered with, you shape much of the personality that will be the outcome of his childhood.

The minimum requirements of the job of mothering consist of providing protection and material care; the fine art of mothering involves providing freedom and stimulation and privacy. As you do a good job and practice your role artfully, your child maintains his healthy development as a person whose liveliness, tempered by contentment, is not blunted by apathy and disinterest.

This aspect of your role as a mother is the one in which you yourself have the greatest freedom, for few external and objective forces constrain you and lead you toward particular kinds of behavior. If you do not provide appropriate freedom and stimulation, your child is not going to die, as he might if left unfed or unprotected, and he will not incur the wrath of society, as he might if left unclothed or uncontrolled and untutored. You have freedom to experiment or make mistakes and yet be able to recover a good relationship with your child, promoting good feelings in him again, because most of the transactions involving stimulation and freedom are the intangible, abstract ones referred to earlier as the most pliable and remediable. Then, too, it is impossible for your child to grow and develop without obtaining for himself at least some of the important freedoms. It is also impossible for you to take care of your child's material needs without providing some stimulation for his developing capacities. Finally, because you can quickly recognize the objective fact that your own life is made easier as you leave your child alone—unless he calls for your help and attention for those few activities he cannot handle by himself efficiently and effectively— you automatically tend to keep yourself from interfering with his privacy. You automatically accomplish, therefore, the important aspect of giving him his privacy.

These built-in assurances, however, do not relieve you completely of all responsibility for consciously and deliberately providing both stimulation and freedom. You must still be aware of your child's pace of development and be deliberate about providing him the freedoms he needs when practicing a new capacity. Also, you must still be aware of the underlying new developments that are only in a kind of embryo stage within your child, so that you can stimulate them and help them become strong enough to develop into full-fledged new capacities. Finally, as you provide this stimulation, as you play with him, you must be conscious of the dangers of overstimulation; you must protect him from the pain that results when play becomes overstimulating and disorganizing.

Fortunately, ill effects are guarded against by the actuality that—unlike protecting, providing material care, and instilling a sense of responsibility and reality—this one function of providing stimulation and freedom to your child is fun, *real fun* for both of you. Although a few parts of this function consist of not doing things—always a chore—most of it is just plain playing with your child, having fun with him, and watching how much fun he has in living.

Your child responds to your good treatment by taking a *creative* attitude toward life. Creativity comes only when childhood is good, when you let your child make creative connections between his body and his mind, between his senses and his will.

Because it is difficult to distinguish when to ensure freedom or privacy to your child and when to stimulate him, you may conclude mistakenly that you must become a walking encyclopedia of what everything means to your child and does to him. This conclusion is unnecessary, for you can rely on two rules to figure out what is what and what you ought to do.

The first rule to follow was suggested in the preceding chapter; as you wonder whether or not to engage in some particular action with your child, ask yourself what the usual conditions are under which people do or have done what you are wondering about. Check to see how much meaningful similarity there is between your circumstances and these conditions. If a particular way of behaving with your child is not appropriate to your living conditions, it is probably unnecessary and should not be included in your behavior.

Whether or not to have your child share your bed with you is a good example of the kind of practice that you can analyze in this way, even should you not know that a healthy infant sleeps best when alone. With almost a minimum of trouble, you can discover that a child and his family sleep together customarily only in cold countries where the absence of central heating and sufficient bedding create a risk that a baby might freeze during the night without the extra body heat, or else in crowded countries where a family has little living space, and women are viewed as possessions to make babies, keep house, and work in the fields. A husband, in such instances, does not seek privacy during intercourse and does not seek to have his children develop attitudes about themselves or about women and love that are different from his indifferent or contemptuous, overfamiliar attitudes.

Since, by comparison, you have enough room and heat and bedding (otherwise be sure to ask for help from a welfare agency), and you are interested in having your daughter grow up to claim respect, love, and attention and in having your son grow up to provide these to his wife, you need not have your child sleep with you; indeed, you *must* not let your child sleep with you.

A second rule covers the situations when you wonder whether or not to exclude some particular action with your child that seems to be standard practice, but appears to be an extra chore that you would like to eliminate. Before you eliminate the "chore," ask yourself why other people who are also likely to be interested in saving themselves work still have carried it out, and focus this question on what it might do for a child. Ask yourself what your positive reactions would be to the particular form of stimulation you are questioning. If you decide that your own positive reactions cannot be obtained in any other simple way, you have a basis for appreciating that the behavior is a necessary and worthwhile activity for you to engage in with your child so he may experience similar pleasant sensations.

For example, in order to reduce the number of demands you must meet, you may mistakenly eliminate bathing your child and so fail to give him the opportunity to sense new things with his body surface, for you may regard a bath as an unnecessary task that gets him no cleaner than using a washcloth. This is an example of the type of activity you must analyze more thoroughly and not look upon only as a means of achieving cleanliness. As you examine the question of baths, you can recognize that only in a bath is your child able to relax the muscles that otherwise are tensed in supporting his body against a rigid surface. A bath to him means the same thing that a plunge into the lake, a shower, or a bath means to you: refreshment afforded by the different body sensations in water, compared to air and dry land. So baths are necessary, not for cleanliness, but for important stimulation.

If you recognize, while reading through the following discussion, that you have been interfering with your child's privacy or neglecting to play with him and stimulate him, you can usually take fairly simple and straightforward remedial steps. First of all, refrain from all the injunctions and prohibitions connected to depriving him of his necessary freedom, interfering with his privacy. Then, let your child play by himself until he signals to you that he is bored with his own inventions and needs your stimulation, or that he is tired and needs your comforting. Once you have met these needs, resume your hands-off attitude—by his crankiness or restlessness, he can easily indicate to you when he cannot take any more play with you, or when he does not need any more comforting.

If remedial efforts do not restore what you believe is a reasonably happy attitude toward life, consult your physician, both in order to investigate the possibility of some physical disturbance at the root of the problem, and also for assistance in obtaining psychological counseling.

Keep in mind that a great deal of stimulation is afforded your child by your example alone if the equipment needed to follow your example is simultaneously provided to your child. As you walk around, for instance, you stimulate your child to think of walking; when he becomes further identified with you and stronger, he can attempt to walk, too, for all he needs in order to put his idea into practice is a floor. Other situations require more equipment; for example, when he is stimulated to use the toilet by the example you provide, he needs not only the toilet, but also a footstool so he can climb to the toilet. Lacking a partner to call your attention to the occasions when you need to provide some equipment, recheck yourself by consulting the books mentioned in Chapter Eight.

Many generalized problems typical of a fatherless home can be better understood in the light of the special problems of each developmental stage, so these nonspecific problems are discussed at the close of this chapter.

## *Problems Connected to Development*

Because the preceding chapter has already discussed many aspects of stimulation and freedom, especially during earliest infancy, only additional points are discussed in the following sections.

### EARLY INFANCY

It is natural for you to treat your new baby with respect and awe, leaving him alone when he is content; you need relief from caring for him almost as much as he needs relief from the overstimulating world. The temptation to overstimulate him in ways that are not connected to providing material cares is very slight; few mothers, married or single, are likely to overexercise a new child (with the exception of the care given to a very ill or premature newborn infant, when all sorts of handling must be reduced to a minimum).

So most of the problems you must watch out for are connected either to failing to provide sufficient stimulation or to intruding on his privacy.

Many opportunities to stimulate new sensations and coordination of his senses may be eliminated by you mistakenly, especially if you are extremely depressed. Thinking mistakenly that an open window provides the same fresh air that an outing in the buggy gives, you may reduce outings to a minimum, combining them with shopping trips, so that your child has only a very little chance to practice coordinating his senses by viewing the changing scene, hearing the sounds of the buggy and of his body against the buggy mattress, feeling the swaying rhythm and the different touch on his skin. The trip will cheer you up, too; so start to provide this stimulation.

The most important stimulation you probably fail to provide—in large part because you are alone and without other adults around—is the pleasant play provided by cooing and talking to your child, rocking him, bouncing him gently, waving his arms and legs to music, swooshing him through the air in your arms so that he feels the wind against his bare skin, or letting him watch his image recede and come back as you move him in front of a mirror.

Because a new baby is so very unresponsive, almost all new mothers find it difficult to learn to play with and make sounds to their babies. Usually, a mother who finds it hard to start up a conversation with her baby is stimulated to play with him when her husband joins her and seeks to share the baby with her. But, alone as you are, there is no one around to help you develop your role as the delighted mother; so you may become accustomed to being wooden and tongue-tied with your infant.

To remedy matters, make a point of having company over when your child is awake and ready to be played with. Once you have broken the ice and learned how much fun you can have as you give your baby his stretches, sights, sounds, and other pleasures, you can dispense with the audience. You are unlikely to sink back into your retreated position. Remember, these pleasures differ greatly from almost all others mainly because they are "free," they do not cost any pain to him first as, for example, the pleasure of having his hunger satisfied does.

## LATER INFANCY—FROM WEANING THROUGH THE THIRD YEAR

The dynamic struggle that is almost synonymous with living comes most dramatically into view as your child develops the inner coordination and strength that permit him to wean himself and to move from place to place. He can finally make the world a different place for himself, because he himself can go to different places in his world.

He can, by himself, make the most of the stimulation he craves; he fairly leaps from your arms and searches out the newness that delights him.

Of course he cannot stand constant change and chaos; but he senses when he can no longer tolerate newness, and then he can return himself to the unstimulating, but reassuring and familiar activities of being fed and rocked.

Essentially, then, your role is to provide him with the freedom he needs: the freedom to investigate.

Your tendency to depression, especially if you have just been left single, may make you inactive and inattentive, and make you irritable when you are distracted from sinking into your own thoughts. Yet you need to make sure that the identification tie between you and your child is better cemented and more sturdy and stronger than that of a child and his mother in a complete family; so you cannot afford to make some of the common mistakes she can that lead to a child's partial estrangement.

At this time of your child's life, you must be, like him, terrifically active and alert. He is getting into everything and learning to identify the things in the world about him by touching and chewing and otherwise coming into contact with them. As the previous chapter pointed out, you need to get to hazards before him, clearing them away; and you also need to provide a series of interesting, but safe, places for him to play and a countless number of safe objects for him to investigate. You need to be alert to signs of weariness of one place, so that you can remove him to another.

In addition, to give him the opportunity he needs to investigate himself, you must be ready to exert yourself constantly and consistently, praising him for everything he tries and does even slightly well, and you must be ready to play "patty-cake" or "this little piggy" with him when he shows you he wants to. You cannot play with him once and expect him to cherish the memory forever—as is true for many stimulating enjoyments for an adult. He needs stimulation, even the same kind, again and again. Do not miss this opportunity to lay a wide and firm foundation for his identification with you; work hard to keep from jeopardizing this opportunity because of your own withdrawal. As Part One suggested, concentrate on the pleasure of watching your child develop, concentrate on the pleasure of all your good memories, and even though a few years later you may choose to get back to dwelling on your problems, at least during this important time make sure you pay praising attention to your child.

As Chapter Eleven pointed out, you must not punish him for getting into troubles you have failed to remove or have been unable to remove. Punishment means pain, and pain forces him to pull away from himself and from you. Thus his identification with you is injured or kept from developing. For the same reason, avoid scolding or criticizing, or even delivering frequent prohibitions. Though your rules make a great deal of sense to you, they make little sense to him, for he does not have your background and wealth of experience. When you deliver a command, all he knows is your tone of voice or that you are keeping him from having freedom to investigate. He still accepts you and your commands, for accepting you is how he has started out in life, but he does not "know" you and he does not "know" himself. He wants only to forget about that person who is doing something that other person dislikes; but it is all unclear. He is not even sure, any longer, what he has done that started the trouble.

In short, he becomes the child described as, "So stubborn he simply won't learn anything, even when he gets scolded good and hard."

So, temptations and dangers must be removed, not just for his safety, but also so that the daily routine with him can be pleasant and not a continuous harangue of *No*'s.

Praise from you makes his identification with you grow and become stabilized. When you praise him, he gets bigger, he gets more like you, he likes you more. And when there is enough of this strong positive identification, he can follow a rule about not doing something, because he knows that he likes you and you like him and for some reason you want him to stop doing something.

Remedying a situation that has degenerated is easily accomplished just by reversing your emphasis after the problem areas have been cleared away. With the sources of contention removed from him—the lamps, the vases, the entire kitchen area, and so on—you can be free to praise him for every tiny thing he does well. As you congratulate him for playing in his playpen by himself, for example, even for only five minutes at a stretch, you make his attitude toward you happier. And the happier he becomes about you and the more he identifies with you, the more he knows himself enough to be able to begin remembering the few prohibitions that are probably still necessary, like the ones against touching wall outlets.

As your child enlarges his vision of his life through his own active efforts, he develops his discrimination, accepting some things and rejecting others, seeking out some things and being indifferent to others. He is showing that he feels confident of finding sufficient satisfaction in the world for him to be able to refuse to have much to do with something that is only partly satisfying.

Like all mothers, you must insure your child's freedom to reject; it is fully as important as his freedom to explore an attractive world safely. It lets him develop his capacity to understand his own reactions, to become aware of himself. As he has found out that he has hands and then feet, he finds out that he has feelings, too, and that he likes some things and dislikes others.

As Chapter Eleven pointed out, forces operate causing you to fail to observe respect for this major growing need in your child, this increasing desire to reject. One is your need to have constant reassurance that you are acceptable to your child in the face of rejection by other people—particularly your former husband. The second is your need to prove to yourself that you can exert control over your child, in the face of the obvious proofs that you have failed to exert control over many other facets of your life.

If either kind of reaction is consistent, you may have a difficult time in helping your child regain trust in you and himself. You must show yourself ready to put up with his misuse of opportunities to discriminate when you finally let him show his displeasures. Misuse them he probably will, for, if he has had his freedom to reject curtailed by you for a considerable length of time, he has probably begun to object to everything just on general principles. Because he is trying to exert his right to reject, he cannot afford to accept even those things he really wants. In your remedial efforts, be sure not to try to trick him out of his negativism, for it is a natural kind of overcompensation for having been forced to accept everything; and it is best treated by respecting it.

As he slowly realizes that you have genuinely turned over a new leaf, that you are not going to force him to take something he does not want and has shown he does not want, he can begin to relax and let you give him a few things. Gradually and slowly, he can once again develop his discrimination; he has but had to take a detour down the pathway set by you.

Treatment that a mother in a complete family can occasionally indulge in with good assurance of being able to recover pleasant relations may easily be too dangerous for you with your fatherless child. For example, you may not, when you are feeling tired of coping with your child's incessant inquisitiveness, dump him in a playpen with his old toys, pay no attention to him until he begins to weary of the monotony, try to cajole him into tolerating more of the sameness by giving him a cracker, and then finally confine him to his crib. This kind of treatment confirms him in his suspicions that no one can be trusted, that no one cares for him. Difficult as it is for you to get beyond your own feelings in order to take care of his, keep in mind that you are your child's major object for identification—his sole object once his father is gone—and so your rejection of him or indifference to him leaves him almost completely estranged and isolated. Not until he is able to form identifications with other people are you, as a mother left single at this time, able to indulge in any habitual neglect that characterizes many women who live imperfect, but generally pleasant, lives.

He needs love + attention

Remember that a child in an ordinary, complete home has many chances to be cared for by his father in small ways, while his mother is still nearby to reassure him if he starts to feel uncomfortable. Seek to reproduce this experience artificially. Stay around with your child and the other person for the first few times that your baby is cared for by the other, and limit to just one or two the number of people who take care of him. Gradually, as he shows that he can be comfortable in the care of a new person, absent yourself and thereby provide him freedom to get to know other people.

It does not make much difference if the other people are men or women; his earliest identifications are less a matter of sex than of temperament and activity. Relatives, friends, or hired baby-sitters can provide the stimulation he needs: variety among people.

It does not help him grow if you arrange to have a baby-sitter come when he is napping; all this does—though you must make provision for this occasionally, too, for your own comfort—is give you a chance to get away from home. Be careful to have the time he spends with other people include being fed by them and being played with by them; these are the most reliable pleasures for him, and as he experiences good feelings when a new person feeds him, he can most easily reaffirm and extend his trust.

When hiring baby-sitters, create a source of pleasure for yourself by paying for some extra time with the sitter so you can talk about your baby with someone who really knows what he is like. This kind of sharing is much more restoring than just talking about your child with people you meet when taking your child for an outing. And with this kind of communication available with the baby-sitter, you can begin to make better personal use of your contact with other mothers. Instead of spending the time talking with them about babies, talk with them about other adult matters, and satisfy the parts of yourself that you need to expand as a woman.

Also arrange to have your child enjoy his bond with you under circumstances different from the everyday home life you usually enjoy together. He can identify with you in your variety only if he is able to observe variety. So, occasionally, when visiting friends or engaging in unmotherly activities that are suitable, like going swimming or square dancing, take your child along.

Always be careful not to expect too much of your child; do not expect his very feeble memory to help him discriminate between strangers and people he has met and learned to like previously. Do not insist that he become acquainted with too many people. Do not turn expansive experiences into pressuring, overdemanding experiences. By all means stimulate his identification with men, but limit close contacts to those relatives, friends, or neighbors with whom you are not romantically involved, people who can sustain the relationship reliably. However serious about remarrying a given suitor you may be, the hazards of courtship are considerable; and you do your child a rank disservice if he is permitted to become attached to a male friend who may easily leave you.

Throughout the second and third year of his life, your child is learning to do a great number of things; so long as he does not run the risk of hurting himself or seriously inconveniencing you, he needs freedom to do things his way.

Ordinarily, a child has an opportunity to watch both his mother and father and to see that they do the same things in different ways. But you, of course, are unlikely to do things in different ways from one day to the next; and in your consistency of behavior, you demonstrate to your child only one way. Furthermore, the people you may let take care of him are trained by you, usually, to take care of him in the ways you approve of, because they are like your ways. Only on the rare occasions when you are unable to control how your child is cared for, as may happen when he is cared for by his grandmother—if you are unable to voice your opinion to your mother or mother-in-law—is your child finally presented with an experience somewhat similar to the typical experience of a child in a complete home. Yet, because of the struggle that may exist under these circumstances between you and someone like a grandmother, this experience is not helpful to your child; he can sense that you believe he has been mistreated, not merely treated well in a way different from yours.

Once he shows, by his vigor and aggressive activity, that he is fairly sure of himself and able to meet the world head-on, if necessary, and once he shows that he is well along in developing his ideas about what he likes and does not like, deliberately arrange opportunities for your child to observe that there is more than one way to be right. These experiences need no longer only be connected to watching other people take care of him; he is no longer so dependent upon learning about the world through the method of "what does it get me?" He can now observe and learn something that is less personally related; he can watch people who are just going about their own concerns and relate their behavior to behavior he already knows. So, for example, in watching another mother who is cleaning her home and caring for her child, he need not be included in the child care—he can just sit and watch and learn enough to be able to conclude that things may be different, but still be good.

This experience is valuable in a more important way than just its value in expanding his understanding and tolerance of the world. It is significantly valuable because it may enable him to develop those tendencies within him that are unrelated to you. He is not just a carbon copy of you; some of his inborn tendencies—leaving his sex out of consideration—are inherited from his father. Yet living in a fatherless home, as he begins to develop and actualize these inherited, father-related tendencies, he can pattern them only upon your ways of behaving; and you may not provide the examples and patterns that enable your child to develop his inborn tendencies as fully as they might develop were another pattern, preferably his father's, available for him to observe.

So, in order for your child to grow as fully as he can within the limits of his inborn tendencies, he needs the stimulation you must deliberately provide for him by artificially arranging opportunities for him to witness persons whose behavior is like his father's.

As is more fully discussed in the concluding section of this chapter, this requirement constitutes a problem for you if your marriage has been terminated by divorce. Presumably, had you and your former husband been well able to tolerate and accept your differences, you would not have divorced. Visiting with his father is an obviously ideal way for your child to obtain the opportunity to see a father-pattern in operation; yet the animosities that have led to the divorce may well make visits very tense and disturbing and may cause you to prohibit certain actions in your child.

Under all conditions, you must discipline yourself to avoid undercutting and destroying your child's chance to develop fully; so strive, in ways you know can work for you, or in the ways suggested in the final section of this chapter, to avoid precipitating arguments or strain of any kind during your child's visits with his father. To the extent that you react to his paternal grandparents in this way, you must also deliberately constrain yourself with regard to them.

If because of the death or desertion of your husband or court orders enjoining your former husband from visiting his child, you are unable to provide this most natural form of stimulation, take additional steps. In making your arrangements, you still need not seek to find *men* who are like your former husband—sexual identification, as you remember from Chapter Nine, is not extremely important until the Oedipal period. But you do need to seek out people who are unlike you, who are more like your husband. Books often provide a valuable resource of characters about whom you can read to your child; television is another means of providing him with this form of stimulation.

In addition to letting him visit at other homes or observe the characters in a story, help your child by carefully observing just how he does things; and when his ways harken back to his father's, call your child's attention to his way. These comments need to be respectful and honoring, of course, not critical or ridiculing or condemning. They are made in order to help him become conscious of himself as an individual who is quite separate from you. These comments must not be made about something he is struggling to learn to do, or else they contribute to awkwardness and self-consciousness—a different matter, entirely, from being conscious of the self.

Praising comments that make real and conscious the activity habits and attitudes a child has developed can be made even to a child just past his first birthday. "You really like to play around in the water, don't you," or "What a great big boy you are, pushing that train all over the room," are examples of the kind of comment that is an effective way of helping even a young child to continue to develop his inherent tendencies, despite the absence of his father.

By the time of his third birthday, your child's body has finally caught up to his activity drive—he is like a well-constructed engine that can push on and forward. Developing in him is the inner control, the brake system, that lets him tolerate delay. With this capacity to defer instant gratification, comes his capacity to learn to use his better coordinated hands, fingers, and eyes in order to play with things like finger paint, clay, sand, and crayons.

Now is the time that, in reaction to the dramatic carryings-on of your child when he has a temper tantrum, you may be unable to keep from incorrectly concluding that other children who can look forward to seeing their father every day are governed by something within them that keeps them from these rages.

Stop to analyze the reality of your life with your child to discover the real sources of the tensions that have become so unbearable they can only be reacted to by tantrums. These are ordinarily totally unconnected to the absence of his father. These pressures usually come from his being requested to use the toilet, to speak clearly and politely, or to obey rules about his conduct that are not obviously and directly connected either to his safety or yours; they are requests or sometimes direct orders and insistence that he stop his natural urge toward wild, free activity. In this way, these requests differ radically from any instruction you may have provided previously; during your child's infancy, for example, your instructions had mainly concerned things that express the activity drive, like banging his rattle or crawling over to you. They were not inhibiting.

At this time, instruction and training, even in using play materials, is still more than your child can bear comfortably. Do not be fooled by his apparent maturity and skill and tolerance for minor delays into thinking that he can do more than he can. The same exasperation, the same temper tantrums, follow too much being expected of him, too much instruction, as follow inhibitions and restrictions. Instructions that may seem trivial sources of tension can constitute very real and significant sources of tension to your child. For example, this happens when he runs into the house to shout for a glass of water, and is told to wait until he has his panting under control and then to ask, in a polite way, "Mommy, may I have a glass of water, please?" Your two-year-old child gets so filled with tension that he is ready to burst, like an overheated furnace that has had the safety valve plugged. And burst he does, either into petulant whining and crying storms or into rages and temper tantrums. In his tantrums, he is not trying to hurt anyone or hurt himself; he is just at his wit's end, and he has to scream, thrash around, and somehow get rid of the tensions that fill him.

To remedy the situation that has led to frequent tantrums at this time, lessen your demands upon your child. It is not usually necessary or wise to make any active attempts to force him to stop having tantrums. Added pressures, especially puni- tive ones, merely magnify his inner problems. Nor is it wise to assume that you must just wait for his storms to pass because they are some normal part of usual childhood development— keep in mind that they are not healthy; they are signs of too little freedom or of more stimulation than he can yet tolerate. So, although it is true that his reactions to unbearable tensions will change by the time he is about four years old, and the tantrums will disappear, do not incorrectly conclude that the passing of tantrums means the eradication of the underlying troubles.

Your child may react to losing his father at this time of his life in ways like poor eating and sleeping, ways that cause a sec- ondary lowering of his tolerance for frustration; with this lowered tolerance, he then becomes more subject to tantrums. So in ana- lyzing your relationship with him, be sure to include observations about his rest and diet habits. Do not jump to the conclusion that his tantrums can only be due to your overexpectations; such a con- clusion might well be as wrong as the conclusion that his tan- trums are due to the absence of the inhibiting effects of a father.

If your child is eating so poorly or sleeping so poorly that he is chronically on the verge of exhaustion, consult your physi- cian for medical advice on limiting these natural reactions. Also deliberately entice your child into restorative and rewarding activities. Be careful, though, to keep from prohibiting energetic activity while trying to get him to accept dependency gratifica- tions, for this only precipitates a tantrum.

If your child has reacted to his loss by a frenzied, almost aim- less kind of overactivity, be careful only to attempt to direct and relate his behavior to his inner feelings; avoid any suggestion that you are seeking to put a stop to his behavior. As he bumbles around, call his attention to his feelings by saying something like, "Poor you, I guess you must be feeling just as unhappy about daddy's being gone as I do, even though I'm not running around and getting myself tired out the way you're doing." Only if he becomes destructive must you exert efforts to stop him. At such times say, "Look, I know you're unhappy about daddy's being gone, but I still don't want you to hurt yourself or hurt my things. That isn't going to bring him back. It's just going to cause extra trouble." If necessary, pick him up and take him away. At the same time that you stop him, in a kind but firm way, from being destructive, be sure to stimulate him to use extra outlets for his angry aggressions. When he has begun to rechannel his anger into nondestructive, but aggressive activity like pounding and messing with paints, you can begin to try to make up for his loss by extra cuddling and other dependency gratifications.

## FOURTH AND FIFTH YEARS

The activity drive is going full tilt by the time of your child's third birthday. Although providing freedom and stimulation are still of great importance, they are mainly connected to expressions of aggression, so they begin to be less important in the over-all consideration of your role than stimulating a sense of responsibility in him. (The following chapter discusses responsibility in detail.) The mother in a complete home can turn to her husband for reassurance as she recognizes that her three- or four-year-old spends almost no time with her; as a single mother, you must handle this rejection alone.

Both his natural developments at this time, his eagerness to run off and play without your supervision and his insistence that you not restrict him (which is what much of his anger is about), must be viewed, not as rejections, but as reassuring proofs that you have successfully given him the freedom and stimulation he has needed all along in order to develop healthily. He is no longer a baby who cries for pity when he is unhappy, and who constantly seeks the reassurance of your presence. He is, instead, confident that the world can be a perfectly wonderful place just because he is so strong and skillful, so trusting of your desire to meet his needs; and he freely expresses by a show of anger the annoyance he feels about restrictions, even those that are naturally unconquerable or those that are obviously, even to him, imposed for his own welfare. During this time, both of you need to learn to regard ostensibly negative aspects of life with a positive frame of mind: your child must learn to value positively the restrictions that work toward his ultimate good, and you must learn to value positively the rejections that prove you have been doing a good job of being a mother.

Like all mothers, you make it easier for him to accept and value restrictions as you make it easier for him to reject you. Thus, in giving him unlimited yet safe freedom to play hard, you make it less likely that he needs to resent necessary restrictions. For example, after a morning of tearing around on his tricycle in the yard, on the sidewalk, in the basement, at a playground, or wherever he can be free and away from you, yet safe, he is worn out, ready to eat lunch and take a rest. He does not need to shout angrily about being taken away from his play for "silly old eating," as he might if you had permitted him only a short play period. By giving him freedom and not insisting on staying with him or playing with him, you also help him to get used to the unconquerable restrictions life itself places on his activity.

As a woman who has become single at this time of your child's life, you may mistakenly feel that you owe it to your child to spend a great deal of time with him; you may thereby corrupt his natural need for this kind of freedom. Only if your child indicates that he wants you, should you stay with him. And even so, prevent additional problems from cropping up by insisting that the time you spend together be limited mainly to gratifications and stimulation more appropriate to earlier childhood. Rather than trying to engage him in rough play with you to console him for the loss of his father, engage him in quiet, restorative play like listening to you read a story or croon to him. In short, demonstrate to him that, if he feels good enough to play like a big boy, he must play like a big boy, and that means without his mommy tagging along; but if he feels bad and wants to play like a little boy again, you are perfectly willing to meet his needs.

Inevitably, however much freedom he has to play hard and thus express his activity drive, like any child he must react with anger to occasional barriers to his freedom, even if these be as generalized and impersonal as the fact that he cannot grab the moon. Usually, because he views you as the person who has given him most of his gratifications and as the person who has the power to withhold some of them, his anger eventually becomes directed toward you.

If you have not resolved your own conflicts about being left alone, his anger, when directed toward you, threatens you. If you cannot tolerate these expressions of anger, if you either stop him from even showing his rage or else give in to him and apologize, you increase some of his tensions, forcing them to be turned inside and not shown directly as anger, or else you give him the false idea that he is king of the universe.

Control yourself, and get back to where you can handle these expressions of hostility constructively. Force yourself to be able to listen to him complain or scold or otherwise blow up, yet listen in an acceptant, but not reactive way. If he attempts to hurt you or himself or others, stop him—by stopping him, not punishing him. Remove him physically, if necessary, and remind him that he may not hurt people, even though he is angry.

Let him express his anger; do not punish him for his feeling angry; you are then handling this kind of situation constructively, keeping him from getting so angry that he loses control of himself and becomes involved in a rage tantrum. By seeing his outbursts as nothing but magnified complaints, you can help put them into a perspective that enables you to tolerate them.

Temper tantrums connected to overexpectations and to overrestrictions imposed because of your natural reactions to vehemence, force, and activity, or because of your sensitivity to rejection, do not cause their greatest trouble because of the immediate conflicts they signify about acceptance of rage as a natural and healthy reaction. Tantrums always mean this; not only single mothers, but all mothers must interpret them in this way. Rather, they cause their greatest trouble because they distort your image in the mind of your child.

Remember what has been said previously about how a child views reality: even if he is quite healthy, he sees the world through his currently developing emotional reactions. The autism of your child at this anal time of life is to assume that, because he is filled with tension and hate when you stop him from running around, you must also be filled with the same kind of hatred for him when you stop him. If such interruptions are only occasional, the over-all attitude is tempered by your child's realistic appreciation of you. But if you chronically inhibit him, your child's autistic impression of you becomes overriding; and seeing you in the light of this autism, he becomes afraid of you. Once his guilt increases, because he is throwing tantrums, his fear is additionally increased.

From this point on, his identification with you becomes strained; yet he is far from being mature enough to tolerate without extreme discomfort any alienation from you. His reactions to being estranged from you are typically demonstrated through such disturbed behavior as troubled sleep, frequent nightmares, or individual rituals that he must adhere to, ones like holding his sandwich a certain way or using a particular phraseology when talking. And these reactions, which signify the breakthrough of his fear that he may lose you, too, in turn place a greater strain on the mother-child relationship.

Should your child show such disturbed behavior, you can remedy the situation by restoring the needed freedoms and stimulation. Stimulating him to increased aggressive activity must also be accompanied by some form of apology to him for failing to see what his need has been. This kind of apology helps him regain his loving trust of you and helps him forgive himself for having hated so much. The guilt that has been mounting along with his tensions is released and done away with.

This kind of apology also stimulates him to take an objective nonautistic view of your treatment of him. As you explain that much of your reluctance to let him run around has been because it has been a long time since you were a child, and no one reminds you that a child needs to run around a great deal, you stimulate him to feel compassion for you. Quite different from guilt, compassion bridges gaps in identification. So the effect of the apology is as constructive as the provision of freedom is restorative in attaining a proper balance.

Exaggerated by your circumstances is the erroneous feeling that you are responsible for everything that happens to your child. This feeling is helpful only when it is tempered by realism, otherwise you are especially vulnerable to your child's assault upon you when he angrily accuses you of not making everything be what he wants it to be. Mistakenly, you can develop especially intense guilts about not giving your child his father.

If you recognize this kind of guilt feeling within you, deal sternly and realistically with yourself and your child, assuming forthrightly the authority you are charged with. Refuse to accept the magical role thrust upon you. So, announce simply to your child that you *are* the boss of such matters as when he stops playing to come in to eat or to take his bath or to take a nap, and none of these things is harmful or bad. At the same time, remind him that you *are not* at all the person who controls such happenings as whether or not his father visits him on time. In a matter-of-fact way, tell him that you are sorry he is disappointed, reassure him that it is understandable for him to be angry, but that, if he is terribly upset, he may want to go to his bed where he can shout and pound the pillow all he wants until he stops being enraged.

At about the time that he has learned the important lesson of expressing his complaints in words and shouts without resorting to physical attacks, be attentive to providing him with the freedom and the stimulation of playing with other children. Such play is especially valuable when supervised by another adult— not you. Unlike the child who has learned that he can be angry with one parent and still find refuge in the other, your child is somewhat isolated in his rages with you. It is therefore reassuring to him to be able to identify with another adult and, at the same time, share, trade, and play with other children in circumstances where he can be provoked into anger with one child and still have others to resort to. In a nursery school, the ideal place for him for part of the day at this age, the teacher provides additional reassurance, because she keeps order and does not let any child bully or be bullied; she therefore stimulates him to trust her.

Although your role seems at first somewhat abstract, you are still providing needed stimulation to your child by sending him to an organized play group, for he is thereby being exposed to opportunities to learn many things learned with greater difficulty in isolation. He learns to express his activity drive in ways that let him conserve some of the effort; for example, after he has finished singing a new song or learning a rhyme, something remains. He can remember something new; his effort has not resulted only in relief. He is also getting more comprehensive fun and exercise, satisfying more of his body drives. In playing a patterned game like London Bridge or tag, his mind has a workout along with his body. Games like these release and gratify more than just running around.

Most importantly, you are providing him with an opportunity to strengthen his identifications with different children, some of whom may provide the patterns for development of his inherent tendencies, as discussed earlier in this chapter. These identifications, in his case, are exceedingly helpful. When he believes that he is like another little boy he is fond of at nursery school, he bases this belief on a realistic evaluation of a similarity. He actually can sing a song or play a game just as well as the other little boy. By contrast, his identifications with you or with other adults, however important, are based on a slightly inaccurate judgment that he is like an adult because he can do some one thing an adult can do.

Some of your reality pressures are relieved, too, by this course of action; your child is being provided with greater opportunity to learn new ways of playing with many materials and kinds of equipment—and at a lower cost than he might easily get at home. Your opportunity to have free time is purchased at a lower cost than if you hire a baby-sitter; and you can confine your demanding role of being a cuddler, reader, cook, washer, shopper, laundress, and games mistress to the fewer hours of the day he is with you. At the same time, you are sure a trained professional is providing needed freedoms and stimulation to him during the hours he is away. As you make the acquaintance of other parents who have children roughly the same age as yours, you can communicate freely with them about your child, sure that they can understand, because they probably have had the same experiences. At your child's nursery school, there is likely to be an organized nursery school parent's group that holds meetings; so you have this opportunity, too, to exchange views and to learn new ideas about raising your child. The teacher can also give you an outsider's view of your child, pointing out the skills and abilities that he has developed that you may not have noticed, and pointing out things that need some extra attention.

During these years of his life, your child is very self-centered in a concrete and materialistic way. Consequently, his natural reaction to the departure of his father at this time is somewhat uncaring so long as his usual routine stays pretty much the same. He is far more likely to worry that he may no longer be able to go to the zoo than to worry because he is extremely lonely in the absence of his father. He is likely to become worried, fearful, tense, depressed, or otherwise disturbed only if he is practically forced to develop these reactions by newly introduced restrictions and deprivations.

Knowing this, you can generally prevent any extreme reactions in your child by providing an ordinary routine for him. If your natural reaction is to try to busy yourself by intensified care of your child—or to put aside most concerns while you retreat into yourself—let your child know that he has not suddenly become the only reason for your continued existence—or that he has not lost your interest and attention in addition to losing his father. Knowing what you are doing, he, too, can become occupied in trying to sort things out for himself, sometimes keeping extra busy, and sometimes just sitting and thinking.

## THE OEDIPAL PERIOD

During the Oedipal period, your child needs freedom to express his exceedingly materialistic, concrete understanding of himself, and he needs freedom to learn about truth and reality. Much of the freedom and stimulation needed during the Oedipal period is connected to responsibility and sexuality, discussed in the following chapter.

Remember how intense is your child's need to try to figure out the truth of human relations. Anything you do, therefore, to increase deception or hypocrisy is particularly disorienting at this time.

Of course, you are no more likely than any mother to engage

in outright deception, but your particular social pressures and your particular status tend to increase your temptation to shade the truth and also increase the likelihood that you may place pressures on your child that lead to his becoming hypocritical.

So, for example, bound and determined that your child is not going to grow up selfish just because he does not have a father—and particularly concerned about selfishness because it assumes significant proportions in your child's behavior during this period—you may pressure him to pretend and show a generosity of manners or courtesy toward others that he does not feel. The hypocrisy strains his relationship with you, however, particularly since he cannot go back and touch first base by intensifying an identification with a father.

Whatever restrictions of this sort you have been imposing, therefore, need to be dropped. It is sufficient that he carry out the usual simple courtesies of "yes, please" and "no, thank you." He must not be required, for example, to pretend that he is enjoying a visit with another child or that he likes and wants to talk with your visitors.

One of the most important nonsexual aspects of reality that he seeks to learn about is your particular status as a single mother; he wants to know why he does not have a father living with him. As you seek to provide him with an understandable explanation, remember that it does not have to be complete, it needs only be sufficiently tied to a reality he can understand so that he can accept it.

That his father and mother argued is *not* an understandable statement. He, too, has had arguments with people, and he, too, dislikes some people; but his arguments get patched up the next day. He cannot truly imagine that grown people can act even more childishly than the children he knows; he cannot understand this as a reason for divorce or separation. In his experience, the obvious solution would be for his mother and father to tell each other they are sorry, kiss, make up, and forget it.

As for the other reasons for his being without a father, most are not much more comprehensible. If his father is gone most of the time because of occupation, your child is unlikely to understand why his father likes being a sailor more than he likes being at home, working in the same way as the other fathers on the street. If he has never had a father, if you are an illegitimate mother, he can come closer to comprehension—assuming you do not make up a fantasy for him, but just stick to the simple statement that his father and you were not able to live together for reasons that he can understand better when he is grown up. He is used to recognizing that there are lots of things he cannot understand until he is grown up; your task is merely to provide enough explanations so that he can leave this question to return to others that he can get an understandable answer for. Even death—from your point of view the least understandable condition—is acceptable to him on this basis.

Essentially, whatever the reason may be for the break-up of your marriage, it is easiest for him to understand an answer that you give if it is limited to two ideas: (1) it is not his fault; and (2) it is so hard to understand that even you do not fully understand it yet, but when he grows up, perhaps he will be able to explain it to you. Do not get involved in trying to convince him that adults argue in a way different from the way children argue; do not try to explain accident or disease to him; do not tell him his father has just gone away for a long visit; do not try to explain careers or other interests and other commitments. Give him the truth, but only a small kernel of it; and reassure him that some day he will be able to know all of it.

All in all, though you cannot provide the constructive and creative aspects of the father-mother relationship to your child, and thus you cannot make up to him for the absence of his father, you can, at least, through your thoughtful behavior, keep the situation from being destructive.

## GRADE-SCHOOL YEARS

With the beginning of formal school, there are only minor differences between your role in providing freedom and stimulation to your child and the mother role in a complete family. Providing him freedom to engage in learning and other activities at school is discussed in the next chapter as an aspect of responsibility.

The greatest area of difference is a special problem in ensuring his privacy and freedom to develop his own interests, while you are also stimulating his interest in those activities that are of special pleasure to you. Ordinarily, a mother in a complete family need not hesitate to ask her child along to a matinee performance of the symphony, for example, or to visit the art museum. She can rely on his father to give a necessary balance to this kind of stimulation, so that her child is not forced to believe he must develop an interest out of obligation to her. If his father enjoys music, the child learns that both parents agree he ought to expose himself to this interest and learn to like it; if his father does not enjoy music, but believes the child should learn to like it, the child can feel his disinterest is supported, and so not feel inescapably trapped into going along with his mother. Even if his father and he both agree they do not like symphony attendance, the child can feel that he is like his father, merely doing something, but not liking it; he need not feel that his mother is intruding into the privacy of his tastes.

But you have none of these checks and balances. Your child is therefore more likely to be intense about rebelling; and you need to be additionally concerned about intruding.

This does not mean that you must forego the natural parental pleasure of stimulating similar interests in your child; any mother has an obligation, in a sense, to introduce her child to the interests she enjoys. But you must be careful to be genuinely permissive about letting him decide for himself which activities he gets pleasure from.

Keep communication lines open for future use at adolescence. As discussed in Part One by cultivating your own engaging and demanding interests and contacts, insure yourself against yielding to the temptation of intruding. Then share leisure time with your child, reporting what you have been doing and giving him freedom to talk about what he has been doing; no longer is there much likelihood that you will demand and insist on knowing in detail all that he does, all about his friends, how he feels about what he is doing, and why.

Remember the cautions discussed in Part One about the hazard of intruding into the privacy of your child's affairs. By making this mistake, you decrease the probability of your child turning to you for important help during adolescence, when his need for stimulation and instruction increases, but when his need for privacy also takes a sharp turn upwards.

Because your tie to your child must be so carefully preserved, you must be careful to avoid neglecting or underrating his interests or friends. Be sure not to give him the impression that he is now on his own, with his own life to lead, while you immerse yourself in yours, excluding him. If you are a working mother, this temptation is increased by the added pressures of your responsibilities; but since those same responsibilities also place additional strain on the identification ties of your child to you, be additionally careful to repair and maintain open channels of free sharing with him.

Your child, in reacting to being left without a father at this time, is unlike the younger child or the adolescent, for your school child does not view separation from his father primarily in terms of his own emotional distortions. He takes a more realistic approach and can, therefore, feel the genuine pain of the loss of an emotional relationship. Thus, for example, he does not feel worthless, as a younger child might; your school child does not autistically reason that his father would only have left him if the child did not merit love. Your child feels lonely; he feels unhappy, for example, that his father is not with him to accompany him to the ball game; and he feels appropriate anguish over other similarly realistic aspects of his loss.

This natural enough reaction of mourning often leads to disinterest in school or other activities. Should you note such disinterest—or the equivalent other extreme of overly intense, almost frantic involvement—stimulate your child to acknowledge the same feelings that you recognize in yourself. Stimulate him to analyze what he is feeling; provide him with the guides you have found useful in Part One, and thus help your child to take an appropriate interest in life again.

The father's role during the latency period is sufficiently varied and bound up in concrete activities so that you can often provide adequate substitutes for it. If his father is first absent during this time, try to find another man who can, under somewhat less spontaneous conditions, perhaps, provide stimulations that are the best available substitute, similar to the ones previously shared with the father. By encouraging your child to join a scout group, for example, you are actually enabling him to enjoy with the leader many of the kinds of stimulation a father in a complete family can provide.

### ADOLESCENCE

During adolescence, you must provide your child with adequate freedom to try out the different roles in which he visualizes himself. As long as he does not become socially unacceptable in his behavior, he must not be limited, ridiculed, coerced, or otherwise interfered with. Within the same limits, he must have freedom for his social activities and school and work activities.

During adolescence, your child is facing so many total changes in aspects that were once familiar, that he frequently needs help and instruction. It is difficult for him to seek this help, because of his internal pressure to be an independent individual. Only if he has had good childhood experiences in knowing that his independence is honored and respected is he able to relax enough to be dependent when he really needs to be. Otherwise, he makes learning about the adult world more difficult for himself, because he usually tries to do it alone first.

Thus, the final results of all the freedom and stimulation you have provided during childhood show up dramatically during adolescence. To the extent that you have avoided pitfalls and mistakes, you can count on having no major problems with your child during adolescence, except for the aspect connected to your child's sexual role that is discussed in Chapter Fourteen.

Because the adolescent child is subject to erratic feelings of being estranged from all that is familiar, be sure you give him every possible opportunity to know or learn that in some of his new aspects he is like his father. Do not, of course, make him feel that he is not in any way unique; but be sure to comment upon resemblances, particularly if he has had little opportunity to know his father or has been out of touch with his father's family.

Like every mother, you must sit back and let your adolescent make his minor mistakes and suffer a little, because you cannot inhibit his independence. But if the natural competition of your adolescent with parental authority has been heightened by your past mistakes in providing freedom and stimulation, be alert to difficulties that are more than just minor mistakes.

As much as his privacy and independence should be cherished, you must not abdicate your position as the person responsible for the final results of his behavior. Thus, if your child is behaving in ways that trouble you—whether or not you are being reasonable in being troubled—insist on the two of you together seeking professional advice. Your child probably is disturbed and needs help if the behavior you object to is something like excessive shyness, sexiness, bookishness, religiosity, or delinquency of all sorts. However, you may be revealing that *you* need help in your viewpoints and your relationship to your child if you are objecting to something like his wanting to spend his allowance on extra new clothes or being anxiously excited about going to a dance. In either case, however, the relationship between you and your child requires the kind of adjustment most easily obtained by seeking and using professional help.

Although his childhood has not equipped him to handle every new aspect of life introduced by adolescence, the sum total of his reactions to good treatment in the past does influence his reaction to being separated from his father at this time. If most of life in the past has been good and healthy, your adolescent need not engage in prolonged and disturbed mournful reactions to divorce, death, or other separation. If things have not been completely good in the past, if he has suffered losses of freedom or distortions in stimulation, his reactions are as likely to be exaggerated as a single mother's can be, as discussed in Part One. Remember, if you notice your child showing these reactions, be sure to seek professional guidance in remedying the situation.

## General Problems

Certain features of the objective situation of some single mothers have importance in influencing a child's reactions, particularly the feelings of identification that are the most important result of the parent's providing freedom and stimulation. Although the effects of some of these situations vary greatly, depending on the age and development of the child, the generalized effects of the following situations are mainly to place strains on the child's feelings about himself and others. As a single mother in any of these situations, you must take account of these special strains (alter the description of them to fit the special circumstances of your child's age).

## VISITS WITH THE DIVORCED HUSBAND

One of the major objective problems divorce causes is the pull on loyalties and identifications. Visits with the father can be occasions for restoring ties and remedying this kind of problem, or they can be occasions which merely aggravate the problem. You have an obligation to attempt to make the visits constructive in nature, not destructive.

As discussed previously, unless the courts have deliberately set aside the father's visitation rights because of some serious defect on his part like chronic alcoholism or cruelty, you have no right to attempt to keep your child from seeing his father and enjoying his company. Even though you believe that your husband is a very bad influence on your child, and even though you dislike his attitudes and principles, you must permit your child to form his own judgment through unprejudiced experiences.

Seek to keep visits free of the wrangling, arguments, and disagreement that the divorce probably sought to end. You can make the visits easier and more pleasant, both for yourself and your child, if you avoid interfering. Arrange to have the visits occur at specific times, then but greet your former husband and leave immediately, letting your child and his father greet each other free of witnesses. If the divorce has been accomplished with a great deal of amicability, so that you and your former husband can spend a few hours together without getting entangled in an argument, occasional visits can be planned as "family" outings, and you can be with your child and his father during these visits. But those two must be free to decide for themselves whether or not they want to sacrifice their privacy to include you; under no conditions must you intrude as a sort of chaperon. Be equally careful to avoid intruding after the visit; do not ask many questions about what happened, particularly if you know you dislike your former husband's ways of acting with your child, and you cannot control your apparent reactions to your child's reports.

Your child's identifications with his father are necessary to his development of an accurate image of himself in line with his inborn potentialities. Ordinarily, if you have been handling the responsibilities of providing freedom and stimulation well, your child is able to correct his relationships with his father by himself, complaining to his father in a forthright manner. If, later, your child complains to you, be sure first to seek, where appropriate, to correct your child's impressions; remind him that his father's different ways may not be worse. If a visit leads to disturbances, you can cope with them, usually, without needing to deprive your child of his freedom of reaction to his experiences. For example, should your child be upset as a result of being taken to a frightening movie by his father, lessen the fearfulness by stimulating your child to talk about what scared him; remind him that you understand, but do not share, his fright; and remind him that it is the movie, not his father, that has caused his reaction. Do not condemn his father for letting your child become frightened; do not condemn your child or ridicule him for feeling frightened. If possible, discuss and plan subsequent visits with your former husband, so that similar activities can be handled in the light of your child's reaction of fright.

If, by behavior he refuses to alter once it is called to his attention, your former husband is actually jeopardizing your child's emotional development, you may be forced to sympathize with your child and to agree with him that his father has not been right. When possible, remind your child that the good qualities of his father make up for his difficult behavior. In some cases, it is also wise to obtain professional psychological or legal advice about the consequent emotional problems.

## VISITS WITH THE PARENTS OF THE DIVORCED HUSBAND

You may have good reason to believe that your former in-laws are responsible for developing in your former husband the personality characteristics that contributed to your divorce; so you may be naturally reluctant to permit your child to visit with them for fear he may develop the same personality problems. But your child benefits from contact with the people who are part of his heritage; he feels supported and comforted by knowing how to like and be liked by more people than just his parents. Also, even if they are unpleasant, his casual and short-lived visits are unlikely to leave many lasting impressions; you can correct the few problems that do arise, using the same ways suggested with regard to visits with the father.

Most of the time, by making a sincere effort to put your relationship with your parents-in-law on an objective basis, by forgetting their role with your former husband, you can form a reasonably pleasant tie with them that permits your child to keep close to them without feeling disloyal to you.

If your former parents-in-law seek by critical comments to strain your child's feelings of loyalty to you, be careful to limit your rebuttal to reminding your child of what he already knows about you; carefully refrain from counterhostility that would merely strain your child's ties to his grandparents. After all, they share your love and interest in your child.

## MOTHER'S REMARRIAGE

If you have remarried, you can best help your new husband and your child learn to trust each other and love each other by being steadfast in refusing to manipulate either of them. Let them take their time; so long as each of them is kind and courteous to the other, you can be confident that, eventually, time and mutual experience will bring them together. If you see signs of any acting out, you can best help by calling this to the attention of both your husband and child and by making appropriate corrective, interpretive comments. For example, if your child belligerently refuses to participate in some activity with his new father, simply say, "I guess you're still angry about my loving two people, instead of only one. But I don't like to see you hurt yourself, you know, and I think you're hurting yourself by refusing to have fun with your new father."

Such a comment is likely to provoke a torrent of words from your child about his inner reactions. And these can be dealt with, one by one, with full reference to reality.

Thus, if he says your remarriage proves you do not love him anymore, reply that it proves that you love another person, of course, but you do not then stop loving him, any more than he stops liking his tricycle when he starts to play with his new blocks. If he says that his new father does not want to play with him anyhow, but is just saying he does, remind him that his new father is no more likely to say something he does not mean than you are: if your husband says he wants to play, it means he does.

Much of this sort of discussion and interpretation of reality can be as effectively carried out by your new husband as by you alone. The very act of searching to correct wrong impressions and autistic viewpoints is sometimes enough to convince a child that he really is cared for and wanted.

The one thing you must not do is trade your love for an imitation of affection between your child and husband. Thus, for example, you must not say, "If you really want to show mommy that you love her, you'll be nicer to your new Daddy."

Such a blackmail attempt only strains the loving bonds that are already being put to a test. If people are at least kind and polite to each other, sooner or later they will learn enough about each other to start feeling affectionate.

### FATHER'S REMARRIAGE

Because he is less identified with his father, your son is less likely to be greatly upset by the remarriage of his father (although you may not be so equable about the altered situation). In his contacts with his father's new wife, your child is likely to react primarily in terms of the direct interaction between them.

If the new wife has a sensible and friendly attitude, the remarriage is unlikely to provoke troublesome reactions that are sustained and long-lasting. And whatever his age, your child benefits from having his intimate circle thus extended. Encourage him to regard the remarriage in this light. Be sure you do not react to the remarriage by expressing some of the critical comments you have previously held back concerning your former husband. You must not try to make your child view the new family ways as being less worthy than his own ways in the family circle he forms with you.

If you can maintain a friendly relationship with your replacement, smooth the works by indicating your child's special likes and dislikes and routines that he is accustomed to. This is especially helpful if your child is setting out on a long vacation with his father and his wife.

If he sees that the new mother is anxious to please him, your child may be tyrannical, dealing out his favorable reactions as if they were more important to her than to him. You may notice such reactions, or you may be informed of them by your irate former husband. In all cases, step in and insist that your child regain a more sensible attitude. Though you may not be able to keep the new wife from trying to curry favor with your child, at least deflate your child's grandiose opinion of his own importance.

### REMARRIAGE OF TWO SINGLE PARENTS

The most difficult problem caused by remarriage between two single parents is, not rivalry between the children of each parent, but rather unrealistic attachments and identifications of the children with each other. This is especially likely if the children are close together in age. Each can easily then identify with the other, and thereby relate to his new parent, without presenting separate individualities and selves and without forging genuinely new relationships. Though such cross-identification makes initial adjustment very smooth and easy, in the long run it works to the disadvantage of each child.

Identifications are ways the self is enlarged. Identification with the bigger personality of a parent or teacher, for example, helps in enabling your child to embark on some of the tasks he sees these people accomplishing. Identification with a smaller personality, as when a child identifies with another child in the second child's regard of a parent, is not functionally helpful. Cross-identification does not permit either child to experience the genuine actuality of the experiences which could, otherwise, give rise to real identifications with the new parent. Cross-identification does not lead to genuine discrimination of likes and dislikes.

Do not increase this tendency to cross-identification by resorting to your understanding of your own child in order to understand your new husband's child. Strive instead to utilize realistic appraisal or recall of your own childhood, and speak to the child about your reasons for thinking he has certain characteristics. Encourage your own child to relate directly to his new father, too, in the same way, by forming a direct tie in terms of his own needs, not by riding on the personality formations of a go-between. Call attention to cross-identifications, no matter how trivial, whenever you notice them. "Don't be a copycat, now David, and say you don't like to, cause I know from your father that you haven't ever tried to roller skate. So just because Johnny doesn't like skating is no reason why you shouldn't try." Or, "Johnny, I don't see how you can be worried about your new father's reaction to your losing your gloves when you've never seen him get mad at you yet. Don't start being a copycat. Just because David's father has gotten angry at him for losing his things repeatedly is no reason for believing he's going to be extremely angry at you when this is the first thing you've ever lost."

With both you and your husband alert and scrupulous about insisting on having a direct and genuine relationship with each child, it is unlikely that burdensome cross-identifications can be long sustained.

### REMARRIAGE FOLLOWED BY NEW CHILDREN

If you remarry and have a new baby, your older child may develop intense feelings of jealousy because of the double competition he is faced with. It is improbable that your child can adjust to his new father in less than a year or so; thus, if the new baby is conceived shortly after the marriage, your older child is still struggling with feelings of competition due to the marriage.

As with the transitory jealousy that may follow any birth, you need to interpret to him his own real conditions. You must insist that he realize that, just as his new father has not displaced him in your affections, neither has the new baby. Point out to him that the new baby does not take any of his gratifications away from him and that he has no real basis for feeling deprived. By being consistent in your attitudes and remarks, you can help him come through his immediate discomfort without lasting damage to his sense of belongingness. Though the need for so many restrictions on your own spontaneity is difficult, it is much less bother than coping with a child who feels deserted and bitter.

### FOSTER HOMES AND BOARDING SCHOOLS

This same problem of feelings of being deserted is encountered if you have placed your child in a boarding school, seeing him only on occasional weekends and during the vacation period. Unless he has had an extremely stable tie to you before going off to school, your child's character is likely, in reaction to his feelings of being deserted, to become increasingly abstract and idealistic or increasingly irresponsible. He may identify with the abstract images presented to him by the school—such things as school spirit, patriotism, "chin-upness"—or he may fail to make even such identifications and instead live precariously in the present, governed only by the vigilance of authorities with whom he does not identify. Many boarding schools serve special purposes that cannot otherwise be accomplished, but a full dormitory and attentive teachers are not constructive substitutes for a father, especially if they mean the sacrifice of the mother-child relationship.

In order to undo some of these developments, after your child returns to live with you and to attend an ordinary day school, you must operate essentially in the fashion characteristic of a mother of a two-year-old. Unhesitatingly praise your child for any special achievement, but be sure to keep this praise sincere, not patronizing. Consult his tastes, without, of course, becoming frantic to please him. When an opportunity arises, speak casually of your reasons for sending him away in the first place. Given a small chance to be slightly free in expressing his confusions or resentments, your child can begin to interact with you genuinely, instead of behind defenses that are both definite façades erected only with reference to you and generalized façades erected as a consequence of the boarding school experience.

Many aspects of the corrective approaches you must take in handling of other relationships that strain identifications are related to how you influence your child's sense of responsibility or of reality. So, the following chapters provide additional suggestions to extend your insight into your special circumstances.

# CHAPTER THIRTEEN

# Stimulating Your Child's
# Sense of Responsibility

THE TWO PRECEDING CHAPTERS have emphasized your role in protecting your child, first, against immediate, present pain from lack of material satisfactions or from injury, and second, against the future pain that can develop if his capacity to accept, search out, and create pleasure and gratification is blunted. You have one other protective role to play: protecting him against punishment by society, by other people, when he fails to be responsible; and you fulfill this protective role best by instructing your child in responsible behavior that is unlikely to provoke punishing reactions.

But, protecting your child from punishment and insuring your child the likelihood of receiving help when he needs it are not primary goals in stimulating his sense of responsibility. The essential goal—one you may not have stated in words, concretely—is the gratification that comes from being responsible. When your child fulfills the biblical injunction, "And thou shalt love the law as thyself," he is able to enjoy what he and it can do together to create pleasure, to make sense out of life, in a continually expanding way. The genuine pleasure of being a responsible person—not merely conforming passively to rules and regulations and not merely trying to take advantage of them—comes from finally getting a chance to assume responsibility and derive real joy out of knowing that, even in only small ways, you can authoritatively make your world and the world other people live in a good place.

This kind of reason lies at the heart of why you, as a single mother, are struggling to make a good life with your child, not just turning the whole chore over to others to carry out. You cannot get any pleasure out of being a mother unless *you* are mothering your child and doing a good job of it.

When you leave this realm of abstraction and get back to the practical question of, "How can I help my child develop a creative sense of responsibility?" the first thing to keep in mind is that in many ways it is easier for you than for a mother in a complete home. A great deal of what a child learns about assuming responsibilities is learned by watching the example of parents. And your child is watching a wonderful example in you; he is watching a woman manage her hardest job under circumstances that are exceedingly difficult.

Moreover, the inspiration you provide cannot be watered down or reduced in any way. Your child must, sooner or later, acknowledge that you have been taking good care of him because you freely and willingly accept and actively assume the responsibility for his pleasure and yours.

Of course, not until your child is in his school years can such concepts about you be consciously thought through. But all during his earlier childhood, as he sees you patiently and cheerfully take care of him, the basic attitudes about responsibility actively assumed are being assimilated.

The special problems that crop up for you and your child because you are a single mother often serve as object lessons to him of why responsibility must not be disregarded. Aside from widowhood, even the basis of your singleness is involved with irresponsibility. When your child is old enough to be able to recognize these irresponsibilities, he has had excellent experience—tough and hard though it is—in understanding why people must not be allowed to hurt other people. Should he have been on the receiving end of things like not knowing when his father is going to show up for a visit, not having a chance to take a vacation with you because you have to work to support him, or watching an open, violent fight between you and your former husband, he certainly knows from direct experience that people really hurt other people when they do not live up to their promises, when they shift their share of responsibility to another person or fail to control their hostilities.

So long as you keep your child from developing the irresponsible notion that, because he has suffered, he has a right to cause other people to suffer, you insure that his experience as a child in a fatherless home is a continual and objective reminder to him of some of the wrongs that necessarily follow when people act irresponsibly.

Be sure, therefore, that you do not let your reactions to being left single corrupt your attitudes and keep you from serving as a good example.

The preceding chapters have pointed out your probable reactions to having become single at different times in your child's life; these need not be repeated in this chapter. But keep in mind that, if in your dependency and insecurity you fail to carry out your responsibilities, you are not a good example; and if in your depression and resentment you grouchily and reluctantly perform your tasks of raising your child, you are not a good example. You have no obligation to anyone to pretend an enthusiasm you do not or cannot feel, but you do have an obligation to yourself to keep your reactions from leading you to sacrifice an extra advantage gained from your position—the example you present as a single mother.

In instilling responsibility in your child, several concepts must be kept in mind. First of all, as pointed out in Chapter Ten, remember that after your child has had enough freedom to develop and practice a new physical and psychological development and stabilize it, you must take over and start to place necessary limits on his freedom, start to stimulate his assumption of responsibility for the activity. Remember, too, that his sense of responsibility grows by steps and stages; and each new step enables him to fulfill a further responsibility, either for himself or for you and society at large. Another concept to keep in mind is that almost every responsibility your child assumes is a control that simultaneously enables him to keep from hurting himself or you or others or property.

Do not operate under the mistaken notion, however, that this happy circumstance—where every increase in responsibility for himself is matched by an increase of responsibility to others—is gained easily, naturally, without any instruction or guidance or discipline and without harsh words or tears or frustration. At times, he is eager to assume responsibilities, does take them over without any struggle at all, and does carry them out without much reinforcement from you for long periods. But generally, a great deal of day-in, day-out work goes into helping your child accept the world of reality where, if able, he is better off taking over a responsibility than waiting for someone else to carry it out.

Though it is true that a child whose needs are satisfied is unlikely to be extremely hostile or directly destructive, it is not true that this satisfaction alone helps him learn to be anything more than just satisfied and self-centered. He may often have no idea at all that his actions are inconveniencing you or hurting you. At times, he may not remember that he needs you and cannot tolerate rejection by you as you react to his actions. Reminding him of these realities is a necessary part of your role in stimulating him to be responsible.

His different childish, autistic views of reality all lead him to hope and believe that somehow he can just wish for things to happen and achieve what he wishes. In his lack of experience and capacity to think very complicated thoughts, he is generally willing to try wishing first, then complaining, and finally, only as a last resort, acting responsibly when he wants to get something.

Of course, this does not mean that he only reluctantly gets dragged into becoming responsible. Disciplining, limiting, and directing, in the setting of love and satisfaction you have created for your child, are not questions of outwitting a wild beast or keeping a raging animal at bay. They are matters of requesting, insisting, and instructing an inexperienced, but eager-to-learn child.

He needs you to point out the long-run irresponsibility of various actions, to bring home to him the world of reality where it is not possible to escape the consequences of his behavior. At times, this is difficult, because a large part of responsibility is involved in upholding rules that are constructed to avoid long-range dangers or to reduce the likelihood of immediate troubles. The kind of thinking that lies behind these laws is often exceedingly abstract and too difficult for your child to understand. He cannot naturally figure out things like the fact that it is safer to cross a street at the corner than in the middle of the block because drivers are trained to look out for people crossing at corners. You must instruct him in becoming responsible for looking in all directions when he crosses a street and in crossing only at the corner, and you must explain to him the benefits of obeying the law.

As a woman alone, you may have additional difficulty in carrying out these disciplining and explaining parts of your role, because your responsibility in this regard is not shared. Neither you nor your child gets any relief. You need to exert all the authority yourself, in a way that keeps from sounding like scolding or nagging, and you also face the total responsibility of analyzing what has happened when you see some breakdown in responsibility. By yourself, you must maintain limits and must face and accept the temporary withdrawal of your child's love and approval when you prevent him from behavior that is potentially or actually destructive. You cannot "pass the buck" to a husband, as might a married mother who pretends that she really does not care, one way or another, but her child's father insists that he carry out some particular responsibility. And you cannot compensate for your child's displeasure with you by getting approval, a pep talk, and a quick hug from a husband.

By way of compensation, however, you need not face the problem of watching your child get away with doing something you have prohibited, but for which he has obtained his father's permission. So long as you carry out the necessary work of being alert and clear in your directions and limits, both you and your child know exactly what is what.

You also have the added advantage of being able to change methods with less difficulty than the woman in a complete home who must also get her husband to change with her. When you see that your child's behavior is obviously irresponsible, despite efforts on your part, you can think through what you have been doing with him, find out what is wrong, change it, and apologize to your child—all with a minimum of time and effort.

You have a further advantage of needing to worry about only one adult's capacity to exert self-control and one person's special foibles. Although the married mother may not share some specific rabid dislike of her husband's, she still needs to uphold it to her child. Your role is simpler in this respect.

When you do lose your temper, especially when you shove or strike your child or make an unfair and frightening threat, you also find it easier to recover a good relationship than does the mother in the complete home. Your child's relatively greater dependency on you helps bring you closer, more quickly, first of all, and then, too, you need only begin to recognize what you are doing, to begin to stop what you are doing. There is no temptation to "carry on," as there is for the mother in a complete home who wants her whole audience to know that she really has been upset, justifiably so.

Just as there is only one adult in your house whose low boiling point about some special subjects needs to be worried about, there is only one adult in your house who needs to know sensible and constructive ways of raising a child. Indeed, once you can keep yourself from acting out your negative feelings, you have put the whole situation potentially under control. In addition, it is easier for you, as a woman, to accept the necessity of removing force and coercion from the methods used to stimulate a sense of responsibility. Your natural aversion to violence, your relative weakness, and your closer identification with your child all make it less likely that you will defensively insist that "there is nothing wrong with a sound thrashing," and act out accordingly.

The books recommended in Part Two contain full discussions about methods of discipline and the use of physical punishment, and should be consulted by you if you have many questions about why physical punishment is not advised. Briefly, psychologists agree that a child learns best how to do things by practicing them; he learns best how to control himself by practicing self-control; and, when physical punishment is used as a method of discipline, he learns little aside from an automatic, sometimes consciously uncontrollable habit of not doing something; he learns an avoidance response, as it is called.

These ideas about learning and discipline have great importance when you consider how to instruct your child in order to help him develop a good sense of responsibility.

Painful punishment, use of physical pain, is not a good method. Its major drawbacks are several:

First, your child's love for law, order, and responsibility cannot be based on ignorance, fear, or guilt; it must rest on his love for you and his identification with you or other primary authorities like his school teachers and minister. Because pain estranges him from you, it shakes the very foundations of his genuine regard for lawfulness.

Then, too, your child views law and order as something that is accomplished by the methods you use, because you and the law are identified. Whatever he feels confident he can do about upholding law and order is likely to involve his use of the methods you have used. But if you have used painful methods for maintaining law and order in the family, your methods are radically different from the ones used by greater society. You instill in him a basic insecurity about believing that he can do anything to uphold law and order in the world since he cannot use the methods he is familiar with. You might wrongly lead him to believe that such weak and puny laws do not also need to be upheld. (Of course, when he tries to keep law and order by use of his fists, he is liable to end in jail; and the same fate is likely if he decides he need not obey the law because the police do not use their fists.)

His trust in you, so basic to his feeling of confidence that most of his wants are likely to be satisfied, is therefore basic to his ability to put up with occasional delay, compromise, and sacrifice cheerfully and without great apprehension and impatience. And this ability to forget about himself is necessary for a genuine sense of responsibility to others. When you hurt him physically, you disturb his trust in you. Indeed, you may instill so much resentment in him that, when he is old enough, he may decide to try to get back at you or society.

Also, real responsibility is a carrying out of cooperative and self-sufficient activities, restoring constructively whatever has been irresponsibly destroyed, and meeting obligations in actuality. It is not just wanting, however sincerely, to do these things. Since pain confuses your child, he does not learn quite so skillfully and well as he otherwise might learn how to engage in constructive action; and there is extra anxiety within him that is never successfully discharged. So because nothing succeeds like success, because people like to do whatever they can do well and completely, he has less desire to meet his obligations than he would have if he did not have this inner anxiety to keep him from feeling he has managed, successfully, to meet an obligation.

Finally, physical punishment tends to make him feel that any irresponsibility can be paid for just by suffering some additional pain, as if pain were a fee for a license to be irresponsible. It links pain to reconstructive efforts, so that, in effect, if no one catches him doing something wrong, and if no one forces him to try to restore what he has destroyed, there is no reason at all to meet this obligation.

As a single woman, in addition to your feminine nature, you have one last advantage in being able relatively freely to give up the ill-advised use of physical pain as a method of discipline: girls do not get beaten so often as boys, so when girls become parents, they do not need to perpetuate and revive physical punishment of each new generation just to make sure they are not the only ones who got a dirty deal.

In short, far from being at a disadvantage, you probably have some unique advantages over mothers in complete families when it comes to being free to raise your child to have a genuine sense of responsibility.

The family has often been called the backbone of American democracy. Although your family is incomplete, you can be as confident as any mother that you can raise your child to be a responsible citizen, a fully functioning member of our democratic society.

## The Development of a Sense of Responsibility

Chapter Nine has already reviewed many main features of the development of a sense of responsibility; additional aspects are easily understood in view of the discussions in the other chapters of this Part Three; and the books referred to previously all contain lengthy discussions of this development. So such material is not repeated in this discussion.

The general dangers you must watch out for that might be caused by *your* reactions to being single at the various stages of your child's growth are also not repeated. Keep in mind the precautions pointed out in the other chapters, and apply them to the question of stimulating a sense of responsibility. So, for example, if at a particular stage of your child's life, you know that you are reacting to being single by being oversolicitous to your youngster, you can assume that you are likely to be failing to stimulate the sense of responsibility appropriate to that time. On the other hand, if your reaction is aloof, you can assume that you are presenting him with but little guidance and instruction, so that whatever responsibility he learns during this time is likely to be faulty and unskilled.

The rest of this chapter concentrates on *your child's* reactions to the loss of his father at various stages of growth and on the remedial efforts that help him regain the sense of responsibility appropriate at each stage. These remedial efforts are much the same as the ones you need to apply should your reactions have caused some disruption at a particular stage. Where your remedial efforts cannot be made, however, because your reaction to your loss is overly intense or because your child's is, psychological consultation is advised. Should you now recognize that some past mistakes have left lingering distortions in your child's sense of responsibility, it is also likely that psychological consultation can help you remedy the situation more quickly and surely than attempting remedial efforts by yourself. (Throughout, whatever the reason for your being single may be, it is referred to as loss or separation or absence, and your child's reaction is called a mourning reaction.)

## THE SECOND YEAR

With some encouragement from you, your child rapidly progresses from infancy on in his willingness and ability to take responsibility for himself; and by the end of the second year, he is often well able to handle many of the mechanical details involved in his care. With praise from you and supportive guidance in appreciating the few limits you place on his curiosity, he is able to develop a genuine appreciation of your point of view. He is also growing in his capacity to tolerate delay when he wants something.

In addition to these signs of his growing capacity to assume responsibility for himself and to respect limits, he demonstrates generosity by the little games in which he gives you something and then waits patiently and happily for you to give it back. The overflowing happiness that leads him to want to share or give in these small ways plays an important part in the foundation of most of what real charity consists of in later life.

Many responsibilities he has been assuming may be closely identified with his father, however, and these may be discarded in the mourning reaction. For example, if it were his father who, in the evening, stimulated your child to assume most of the responsibility for washing himself while Father read the evening paper in snatches between leaning over the tub, your child may refuse to wash himself now. In your remedial efforts, avoid making much fuss; wash him yourself. Gradually, after a few days or a week or so, try to duplicate part of the old ritual by reading the newspaper at bathtime and suggesting that he take a bath the way he used to take one. Explain that you know he liked to have his father with him during his bath, but you hope he will also let you be in there the same way. If his reaction is to insist that he wants to be alone, respect this desire; should he finally decide that he would like your company, he will let you know. In either case, help him draw his bath water, then help him in and out, with a flat insistence that he be responsible for coming out as clean as he likes to be.

Many of the little chores he has been providing may be identified with his father, too. He is comforted by your remarks that he is doing these things as well by himself as with his father; they strengthen his ties to you and also remind him that he has not completely lost his ties to his father. Remember, though, that this assistance is freely chosen; he is far too young to assume any chores that are not connected directly with himself. So, though you may finally have become accustomed, for example, to his doing little jobs around the house like being willing to go get your cigarettes, you must remind yourself that these were favors, not obligations. If, in his reaction, he now does not want to do anything of the sort, give him the freedom to refuse. When his allegiance to you is again stronger and his inner reserves of enthusiasm are rebuilt, he will be back at helping you.

Impatience and intolerance for any delay, if these are his reactions to separation, are probably harder for you to put up with; do not let yourself be provoked into equally impatient and intolerant responses. Instead, at first try calmly to meet his demands, letting your own chores go for the time. But be sure to tell him that you know he is unhappy, and that is why you are paying so much attention to him. As you notice that he is gradually becoming more relaxed, carefully, but in a matter-of-fact way, start requesting that he wait until you finish some task. He is not likely to turn an initially honest mourning reaction into a neurotic power struggle, for he is still getting needed gratifications and does not have any sharp animosity to you. But, like any child this age, he needs your encouragement to tolerate the momentary delay.

If the limits that he has previously respected now become a source of discord, again keep in mind that this is his way of trying to find out what is still stable and what has changed. Do not assume, for example, that he is refusing to stay away from the wall outlets because he feels suicidal or because he wants to plague you, since he thinks you took his father away. He probably just wants to find out if he still may not touch them. So, provoking though his behavior may be, respond calmly, reminding him that you do not want him to hurt himself any more now than before when his father was with him. Think of this as mainly a re-education; he has been shocked, he has forgotten or is not sure of what he once knew; so he needs help in relearning. A large measure of responsibility to others all through his life consists of knowing what he may not do, and his important beginnings in respecting limits must be strengthened by your friendly but firm support.

## THE THIRD YEAR

A great deal of responsibility to others, of course, is learned as part of your child's learning to control his temper. This engages much of his attention through his third year of life, but many other aspects of the sense of responsibility also develop rapidly at this time. He begins to control his inner fears and dislikes, and from this develops his later capacity to do things that are distasteful simply because they are part of duty; he increases his assumption of helpful chores; he takes almost full responsibility for his own care, from being able to pick out his clothes and dress himself almost completely to cooperating with you as you are straightening up his toys. With his increased capacity to be productively effective, he is well on his way toward becoming the person who does not need to *pretend* that he is accomplishing something, but who, instead, actually gets down to the substance of work, taking real care of many responsibilities.

Aggressively active at this time, viewing impediments with reactive hostility, his reaction to the loss of his father is likely to be either an abrupt cutting-down of his activity drive or else acting-out, hostile reactions that may range from frequent tantrums over minor inconveniences to deliberate attack upon you or upon your belongings.

As pointed out in previous chapters, he needs your help in sorting out his anger. It must be kept separate from the fatigue that is an ordinary part of life at this time anyhow, and that usually is increased if his mourning reaction has led to upsets in sleep and diet habits. He needs help in keeping his anger from getting mixed up with his growing awareness of his toilet needs. He needs help in keeping his anger from being acted out; hostility just leads to his feeling additionally guilty and worried—particularly if the hostility has been directed toward you.

Usually, his increased fatigue shows up in increased minor accidents. As you would even were you not aware of his extra troubles, comfort him. Do not belabor him with a scolding about how he has to be more careful; just remind him that it is very easy to trip when he is tired, and suggest that he rest for a little while. If his pain has led to an angry outburst, your sympathy is needed. Tell him you know how angry he must be about his father's absence and how angrier he must be when he gets himself hurt. Remind him that you do not want him to hurt himself, that you are sorry he is angry with you, and that you wish he would just give himself a chance to relax for a while. Suggest a quiet book-reading time together. As the days pass, and he gradually connects his fatigue with his extra anger but sees that you are not blaming him for either, it becomes easier for him to express his basic unhappiness and rage about being left without his father; he needs no longer run himself ragged in order to have a chance to blow up.

So, too, deal with any changes in toilet behavior. He may have been using the toilet and may now give it up. Do not blame him, do not shame him. Clean him up without much comment; then, when you two are quiet together, bring up the connection between his inner anger and the altered toilet behavior. Suggest that it is always difficult to go on being a big person when he is angry inside, but that you really do not think it is as easy to show you how angry he is by wetting his pants as by just telling you. Suggest, too, that maybe he is just unhappy, and wetting his pants may remind him of how much nicer it was when he was a little baby and his father was with him. Remind him that you will cuddle him whenever he wants and, after all, it is not very comfortable for him to have to stop playing to get his pants changed. As you avoid reacting to him negatively, he can more easily express his feelings in talk and crying. The toileting can then go back to normal.

Should he, in his reaction, destroy his toys or some of your property, you must first of all make certain that his act has been destructive because he is hostile; remember that he may also be reacting to separation by trying to be more mature than he is able to manage. Do not confuse lack of skill with hostile destructiveness, any more than you would confuse his need to be active and energetic with being hostile. It is hard to tell if he is being willfully destructive or just active and curious when, for example, he cuts up his overalls with his new scissors, but he deserves the benefit of the doubt. And though he may break the sugar bowl carrying it over, unasked, again this may just be a sign that he wants to be helpful to you. So unless his actions are accompanied by definite statements that let you know he is trying to destroy something, deal with these episodes as if they were unconnected to any possible anger. Remind him his scissors are to cut paper with, not his clothes; thank him for trying to help you, but suggest that it is not so safe for him to carry big glass things as something like the silverware. Even if you are fairly certain that some destructive acts are his efforts to provoke, treat them, initially, in a matter-of-fact way. Remind him that he can mess around with the sand in the sandbox or his clay and his paints, but not with his food, since his supper is to eat, not to play with.

If, however, he warns you that he is going to break something, stop him, right then and there. Do not get provoked into threats of what you will do if he dares to carry out his threats. Do not provoke him by telling him he does not dare. Just stop him. As you either remove the particular object or remove him, tell him that you will not permit him to destroy things because he is angry over the fact that his father is gone—or because of any other reason. As calmly as you can, tell him that if he is angry, he can shout and scream and even go to his room and bang his toys around, but he may not break things, any more than he may hurt himself or try to hurt you. Remind him that you know how angry he is, but remind him, too, that you do not think breaking anything is going to bring back his father. Ask him if he wants to tell you how he feels—the reaction is usually a vehement refusal. But the suggestion and your manner of responding eventually sink in. He may not ever tell you anything about feeling angry, but at least he knows that you do not blame him for feeling angry, so some of the tension inside is reduced.

If you discover that some object has been deliberately destroyed, confront him with it in much the same manner, but remind him that you do not want him to break anything again because he is angry at the world. If you can let him know, without raising your voice, how angry you are that he broke the object, fine; if shouting when you are angry is more natural for you, great. Keep your anger within the same bounds as always—no physical punishment—but do not try to cover up the fact that his action has angered you. He needs to know that destructiveness is not accepted, although anger is. By your example, you remind him that a person can be angry and still not seek to hurt or destroy; you can call his attention to your behavior, too. By all means, express your own genuine reaction, so do not seek to make him think he has hurt you or disappointed you, for these are not your reactions.

If he becomes deliberately hostile toward you, much the same reactions are called for. Handle this tantrum just as if it were any other tantrum. Pick him up and place him where he cannot hurt himself or bother you too easily with his continued efforts to hurt you. Keep in mind how frightened he must be if he believes he must hurt the person who is most responsible for taking care of him and protecting him. But do not call his attention to his fear of you, for he may then be provoked to attack you again in order to prove to himself that he is not scared of you. Remember, though, that anger and fear are not natural feelings—they only come when he is so convinced he is weak and vulnerable that he must attack in order to reassure himself.

Be sure, at the same time, to try to increase his opportunity to be as active as possible. Any of these rage reactions can also come about, almost as easily, as a natural consequence to something so simple as that he has been spending most of his time indoors and he has not had much chance to play.

If his reaction to his father's leaving is a radical cutting-down of activity, if he is just moping around indoors, listless and uncaring, you can be helpful by suggesting to him that he may be feeling scared; he may have the wrong idea that somehow he has been responsible for his father's absence. Reassure him that even if he had been very angry with his father, this was not what caused his father to leave. Try to stimulate him to go outdoors and run around. Once he has had a chance to work off some steam, he may feel freer to mention some of his inner reactions to you. Remind him that you are still with him to protect him, and that you do not want him to hurt himself, any more than you want anyone else to hurt him.

In all these efforts, essentially, you are striving by being open and acceptant of his emotions to help him express his anger and then reduce his tensions by the normal process of talking and playing.

### The Fourth Year

As he gains additional control over his temper, he learns to express his activity drive in constructive ways; so by his fourth year, your child is really well able to work very productively. In addition to this basic essential of the sense of responsibility, he also is able to conform to rules that are set up by arbitrary authorities—with a person like his nursery school teacher, for example, who has never been identified with in the course of actual physical care and who is known only as someone who is supposed to be in charge of him. He is able to trade and bargain, to make promises and deals, to carry out projects jointly with other children his age, working with them cooperatively and not trying to become their junior-sized straw boss.

All this capacity for genuine obedience, cooperation, and self-restraint rests on his capacity to extend his identifications. Thus, the teacher is considered by him to be a part of you, and the other children are considered to be a part of him.

His reaction to the loss of his father at this time may be a re-emergence of the unconstructive behavior described in the last section. In his way, he is saying, "I cannot completely trust myself to control my anger. One of the people I have been counting on to help me, inside myself, is gone." If his behavior only becomes unconstructive and not hostile and destructive, little need be done to remedy the situation, aside from giving him time to reassume his constructive responsibilities. He needs to be a baby again, so permit him to be a baby again, at first. Indicate to him that you understand what he is doing: "I guess you're so upset about not having your father here that you don't care much about being a big boy and putting your books back in the book-case by yourself. So help me while I do it for you, okay?" Be sure you do not shame him about his wanting to be a kind of baby again. There is a world of difference, for example, between the kind of comment just described and one that goes, "You mean you're a little baby again and can't even put away your own books? You weren't a baby when your father was here, were you, so why are you being so silly now?"

His conviction that he is a big boy and like you and like his father is the source of his strength. When you take it away from him by ridicule and shaming, you actually turn him into a baby, a very angry and self-doubting one.

Be sure, too, not to slip into a system of bribery because of your awareness of his need for extra reassurance and cuddling. Bribes make him trade something that, under the circumstances, is an overexpectation, in exchange for something else that, under these conditions, is no longer legitimate. For example, do not say, "Honey, pick up your books and I'll give you a big hug for being such a big boy."

After a few weeks, start back at the constructive, disciplining requests that he pick up his books because he is a big boy. Remind him to practice doing the right thing. Here is the kind of reminder that, under usual circumstances, often starts to resemble nagging, and that often brings forth angry refusals, deliberate inattention, forgetting, and tearful complaints. You need to stand firm and remind him that adults do not always enjoy cleaning up a mess, but because they are grown up, they still take care of their responsibilities. It helps to point out the benefits he obtains. For example, with his books picked up, he can play with his train on the floor.

Remind him that his possessions need his care, and so when he does not care enough about them to take care of them, you will assume he does not want them for a while. Here is the important time in a child's life when he finally learns that irresponsibility usually carries its own penalties. He needs support and reassurance from you that you are not putting his books away in his closet for the next week in order to punish him. You must be sure that you make clear to him that it is your way of keeping him from needing to be bothered by those old books that he has shown he does not care about.

Although you may feel that this is a funny trick, it is exceedingly serious. It would be wanton and conducive to irresponsibility if you merely let him keep his books on the floor for so long that they fell apart as they were stepped on, or that he tripped as he attempted to hop over them. He needs your reassurance that you are positive he can stand the unhappiness of not having his things when he does not care for them. Honesty of emotion, not hypocrisy, is thereby encouraged.

If his reaction to his separation from his father is to attempt a maturity beyond his age, to try to take over many responsibilities for your care in addition to his own, you must prohibit him from this guilt-laden kind of overextension of himself. Get to the heart of the problem fast; tell him you know he probably feels bad about all the times he resented being bossed around by his father. Remind him that you do not condemn him for it, though. Remind him that he is only supposed to be responsible for himself, and that your job, because you are an adult, is to take care of him in some ways and to take care of yourself.

As he sees that you will not let him "work off his guilt," that you accept his right to be angry, and you do not think he needs to hurt himself by feeling guilty, he can be more free about expressing, at first very tentatively, his resentments. Reassure him that adults seldom ever manage to be able to feel good about everything they have to do and often feel the same kind of resentment. Point out, though, that it is bad enough to have to do something he does not especially like, in order to get to do something that he does want to do, without making it all the worse by hating himself for being so weak in the first place. Remember that his autism dictates what he feels and how he reacts. Even though you may never have told him in any way that it is wrong to be angry or wrong to be weak, an automatic process within him leads to these conclusions, and he needs reassurance and help in correcting the autistic views. When something like the loss of his father occurs at the time when he is most intensely resenting all authority, the guilts easily become truly fantastic.

If his reactions involve loss of sphincter control, becoming accident-prone, genuine terror about going outside, or any other similar severe, self-imposed restrictions of his freedom, be absolutely firm about discussing both his anger and his fear. Reassure him that you do not believe he needs to hurt himself; point out that you do not believe it is wrong to be angry or to get scared when he feels so weak. Keep in mind a generalization that many psychologists find useful: people are frightened by the things that represent what they want to do angrily to others; and people usually hurt themselves by the same methods they wish they had enough courage to use on the people who are making them angry.

For example, if your child returns to wetting his pants now in reaction, he is first of all reassuring himself that he is just a baby and so cannot possibly hurt anyone even if he tries; therefore, he need not worry about losing his self-control. Backwards logic, isn't it? But still, it makes a childish kind of sense. He is also acting out, symbolically, what he views as an exceedingly angry way of hurting you and his father for making him so unhappy—only he does not quite dare tell you how angry he is, so he feels worried, guilty, and thus punishes himself, instead of you, by shaming himself with his wetting.

As you remind him that he does not need to feel guilty, that you think he has a perfect right to feel angry, but not to hurt himself, and as you show him that you are not angry or hurt or disappointed—so that he can see he really has not hurt you at all—you help him get himself out of the trap he is in. The more you stimulate him to talk about how he has been afraid that he really did cause the trouble, and the more you reassure him that everybody has very angry thoughts at times, but that thoughts cannot hurt anybody, the more you help him relax. You can eventually turn it into a game—let him bet you that you cannot guess what he is thinking. As ridiculous as this is—by the way, it is one game you can always be certain you will lose—it reassures him that his thoughts are private and, more important, powerless. As you pretend to guess what he is thinking, you also have a chance to slip in a little extra propaganda about loving him, "You're thinking that I love you sixteen pounds and eleven inches"; "You're thinking that I think you're a very good, very big boy."

Throughout your remedial efforts, remember that responsibilities carry privileges; so that as he is excused from carrying out his responsibilities because he is unhappy, privileges also disappear. As a concrete example, if, in his reaction, he becomes unwilling to assume without fuss and bother his responsibility to take a few bites of everything served to him at mealtimes and to drink his glass of milk, he also then forfeits his right and privilege to have any snacks between meals. This is another version of the important understanding that irresponsibility involves its own penalties. A couple of years earlier in his life, you would be unfair to impose this kind of restriction on him; at his advanced age of four, however, he is more likely to be hurt and confused if he finds that he can get lots of privileges for nothing than if he is helped to see clearly the realism involved. The only unfair treatment and unhelpful insistence would be if you made the mistake of insisting that, whether he wants to or not, he continue to assume all his responsibilities.

If his reactions lead to complicating troubles in other settings, it is helpful to suggest that he may want to give up these activities for the time being. For example, if he is made fun of by his nursery school playmates because he wets his pants, remove him from school temporarily, so that you both protect him from feeling ashamed of himself and from feeling all sorts of mixed-up animosities and guilts toward his playmates. Tell him you are sorry the

other kids do not know how unhappy he is and cannot understand that that is why he wets his pants. If he feels able to tell
the other children that it is not their business because he is not
bothering them, he can, of course, be allowed to continue in
school. But he must be helped to see that attendance at nursery
school is another privilege that, at this age, he gains because he
assumes various responsibilities. He must not be allowed to expect
special treatment for long; the same thing goes for all the other
manifestations of unhappiness shown by him in the school setting: fist-fights, crying spells, unwillingness to share, withdrawal
from the group activities, and so on. Ask the teacher to cooperate in keeping the other children in hand for a week or so and
in pointing out sympathetically to your child that she understands his reaction. But after a week or two, both she and you
must request that your child either begin to control himself or
stay home until he gets himself back under control.

What he is able to do, as a basically healthy and energetic
child, he tries to do and does do. As you help him relieve his feelings of guilt and fear, as you help him express his anger and resentment through talk, not through body english or other forms
of acting out, you can help him reorganize himself without being
left the worse for his initial reactions.

## THE OEDIPAL PERIOD

The loss of his father at this time, whatever the reasons for
it may be, arouses tremendous guilts. His reactions to these guilts
can be extremely varied, as the next chapter illustrates.

You relieve his guilts as you work to correct the Oedipal
problem itself; so that relatively little, directly, is required of
you with regard to the sense of responsibility, as such. Whatever
the irresponsibilities may be that he shows in his reaction, you
need to handle it both as a problem in responsibility, following
the preceding suggestions, and as a problem in his assertion of an
incorrect view of himself as a sexual adult. A few new ways of
acting out irresponsibility also occur at this time.

For example, when he attacks your dignity and status by
teasing, be just as alert to stopping the teasing as you ever were
to stopping a physical attack; he seldom teases about something

he really wants to know. He teases by asking about something he already knows. So do not let yourself be fooled into giving lengthy explanations time and time again. After the first or second time, tell him flatly that he knows how things are, he knows they are what they are because that is how things are, and he also knows that he annoys you when he teases. Remind him that even if he can get you angry by his incessant teasing, it no more makes him bigger than you than if he were to break something belonging to you and get you angry. Tell him that you want him to be in control of himself, not you; when he is older, he may be able to boss other people around, but not while he is a child. Reassure him that you do not blame him for wanting to be in control, but you do blame him for the teasing and want it stopped. Remind him that you are sorry he is so angry about being a child, but that you like having him as your child, so you do not agree with him at all that it would be nicer if he could grow up in a hurry.

Surliness, rudeness, and contempt are also new developments that can be treated the same way. Require basic courtesies from him as you have done in the past few years; remind him that if he cannot be with people pleasantly, he need not stay with them. If his discourteous behavior continues, request that he leave and go off by himself, alone, to be as rude as he likes.

As is necessary during earlier childhood, keep separate his open expressions of anger and his distorted, acting-out release of anger. Remind him that he may tell you he hates you, but he may not be sassy. As embarrassing as a loudly spoken declaration in public that he hates you may be, you must not react to it as if it were the same as being rude. Tell him you are sorry he hates you, remind him that you love him, and continue to insist on whatever it was that started him off. Should he go off on a tirade about how much he hates you, ask him to stop. Reassure him that you do not mind his telling you once or twice, although you are sorry to know he hates you so much, but that you are a grown-up person and not likely to forget what he has already said. So since you already know how he feels, you want him to stop telling you.

An additional new kind of irresponsible reaction is pilfering or outright stealing. (In earlier years, when he walked off with things that belonged to others, it was probably because he did not understand clearly that he was not to take things that belong to other people. And lying, when he was younger, was also mainly due to his difficulty in distinguishing wish from reality. In earlier years, too, any increase in walking off with things belonging to others, following the separation, may result from his confused idea that nothing is sacred, everything is mixed-up. Do not leap to the conclusion that it is an attempt symbolically to gain a substitute for the lost love.) But during the Oedipal period, with all the instruction and understanding he has previously experienced about property rights, stealing must be viewed as a real symbolic act, an effort to get something to replace love. Explain to your child that you will not allow him to steal things and that you will not shield him from the anger of others, should he again decide to steal. Remind him that you know he is upset because his father is gone, you know he is angry and feels cheated, but that money or property are not good substitutes for affection and closeness. Point out that, even if he ends up by hurting himself so much through stealing that the police are called, he cannot bring his father back. Keep in mind that he is probably not stealing in order to embarrass you, so control your reactions when you accompany him to restore the property and apologize. Meanwhile, try to reassure him that you love him and want to help him.

Because so much of what is regarded in America as adult responsibility rests in a firm respect for property rights, this particular symptom—while perhaps no more significant in itself than rudeness or teasing or any other symptom of disturbance—requires prompt and additionally thoughtful attention. If your initial remedial efforts do not bring a fast stop to the pilfering, should more than one or two additional episodes come to your attention, be sure to obtain professional help. Chronic lying, running away from home, and hostile attacks on you at this time, too, are signs of danger, and must be treated like stealing.

Of the many different characteristics of adult responsibility, only one aspect is absolutely required by law: an adult must be able to tolerate enough delay of his impulses so that he does not attack people or property. An adult can be a bum, living on handouts, never assuming support of himself or others; he can be miserly and uncharitable, unsociable, and discourteous to the people he has contact with—still the law will not seek to restrain him. *But*, basic control of impulse, sufficient so that he does not steal or rob or murder or commit sexual offenses, is mandatory.

Your Oedipal child has had far too much opportunity to learn the general rules governing social behavior—we do not steal, we do not lie, we do not hurt people—to be repeatedly breaking these rules as part of a relatively uncomplicated reaction to the loss of his father. More likely, he is demonstrating some deeper disturbances.

So when he shows these reactions after he has already had four or five years to learn to govern them, and after you have reinforced his understanding by your reactions to his first or second offense, remedial action is mandatory—lest he continue to get himself into trouble or bury these impulses within him, not comprehending them or their cause, afraid of their consequences, afraid of his possible loss of control over himself in the future, and hating you because you have failed to help him regain control of himself and thus of what happens to him.

As stated previously in discussing nursery school behavior, your child's reactions must not be allowed to claim long-continued special treatment in any group; this is still true for him in his kindergarten class. Remove him until he calms down.

If he should be so unfortunate as to be picked up by the police for his very first episode of stealing, it makes sense for you to claim special privilege for him as a consequence of his special circumstances. Usually the law understands this and has special limits for first offenders who are so very young. But leave it up to the Court if your son is caught after a second episode— you have told your child you will not protect him from the consequences of his actions should they be repeated. Work with the social workers attached to the court or detention home, and cooperate with their suggestions.

## THE GRADE-SCHOOL YEARS

Your child's capacity to take care of his responsibilities for himself, to be courteous and sociable, to tolerate delay, to work productively, and to join with a group in providing for its welfare are all decidedly increased by the practice of these responsibilities characteristic of his grade-school years. Up to his entrance into regular school, he has had his hands full merely learning to take care of himself in a responsible manner. But as he now begins to need less from you, he can offer more to you, and his offerings can be structured by you as chores that become his full responsibilities. He also learns how to use money and receives an allowance from you—an important step into the grown-up world of responsibility where money can buy privileges directly because responsibility has already been discharged in earning the money.

He also learns the responsibility of maintaining the comfort of others by keeping his feelings to himself. At five or six, he could say he hates you and reflect no failure in the development of his sense of responsibility; but at seven or eight years of age, he can legitimately be charged with the responsibility of simply telling you what he dislikes, without the judgmental comments. He is also expected to exercise tact and self-imposed restraint with his teachers, schoolmates, and all others.

Just as play is the work of the preschool child and a job is the work of the adult, learning is the work of the school child. So by learning well at school, your child is practicing the skills used later in full assumption of his responsibility for himself.

In reaction to the loss of his father during these years, your child is most likely to show adultlike mourning reactions that involve his loss of interest in the activities connected to all these responsibilities.

Of them all, only his conduct at school and the maintenance of his preschool responsibility for himself are serious problems. Other reactions can be left alone, most of the time, to handle themselves as time wears away the intensity of his initial mourning reaction. So let him drop out of the cub scouts, stop taking piano lessons, and be only minimally responsive and courteous to others. But take steps to remedy school or personal reactions.

Discuss his school problems with his teacher, requesting her help in re-stimulating him to assume his responsibilities. Point out to your child that you can understand his reactions, and so you are not requiring that he be able to carry on with his chores at home, for the time being, or continue his extracurricular interests. But remind him, emphatically, that you cannot permit him to hurt himself by failing to do his school work.

Be especially careful to avoid any suggestion that you really do not think school work is important. Although many adults may feel that the grade-school years are not objectively meaningful, learning at school must be respected as seriously by you as you respected his earlier efforts at play. (Make sure, too, that you do not complicate matters by objecting to the content of the material taught at school. This is no time, for example, to get into a fuss at school because the teacher starts the day with a minute of silent prayer or tells the children that people are descended from monkeys. Ordinarily, the teacher, not your child, is the one to voice your objections to anyhow. At this time, because you are asking for special help from her, it is not sensible to make it more difficult for her to feel generous.)

Even if you know that your child is capable under usual circumstances of doing top work at school, do not continue to insist that he perform to top potential now. Think of his mourning reaction as if it were a lingering lowgrade fever; it cuts into his efficiency. So if the teacher reassures you that your child is doing at least passing work, do not place pressures for doing better than just passing. When the mourning passes away, just as when a fever passes away, his grades and learning will increase again.

If, however, he is still passing only because his over-all brightness in class discussions offsets his failure to carry through routine responsibilities for things like homework, library assignments, and special projects, you need to remind him that all of the teacher's work assignments are his responsibility. If necessary, curtail additional privileges until after he proves to your satisfaction that he has finished his homework.

Should his responsibility for himself take a sharp nosedive and stay low for more than a week or two, explain to him that his responsibilities for washing himself and carrying out his other self-related chores must be assumed. Suggest to him that if he finds himself too unhappy to bring himself to carry out these minimal tasks, that he ask you for help with them. If a few weeks of return to the kind of sharing that was characteristic of the time when he was two or three years old does not bring him back to being fully able to carry on by himself, obtain psychological help. Your child's self-respect is not ordinarily reduced this seriously for longer than a week or two, unless older, deeper problems are being revealed.

Once he is back to being a good learner at school and clean and orderly at home, start requesting that he assume additional responsibilities like chores or tact at home and group participation or other extracurricular activities. All of these are alike; they are all ways of practicing sociability and responsibility. It does not matter which one he reassumes first; none may be used as a bribe for the others. So even if he is still not carrying out his chores, let him attend his cub scout meetings. After a few more weeks, you can start insisting that he evenly distribute his activity and assume more of the responsibilities that help you out, or else forfeit some privileges.

Your child may react to his loss by becoming very money-minded, as well as becoming very greedy and insecure about his friendships. If you notice the combination of these two facets, interrupt and interpret. So, for example, if you learn that he has stopped liking one child because that child never buys him any treats, remind your child that gifts are not a responsible basis for friendship. In the same way, handle his reaction if you notice that he is now spending all his allowance on his friends. Be sure you have not contributed to his misunderstanding by too much emphasis upon your money problems as a single mother. Be especially careful, if you have divorced and a cause of continual strife is the matter of support payments, that you do not indicate to your child that you hate his father because his father is not sending his payments regularly. This kind of comment can lead to your child's misconception that the only way to have security in friendship is to purchase it. Be sure, in fact, that you do not place undue emphasis upon the matter of having friends at all.

Very often, because any emotional suffering can broaden and deepen understanding and general attitudes about life, a child's interests can be radically altered and advanced following a loss at this time. But each such expansion must be carefully scrutinized. For example, it is reasonable for your ten-year-old child to stop playing cops and robbers and start spending more of his time with some other friends that have more complicated interests like building model airplanes or radios. But it is not likely to be helpful if he switches to carrying out these advanced interests with a pal many years his senior, for he may be trying to substitute for his father, carrying out these interests only because there is no other basis on which he believes he can manage to get the companionship. You can help by reminding him he need not purchase companionship by straining to maintain an interest in an activity that is not personally gratifying. Help him establish his friendship—if it is otherwise helpful and wholesome—on another basis. If this is impossible, help him return to friends with whom he can at least have a fair trade, playing with them on an equal give-and-take basis.

If his interests mature and he can find no one with whom to share them, refrain from showing concern. Many a child, for a few years at a time, is unable to find anyone else equally wrapped up in science or music or mechanics and so has only a few friends that he spends a little time with at group activities, remaining solitary in pursuit of his interest most of his leisure time. By no means must you regard his friendlessness as a continued negative reaction to his loss, unless it is accompanied by other signs of deep disturbance like poor eating and sleeping, eccentric mannerisms, poor school work, or unoccupied withdrawal and solitude. If these signs are present, psychological consultation, of course, is indicated.

Be sure that you do not confuse your child's natural mourning reactions with other efforts to attempt to dominate you or escape his responsibilities. For example, even under ordinary circumstances, it is natural for your child to be unhappy about accompanying you on an afternoon visit to one of your adult friends where he has no company. His mourning makes it even more likely that he is not able to sustain this kind of pressure. But once he has recovered enough emotional strength to be interested in his own activities, do not let him dominate you by a continuance of the unwillingness to accompany you or by an insistence that you stay home with him. Give him a fair shake. Do not impose much of this kind of inconvenience on him; but remind him that occasional inconveniences are part of living with people, and he is as able to handle his responsibilities with you as with anyone. So insist, as before, that he accompany you and that he be pleasant and courteous.

After several months have passed, any continuance of your child's extreme mourning reaction is unreasonable. The responsibility for continuing with extracurricular instruction, for example, ought to be reassumed if he had previously shown talent and skill. Do not let him become irresponsible about the continued practice involved in something like music lessons. Do not mistake the natural and expected loss of enthusiasm for music, which any child experiences when he discovers that hard work is involved in developing a skill, for a lasting effect of the loss of his father. Stimulate him to be responsible; if he cannot cooperate, obtain some outside help with your problem. Although you may be tempted to drop the whole struggle because you do not consider it worth the effort, your responsibility in this kind of matter is as clear as it is for any mother: if your child has a potential skill, he owes it to himself to work to develop it. You do him no favor if you permit him to escape his responsibility to himself with a misconception like, "His loss has left such lasting sorrow it prevents him from being able to enjoy the piano any more."

As mentioned in preceding chapters, your child must also face up to his responsibilities in the groups to which he belongs. Attendance at the church group's father-and-son meeting, for example, is a part of belonging to the group. Even though he may feel little enthusiasm for attending with a relative, the leader, or with another boy and his father, put this responsibility on an open, either-or basis. If he cannot carry out his responsibility by attending the special event, he may not attend the other regular events. He needs protection from the possibility of being embarrassed because he does not have his father with him, of course, as pointed out previously; but he also needs encouragement in recognizing that associations carry responsibilities just as friendships do.

In many ways, the school child is similar to an adult. Just as it is reasonable for you to expect your own mourning reactions to pass with time and leave you free to assume all your responsibilities—not just the few major ones that you did not relinquish even at first—it is reasonable to expect similar behavior from your grade school child.

## ADOLESCENCE

The development of the sense of responsibility in the variety of ways just discussed continues without any decided break through high school. But the startling changes of puberty and the many demands of adolescence involve the assumption of additional facets of responsibility, among them your child's opportunity to hire himself out on a job, to drive a car, and to assume his own social responsibilities. (Those involved with sexuality are discussed in the following chapter.)

The usual reaction to loss in adolescence is increased self-centeredness and irresponsibility; your child, however, may react to separation from his father at this time by a heightened sense of responsibility. The general adolescent tendency to make melodrama of even the most ordinary experiences often confuses the picture, making it difficult to determine if a straightforward mourning reaction is operating or if some particular behavior is a way of dramatizing the situation.

In certain instances, you are unlikely to know if such behavior occurs. For example, it may operate when he is on a date, taking advantage of his girl's sympathy and listening-ability, spending the evening talking about his own reactions to being without a father. In so doing, he leaves the girl emotionally worn-out and unrefreshed by her date with him, although he has had a great time being inconsiderate, irresponsible, and selfishly exhibitionistic. Should you happen to learn of irresponsible behavior like this, be sure to offer him a simple choice: he can stop dating until his sorrow is reduced and he feels able to assume his responsibility to be pleasant, courteous, fair company—obtaining psychiatric help in reducing his sorrow, if necessary—or he can stop the irresponsible acting out immediately and make an apology as soon as possible to the girl he troubled by his discourteous failure to pay attention to her needs.

Other kinds of acting out more easily come to your attention. For example, it is reasonably difficult for your teen-ager to disguise the fact that, against the orders that you, like any parent, have wisely laid down, he has been drinking alcoholic beverages when out on a date. (Drinking at home is not considered being irresponsible. In fact, many psychologists agree that it is wise for the teen-ager to have had commonplace contact with liquor at home throughout childhood.) Your teen-ager may seek to excuse his irresponsibility to his date and his disobedience to your rules by summoning the hoary cliche that he "got to feeling so depressed about you and about dad that one little drink was taken to see if it would make the gloom disappear."

If you fall for this once, you might as well cease all efforts to help your teen-ager. As this book stresses, you have an absolute obligation to your child to call a spade a spade. You do him no service by letting him make himself feel guilty about the basic rebellion against your limits and then guilty about traducing the meaning of separation from his father, bothering his date (assuming she was distressed by his drinking and did not join him), and lying to you.

The same considerations apply to all minor acts of irresponsibility. He may seek to excuse reckless driving as being due to his attempt to forget his sorrow by trying some fancy driving; he may explain a parking ticket as due to the fact that he was so bound up in wondering what you were going to do now that you are single that he did not even realize he was parking overtime. He may seek to justify heavy smoking in similar ways.

If you have reason to believe that all these instances are efforts on his part to work a racket, with his friends as well as with you, get right down to basics. Tell him you are sorry he is so insecure; tell him you are sorry he has so little respect for you that he believes he can convince you of a cock-and-bull story. Remind him, however, that he has been given dating privileges and driving privileges only within certain limits, and he has passed them. So lower the boom. Whatever your original agreement was, put it into effect. For example, if you agreed he could drive the car only if he obeyed the traffic regulations absolutely, and that one minor infringement would lose him the privilege of driving for a month, now is the time to start counting the thirty days.

As you can see, this is outright punishment. Unlike the responsibilities your child has assumed in all preceding stages of childhood, many of the responsibilities he assumes in adolescence are really privileges often reserved, in most other countries, to the adults. He may have these privileges only so long as he carries out the responsibilities attached to them. Hence the punishment—usually, of course, the loss of the privilege.

Criminal and sexual delinquency are not likely to be sustained reactions of loss; but in each case, only once may be enough to get your youngster into serious trouble. You can avoid this likelihood by being particularly alert to early signs. If he begins to spend much time away from home—particularly if his studies begin to suffer—be sure to set limits. Require that he complete all homework assignments before going anywhere in the evening, and require that he drop extracurricular activities unless he maintains at least a good C average. Usually, his own basic insecurities are sufficiently strong to enable him to accept the limits you place on his behavior; you need not anticipate a scene that ends with his leaving your home forever just because you assert your authority. Rarely do head-on clashes of any importance take place. Even if they do, stick to your guns.

Your own special situation may become a source of trouble when you assert limits, especially if you are an illegitimate mother or divorced because of infidelity and you seek to restrain your child from sexual acting out, or if your husband is separated from you because he is in prison and you attempt to restrain your child from criminal acting out. However, by your very willingness to risk hearing this charge and to disregard the competitive challenge to defend yourself and, instead, use his charges as exactly the reason why you refuse to permit him to hurt himself, you make of your marital difficulties the object lesson they can be. Hold your ground. Even if your child becomes a resentful, neurotic adult (obviously a very far-fetched possibility), he is better off than if trying to reconstitute a good life for himself after he has a jail record or has gotten married and been forced to leave high school or other equally unfortunate outcomes.

You can help your child strengthen his own tottering emotional resources by helping him understand that you do not want him to hurt himself and by indicating that you will gladly risk incurring his resentment and animosity in order to prevent him from hurting himself.

Keep separate, however, such ways of acting out conflicts and the ordinary, rebellious ways that typify adolescence. For example, whether you want him to or not, whether you know about it or not, your adolescent is likely to start smoking cigarettes. You would be foolish indeed if you viewed this as proof of any intense inner disturbance about being left without his father. Too, he is likely to get drunk once, possibly twice, and be very ill because of it; again, this is par for the course. There may often be times when he seeks to butt in on your conversations with your friends or fails to ask a visiting friend of his to have something to eat or drink; this erratic social irresponsibility is mainly something to be tempered and suffered, too.

However, your child may react much more intensely to the loss of his father. Rebellion, sheer flouting of your authority or of all authority, is not uncommon. It requires the same serious and immediate care that acting out by stealing, lying, truancy, or physical attack in the Oedipal period requires. In many ways, the two processes—the Oedipal and the adolescent developments—are similar, although the law, of course, views the adolescent's in a different manner than it does the six-year-old's.

If the law or nature catches up to him before you do, try to give him emotional support to make it easier for him to bear the consequences.

If you sincerely believe that his criminal offense is causing him sufficient suffering by itself, and that it was due to something unlikely to recur, just as with a younger child, ask for special consideration from the court. But do not help him avoid the consequences unless you are very sure. If you are prepared to help provide psychotherapy for him, in exchange for special consideration, you can feel fairly confident that his self-control is going to be strengthened.

If your daughter or if your son's girl friend becomes pregnant, it is usually wiser for you to arrange for her to bear her child out of wedlock and have it adopted, legally, than for you to consent to or force a marriage or to attempt to secure an illegal abortion. You can obtain help from the social workers at welfare agencies in finding a home for unwed mothers in another city for the time being. Although you may worry that people will talk, people can only talk about things they know about—all else is guessing and gossip and usually soon stops. So be sure to keep your knowledge to yourself; insist that the girl now recognize she has already hurt herself sufficiently and, therefore, now needs to bear her own secrecy.

If your adolescent child shows little overreaction to the loss of his father, you may become apprehensive that his tensions are all steaming up inside of him; you may even worry lest your child be thinking of killing himself or running away. But it may be that his apparent lack of emotion is only his adolescent way of keeping from being too emotional. If he shows no other symptoms—no withdrawal from people, no lessened effectiveness at school, no unpredictable outbursts of emotion quite out of keeping with the events surrounding the outburst—your fears are probably groundless, particularly if you two have had a generally good relationship. If he shows any such bizarre symptoms, however, seek psychological evaluation immediately and, of course, avoid letting him drive or engage in any other activities that demand great self-control. Explain to him in a matter-of-fact way that you are worried about the way he is taking the family break-up; tell him you do not want to make him additionally uncomfortable by being pointlessly concerned or restrictive, but you need reassurance in order to be more calm. Although he probably resents the idea, follow through; serious or not, his reaction needs to be understood by you.

Less frightening ways of reacting to the loss of his father are his taking a job and insisting that he is going to carry a bigger portion of the responsibility for the family, or his giving up plans for college in deference to taking a job in order to support the family.

If you believe that his very impulse to take a job—either as a part-time position or as the beginning of his full-time occupational career—is only a means of acting out guilts and shames, be sure to stop him. If he has had a reasonably good high school record, insist that he take only a part-time job while finishing high school. And if you have the financial means, insist that he try a year of college before carrying out his plan of foregoing college to support you. Point out that you do not want him to hurt himself or feel in any way responsible for the absence of his father.

Remember that when your child was a one-year-old, he thought everything in the world was for him to grab and put in his mouth, and he resented your protection and intrusion when you took away the lamp cord and gave him his uninteresting old rattle. He is bigger and wiser now, but his impulses pull him just as they did in the past; he still needs you to remind him of his limits and his responsibilities. So, though the autism of his age dictates that he view your insistence on the value of education as an old-fashioned fairy tale that only old folks like you believe in, stick to your guns. Remind him that his friends are *not* the only ones who know the score—remind him that they are being foolish to leave high school to take a job, however much more money they can make in a week than their fathers did for a month's work a generation ago. Your responsibility is to go right on being old-fashioned.

Once you agree to a part-time job, remind your teen-ager to give full consideration to the responsibilities of a job. Help him analyze the potential job in an objective way, examining what he can offer to the position, what rewards besides money he will receive, what drawbacks there are. If you discover that he really dislikes the job but feels compelled to take it, be sure to point out to him that a major adult responsibility—one he must assume—is to make certain that a job is to his liking. Otherwise he will sooner or later give less to the job than he ought to, falling down on his responsibility to himself as well as to his employer. Prevent him from romanticizing a position; if he is really mature enough to help take over family financial responsibilities, he is old enough to be realistic.

Your child may react to his loss by showing a casual disregard of the kinds of precautions that are trivial, but whose disregard is potentially dangerous. He may be careless because he has insufficient emotional stamina to take care of all details claiming his attention, or he may be genuinely indifferent to minor concerns when so much that is important has altered. But he must be called upon to exercise the same protection of himself that he learned to carry out when he first started to look where he was walking; he must not be allowed to trip himself, figuratively. For example, he must not let others exploit him; he must not make free-and-easy agreements with his employer as to pay and hours so that he ends up being victimized. He must be helped to recognize that dignity and insistence on justice are equivalent to a genuine sense of responsibility; so, for example, he may not "show his appreciation" for being on the first team by agreeing to wash the coach's car every week. He must learn to take his chances on the basis of his athletic prowess alone. However much he may seek a particular goal, he must be kept from irresponsibly shading corners and running risks in order to gain the goal. So, though he may not deliberately be seeking to embezzle, for example, he must not borrow from club treasury funds, however temporarily, for his own purposes. He must be helped to see that it is not just being stuffy and suspicious to worry about things like reputation; he needs encouragement and support in learning that long after people have forgotten the justifying particulars and explanations and circumstances of an act arousing thier doubts, they remember the act and attach ordinary interpretations to it. He must assume responsibility for maintaining and protecting his good reputation; he must not irresponsibly "just not care." He should not agree, for example, to drive his girl, unchaperoned, for an overnight visit to her relatives out of town.

In reminding him of all such responsibilities, be sure you distinguish between ideas that have not changed since your day and ideas that have. General morality has not changed much; we are as good or as bad today as ever. But material circumstances have altered radically. For example, your child is not likely to jeopardize his future professional career—should he have chosen this goal—by taking a menial job during high school. Thirty years ago, if he intended to go to medical school and return to his home town for practice, a child would have been irresponsibly creating future obstacles by taking a summer job as a factory hand; his future patients would always remember that he had once worked as a common laborer. But today these considerations make little sense, particularly with families moving around a great deal, with neighbor groups breaking up and changing drastically, and with little likelihood that he will be spending his adult life in a community comprised of people who knew him when he was a child. So do not interfere with job selection on the basis of this kind of outmoded consideration.

By the end of his teens, your child has learned almost all he needs to know about being responsible and sociable. Almost all of his attitudes are so stabilized that he automatically assumes appropriate responsibilities and then fulfills them. Honest and confident, he regards his social duties and his duties to himself and his family as intermingled, all equally important, all ones he wants to fulfill, and all ones he works to fulfill. Not at all a person who must be held back from antisocial and irresponsible behavior by fear of punishment, he can be a person who likes himself and likes other people and, thus, is willing and able to participate in a group that promotes the well being of the majority.

# CHAPTER FOURTEEN

# Stimulating Your Child's Realism
# about Sexuality

As THE PRECEDING CHAPTERS have indicated, your daily interactions with your child throughout his development allow him to form attitudes about bodily sensations that can involve both positive and negative feelings, that permit him to view his natural bodily tensions and gratifications with either pleasure or anxiety.

Though he does not become an adult biologically until he reaches puberty, and though he does not become an adult emotionally until he reaches his twenties, the attitudes about sensuality and bodily pleasures that he develops during his long period of immaturity are all connected with his later regard of adult sexuality.

Unlike the ease with which you can observe, almost daily, how your child develops his sense of responsibility and how he grows to share your general values in living, difficulties are faced by you in viewing the development of your child's sexuality, for his sexual attitudes are seldom fully directed toward you in actuality.

## Sexuality in the Pre-Oedipal Periods

Any mother, single or in a complete home, can provide to her child the experiences necessary for him to develop healthy pre-

Oedipal attitudes regarding sexuality. A father's presence is not necessary for a child to develop the healthy pre-Oedipal realism about sexuality that contributes in his later adulthood to love-making that is appropriate, spontaneous, and happy. As Chapter Nine pointed out, your child's realism about his own bodily sensations develops from the care and experiences he has as he goes through the various stages of physical development; for him to have realistic attitudes, he only needs to have had nonneurotic, undistorted experiences. As you implement the good and healthy interactions that have been described in previous chapters, and as you avoid the ones that detract from your child's happiness and health, you pave the way for your child to develop healthy adult sexuality.

Because so many examples have already been given of these kinds of interactions, only a few generalizations are reviewed at this time.

If your child's earliest experiences are chronically overstimulating, he develops basic anxieties about all intense stimulation. In later life, sexual excitement may be viewed with anxiety and withdrawal, because it is a preamble to even more intense stimulation. So, by insuring your child a modicum of pleasant stimulation and a minimum of disturbing discomforts, you are increasing the likelihood that he will find sexual intercourse and other intensely exciting, playful experiences gratifying.

Bad experiences in receiving care and protection lead automatically to anxieties connected with feeling a specific body want and being dependent on others for relief. From the anxiety, develops a lack of trust in both the self and in others; brittle self-sufficiency may be substituted for dependency in the effort to keep the frightening intimacy away, or a very passive, defeated attitude may develop that makes all forms of intimacy as worthless as isolation. If the bad experiences include a pattern of providing care only after severe pain or injury has been experienced, all pleasure must be combined with pain or else viewed with guilt and fear.

These anxieties interfere drastically with the give-and-take of healthy adult sexual intercourse. A person who has had these bad experiences may give love and pleasure drearily and without joy or may give very little or none, because he is unable to trust that he will receive in return any love or pleasure. He may even deliberately seek out situations that his common sense tells him cannot possibly involve a return of love or pleasure; by making certain, in effect, that there is nothing to hope for, his anxieties are reduced slightly. Purchasing sexual intercourse from a prostitute is an example of this sort of behavior, as is making meaningless, hasty, unemotional "love" with a frigid, unresponsive, or reluctant partner. A man may forego the active male role and take the passive, receptive role instead, not initiating intercourse, sometimes not consummating it, for fear of being as unsuccessful as he once was when he signaled that he was hungry and wanted to be fed. A woman, careless because she dares not really care, may either reject sexual intimacy or be so uninterested that she does not respond to intercourse with her husband, a lover, or a stranger.

By insuring your young child the peaceful, happy, pain-free cuddling and cooing and caressing and material care he needs, you permit him later to find sexual intercourse a way of expressing his tender, warm, loving feelings in an intimate and immediate way.

Bad experiences in enjoying variety and change and freedom also cause later troubles with regard to sexuality. Even when attention is not paid specifically to sexual exploration, the limiting of freedom leads to negative feelings about having inner impulses and about expressing these. Many times, a child's freedom to explore most of his world and most of his body may not be trammeled, but his right to explore his own genital region may be completely taken away. The mother who may otherwise trust her child to poke his finger in his nose, sure that eventually he will learn to use the more efficient and satisfying method of blowing his nose in a handkerchief, may not extend the same complacent trust to her child when he wants to poke around in his phallic and anal areas. Often combined with this form of restriction are moral condemnations for what she regards as her child's licentious, immoral, and repulsive curiosity.

Adult sexual desire is exactly the kind of "unjustifiable" impulse that easily becomes linked with the inner burden of guilt. It is not "worthy work," it is mere pleasure; so it is easily regarded as contemptible. The ideas of being good and being sexual may become incompatible. A man, for example, may feel contempt for any woman who indicates she enjoys sex, or he may have contempt for himself because of his own sexual wants; he may be able to respect only a woman who disappoints or frustrates him sexually. He may impulsively fall in "love" with a "fallen woman"— not always a prostitute, sometimes just a woman who enjoys sexuality—because she overwhelms him, temporarily, into believing that it is reasonable for him to feel sexual excitement. Unable consciously to accept any sexual feelings, the person may resort to artificial releases of inhibition like alcohol or drugs, in order to become free enough to release some of the pent-up sexual impulse. Having grown up with rigid standards about what is right and what is wrong, always and in all places, the inflexible adult may not accept sexuality unless it is according to a set pattern; the whole pleasure of sexual intercourse may be destroyed if the partner alters the pattern.

By giving your child his necessary freedoms, by avoiding inhibition or condemnation of his curiosity about his own body, by sharing with him your likes and dislikes but respecting his right to formulate his own, you lay the basis of his ability and desire to give pleasure to his loved one as he himself desires to obtain pleasure. He can then identify with his beloved and truly join in the act of love, not engage in mere sexual exercise.

If he is severely punished, physically, for being active, or if he is prohibited from being aggressive, he develops tensions, hostilities, and fears. These same troublesome feelings develop if he is forced to be more independently aggressive than he is naturally prepared to be (as when he is forced to use the toilet). These negative feelings often are associated with anxiety and restlessness over any form of confinement and can lead to the use of sexual intercourse, not as a way of expressing love and concern, but as a way of releasing hostility or the activity drive. Intercourse so becomes an act that is compelled by inner tensions, not a freely chosen play activity. It can take on the character of a crude gymnastic performance. Brutality intermingled with sexual practices can become the major focus of attention, while all feelings of tenderness become submerged until enough guilt over the brutality has been accumulated to reassure the neurotic person that he has suffered enough from his guilt to be free to enjoy himself. The feeling of being exhausted by sexual play may become paramount, and the refreshment and invigoration that are healthy aftermaths of sexual intercourse may not be felt. So much tension may be built up by past delay and discomfort that the control mechanisms may no longer be trusted; sexual intercourse then may become an act to be sprinted through, as if the devil were in pursuit, or may become an emergency that cannot be resisted or delayed whatever the circumstances—intercourse is not enjoyed in relaxation and leisure and ease.

If bad experiences of childhood overemphasized the importance of self-control, sexuality, like any impulse, may just be terribly frightening, a force to be avoided at all costs. Its orgasm may be the only aspect that is resisted, so that intercourse becomes a drawn-out, teasing, tiring experience, but not a successfully gratifying one. Or, because he feels he has paid for it by tolerating the frightening sexual impulses, he may feel free to act out old hostilities; so intercourse may become only an aggressive and hostile act —the sadism a goal in itself, not a means of accumulating guilt so that sexuality may be enjoyed.

As you permit your child ample expression of his activity drive, as you provide ample praise and justification for self-control but avoid asking too much control of him, you provide the necessary foundations for vigorous, constructive attitudes about sex. (You also provide the foundations for handling anger realistically—not in bed.)

As you can see, experiences that later relate to sexuality are really learned in the context of experiences related to privacy, succor, mobility, responsibility, and sociability. These merge with the attitudes he learns in the course of his Oedipal period, his school years, and his adolescence. Aside from minor difficulties that are discussed in the next section, your singleness does not alter your ability to provide the basis of healthy pre-Oedipal attitudes.

### SPECIAL MINOR PRE-OEDIPAL PROBLEMS

General principles that guide any mother govern how you handle most of the minor problems concerning pre-Oedipal sexuality—problems like nudity, questions about babies and sex, and sex play with other children. Thus, consult the books recommended in Chapter Eight for advice on how to be truthful, accurate, and helpful in giving answers on a level your child can understand. Some questions that relate to your unique circumstances may cause you occasional difficulty, however.

For example, as your child has noticed the increasing size of another woman who is pregnant and has learned that "little babies grow in their mothers' stomachs after a mommy and daddy put together the tiny first bits of a new baby," he may be bewildered about his own existence. He may ask how he came to be when he has no daddy. But all he is really asking is, "Did I start the same way, or not?" And all he really needs to know is that he was not any different, that when he first started to be alive, he did have a daddy. So do not overwhelm him with talk about divorce, widowhood, desertion, and so on; just reinforce his understanding of how babies get made.

If your child is a boy, your attention to the question of nudity must be sharper than is required of the married mother. Your son has no adult male to compare himself to for reassurance about what his body will be like when he is grown up. You can help him be more relaxed about himself if you avoid letting him see you nude, for you differ from him in size and shape and detail, and his comparisons are not easily integrated. During his childhood, he can get around enough to see other little boys undressed and receive some reassurance that he is not unique. (Once he is in school, of course, he may also have the opportunity to see grown men, his teachers, undressed; at that time, he will need to learn from you explanations about the differences in general body size and shape, hair distribution, and size of the phallus.) In a sense, your goal is to avoid confusing him by your nudity; he will need to obtain further reassurance about his own body from comparisons and evaluations made when he is older, for, unlike the boy in a complete family, he cannot grow up with a day-to-day acquaintance with such information.

Do not mistakenly conclude that it is necessary for you deliberately to show your child how other children are constructed, or that your child ought to be encouraged in open sex play. You still need to protect your child against the dual dangers of infection and injury and of tension and guilt caused by open sex play; you still need to prohibit this form of acting out, for as the books previously referred to indicate, all children—including those within whom the parents have strived deliberately to instill a healthy attitude toward sex—are subject to feelings of constraint and anxiety when engaged in sex play. And, the ordinary course of events in places where children undress—bathrooms and at the beach—usually allows a boy to note that little girls have flat nipples like boys but no penises, and allows a girl to note that boys have flat nipples and have "wee-wee makers" where she has her "'gina"; so no special viewing occasions are required for your child to learn these realities. Indeed, such artificially arranged situations usually only promote added tension.

The same constraint is required of you in your toileting habits if you are to prevent undue confusion in your son. He does not—contrary to popular belief—need a father or other man as an example of how to urinate; he can learn simply upon your verbal instructions to urinate standing up. But spare him the confusion of watching you urinate sitting down.

In short, practice more constraint about sexual matters than might a mother in a complete home.

## Oedipal Period

With the advent of the Oedipal period in about the fifth and sixth years of your child's life, your task and his development are no longer similar to the ones characteristic of life in a complete family. The Oedipal period is the one time of a child's life when he definitely needs *two* parents living together. Otherwise, he cannot develop essential attitudes about sexuality at the time and in a way that is natural and usual.

This does not mean, of course, that your child without a father at this time is turned into an emotional cripple, unable ever to develop sensible and healthy attitudes concerning the pertinent matters of this period. And it does not mean that his only hope of avoiding remaining such a cripple is to enter into psychotherapy when he reaches adulthood. It merely means that his childhood is altered from its natural patterns.

Chapter Nine reviewed the healthy development of a child in

a complete home; but since most of this development is altered because of the absence of your child's father, it is also necessary for you to keep in mind the unhealthy developments that can occur. In many respects, each of these is more easily lapsed into if you are not alert in your incomplete home; consequently, these are the developments you must be careful to avoid.

Nothing that can occur in a fatherless home is unique, because a poor marriage—witnessed and reacted to by a child of a complete home—gives rise to the same distortions that can develop in a fatherless home. In many ways, you retain greater control over your interaction with your child during the Oedipal time than does a mother in a complete but unhappy family; so your child's reactions—even uncorrrected by you—often tend to be less confused and complicated than those of a child who is buffeted between two unhappy adults. Even if you are reacting highly neurotically and foolishly, your child is still subjected to a form of consistency that has some positive virtues. Of course, this saving fact does not excuse you from the necessity of curbing all such neurotic interaction, but it does provide some consolation and encouragement. In short, keep in mind that though your child's development is, of necessity, different, it need not be lastingly distorted; and though it is easy for you to fail to correct his Oedipal misunderstandings, you still provide a consistent pattern that offsets some of your failures.

Remember, the Oedipal period is the time when a child's capacities for fantasy and dreaming take a great spurt; gradually, as he goes through various fantasy developments, his thinking process becomes what adults call "genuinely realistic." He evolves from viewing himself as capable of becoming an adult almost instantly—as soon as he but adds a few final touches to the ways in which he is already behaving, ways that are highly similar to ways adults behave—to finally viewing himself as a child, but a child who will continue to grow and mature and eventually become an adult. He goes from being caught up in his erotic body sensations and sexualized concerns and fantasies, to setting sex aside as too much to handle, too much discomfort. He also goes from thinking that wishes are realities, to recognizing that he does not get what he wants but, rather, what he is able to work for and manage successfully. As a child views his parents interacting with each other, enjoying each other, enjoying him, reacting to him, not as adult to adult, but as parents to child, he slowly develops the idea that marriage is for these two parents and is not for him to break up. With the real, working model of good marriage as the screen against which he projects his Oedipal fantasies, the child recognizes the disparities, the grotesque incongruities and differences, between himself and his parents. There is no way out for him; he must grant that children are children, not adults. And, viewing his parents as separate people—male and female, intimate, contained, self-assured, responsive, responsible, and affectionate— slowly and gradually he develops the concept of what a man is like to a woman and what a woman is like to a man. He gives up his exaggerated ideas of what sexuality is and instead identifies with the realistic images presented by his parents. These identifications are not at all like earlier identifications; these are more specific, focused more on emotions and less on action patterns. Most importantly, these identifications encompass concepts about the object of the emotions—not just the man, but the man in relation to a specific kind of woman, a wife, is identified with, and the woman in her attitudes toward and her expectations of a certain kind of man, her husband, is likewise identified with.

When a good marriage and the relationship that binds it is not available for the child to observe and identify with, he cannot develop the same full understanding of his immaturity. Friends, relatives, and lovers all have different roles to play, all have different ways of relating to each other. Consequently, no other relationship but a marriage of healthy parents affords a child the opportunities and pressures he needs in order to correct his immature versions of reality.

In a complete home where the parents—separately or together —react to the child as to an adult, the child finds no correction to his distorted idea that he is an adult already. In a complete home where the parents—separately or together—make the child's discomfort over sexual tension preferable to discomforts that might otherwise be suffered if sex were put aside, the child finds no reality support for his need to set sexuality aside. In either case, the mistaken, yet unshaken, belief that he is an adult subjects the child to other rebuffs and failures that are exceedingly confusing. The boy, for example, still positive that he is actually a man, cannot understand why his mother only teases him about marrying him, why she continues to stall him off. The girl cannot understand why she fails to win her father for herself.

When the parents go so far as to become foolishly dependent, themselves, upon the flattery and seductive pose of the child, the child must sustain this pose, despite all the tension it produces, lest the parents reject him completely. For example, a vain mother who is intensely (and foolishly or neurotically) flattered when her child starts to flatter her, may react negatively to the absence of such flattery: "Why didn't you notice the new way I fixed my hair for you? If you're not going to be nice to mother, mother isn't going to let you have the surprise she brought home for you."

No child has the fortitude to withstand the pressure of a parental rejection that can be remedied by something so little horrible as being plagued by sexuality, putting on an act, and handing out a line—especially when no surcease from the sexual tension is afforded by the parents, when no love for his childishness is forthcoming, when he does not even know that his ideas are unrealistic. Consequently, the sexual pose is readopted; the child becomes enslaved to the Oedipal problem.

Were this only a temporary problem, it might not be exceedingly troublesome; but when the parents fail to be wise, the child's reactions continue and produce extensive distortions of all later personality growth and function. The latency period is interrupted by sexual fantasies, and it is kept from being an unemotional time in which learning of factual information in the school can be concentrated upon. Thus, behavior problems and learning problems are common for the school child who has not been able to put his sexuality into the background, seldom examined.

Adolescence, too, is distorted; its huge surge of sexuality is viewed by the still-Oedipal adolescent as the same old stuff, not at all seen in its newness and power. The controls that serve to contain Oedipal sexuality are resorted to, but they are not effective against the pubertal sexuality. Promiscuity or substitution through other forms of delinquency often result, because ineffective controls are resorted to. Or the adolescent, in the effort to back away from the overwhelming stimulus of his newly emerging biological maturation, pulls away from all reality, seeking solace in dreams or bizarre fantasies.

Finally, adulthood, too, is affected; the childish attitudes about sex remain and keep sexuality from being fully enjoyable as a means of expressing love and affection. The still-Oedipal person continues to think he is unique and wonderful merely because he feels sexual excitement; he expects this one aspect of adulthood to be sufficient to establish his claim to being mature.

### OEDIPAL PROBLEMS TYPICAL OF THE FATHERLESS HOME

Exactly how your child reacts to his Oedipal situation in his fatherless home is related to the time when he is first fatherless.

If his father has been absent throughout much of the pre-Oedipal time, and if you are reasonably certain you have given your child good care throughout the pre-Oedipal period, any disturbances that show up later in the latency period must be viewed as ones produced by Oedipal mistakes or mismanagement.

If he is first separated from his father during the Oedipal period, definite disturbances are likely to occur, and must be distinguished from possible pre-Oedipal problems.

Unless you take definite steps that are positively corrective, your Oedipal child automatically reacts to two forces associated to being without a father:

First, your child is not required to face and integrate the disillusionment that comes with recognizing that you cannot be competed for and won; so the battle, by default, is regarded by your child as won by him. Notwithstanding what you may do to encourage or discourage this belief once it is established, your child assumes you are really conquered—you just have not given in gracefully yet.

Second, your child has no real image or pattern of the man or of the relation of the husband to his wife to guide inner concepts and to help him face and integrate disillusionments and frustrations that emerge as you fail to give in completely. The critical absence of a man in a marriage results in your child's inability to focus a realistic identification. He cannot, therefore, compare his various attitudes to the image of such an identification. He cannot practice flexible attitudes with regard to who in a marriage is active and who is passive, he cannot comprehend fully the fixed relationship of mutual love and respect that pervades a marriage.

Remember that your child, either boy or girl, needs this male pattern. In its absence—and in the absence of definite corrective influences exerted by you—your boy can develop one of many different bad attitudes, each accompanied by confusion or anxiety, each causing trouble during the rest of childhood and during adulthood. Your girl reacts in different ways but with similar problems—unless you exert corrective forces.

As one such bad attitude, your son may just retain his inner belief that even without any proof in reality, he is still the most manly man ever created. Operating with this idea, he may remain chivalrous and courtly toward you, awaiting the great day when you will finally recognize his manliness. He may, however, give up hope that you will ever exercise the good judgment and fine appreciation that his manliness deserves; so he may become contemptuous of you for your timidity and hypocrisy. He may then develop a compensating ideal of a perfect woman who can see him in his glorious manliness, and so become aloof toward you, for you do not fit his ideal.

Each of these examples of common reactions has its effect upon adult attitudes toward women. The first causes him to remain a boy forever, a momma's boy, who has no use for other women because he is still waiting for you. The second causes your boy, contemptuous of you, to continue to flirt with other women, of any age, yet basically to be disappointed by them because they are not you—this despite his underlying resentment of you. The third leads your boy idealistically to evaluate all women against his perfect ideal and, finding that they fall short, to react intensely in his continual disappointment.

Other basic patterns not quite so benign can also be developed. The three reactions just described merely involve a continuation of relatively simple confusions that can later be corrected without intensive efforts. But your child can also react by relinquishing his belief that he is a superior male; then, not knowing what to do with his boyish manlike qualities, he feels as if he were cast loose without any firm idea of himself to hold on to. He may then resort to an intensified identification with you as he tries to find a self, and so end up passive and feminine in his behavior. Or he may react by creating or latching onto an ideal of the perfect man, which he continually measures himself against; as he necessarily fails to measure up against this ideal, he may become intensely ashamed of himself, feel decidedly inferior, and resort to isolating himself from others, refraining from competing with others, so that he is not discovered in his inferiority. If his ideal is based on shallow images like the ones provided by television and movies, he may assume the same shallow characteristics and become an unruly, rough, and tough boy and man; or he may just yearn within himself for the day to come when he can act this way.

All of these reactions have in common the pointless belief that he is unique because he has sexual desires. His conviction of his manliness springs from this notion. And once solidly rooted in childhood, it is difficult to erase, even by later experience that proves other people also have sexual desires.

Whatever his reaction may be, in short, it is a travesty on truth and reality.

If your child is a girl, she, too, suffers in her development because of the absence of a father, whatever your reactions may be, however innocuous, nonneurotic, or sensible. Because a girl needs to take more steps in her Oedipal development after the second step in which, like a boy, she is identified with her father, your girl is several additional steps behind in her development—compared to a boy.

In her basic difficulty, she, too, remains convinced of her essential manliness. She can continue through her life convinced that she is a better man than any man she meets. Or she can dream up an ideal image of what a perfect man is like. Because she has so few characteristics of the man in herself, actually, she tends to take this idealistic path. She may then seek to identify with her image and, when she fails, be unable to understand whether her failure is due to inadequacies in her image or to inadequacies in the extent to which she has lived up to it. In behavior, she thus grows to distrust her capacity to imagine, becomes very uncreative and factual, and emphasizes her manlike qualities. She can also try to regain some solidity in her confusion by once more identifying with you but be intensely infantile in her efforts to restore the situation that existed when she made her first identifications with you.

The different complicated patterns generally lead to similar behavior during the school years and later adulthood: either emphasized manlike striving, infantilism with almost complete burial of sexuality, or a placid, matter-of-fact, and practical kind of asexual, mechanical behavior.

The one result that fails to come about is the one that *cannot* come about: she does not become a girlish girl who has thrown aside as pointless any desires to be a man, who has thrown aside any desire to win a man immediately, and who retains her affection for her mother and retains her vision of herself as a girl who will become a woman some day.

## INEFFECTIVE APPROACHES TO SOLVING PROBLEMS

Although all these problems are directly related to the absence of a father during this time, you cannot attempt to solve them by providing a male substitute for a father or by remarrying and providing a new father. Each of these approaches produces many additional complications, yet neither produces any help for your child.

This is easy to see by analogizing the Oedipal problem to something as concrete as a situation where a woman wants to breast-feed her child but is not permitted to for medical reasons. Because her basic goal is to implement a warm, close relationship between herself and her child, she does not want her child to have a nursing relationship to another woman and thus become exceedingly confused and tugged between several loyalties; so she does not seek out a wet nurse who will provide breast feedings. What she does, instead, is to provide her child with a different form of feeding, a bottle, which still lets her, the mother, have a close tie to him, still cuddling him, still keeping him warm and close, still giving him the challenge of a good, though artificial, nipple.

This kind of situation can be equated to the fatherless Oedipal situation by regarding the possible wet nurse as the potential new father. Although it may seem that a father ought to be exactly what is needed, your remarriage at this time provides your child with a very different relationship to observe than the one that is characteristic of a marriage that has existed for five or six years. The usual family relationship in the ordinary Oedipal situation is not one including the newness of romance and just getting to know each other. It is grotesque, in fact, for the same romantic, heightened alertness to each other that characterizes a new marriage to be continued through more than a few years—it is as if the intimacy and living together still had not produced any knowledge of each other, as if the two married partners were still but attractive strangers to each other. Remember that it is not excitement and attention between man and woman that your child needs to observe, but rather the give and take, the acceptance, the ease, the lack of tension that come as marriage stabilizes.

In short, the only thing your child can learn from watching a new marriage is exactly the same distorted picture so correctly criticized in most Hollywood versions of marriage. For the good it might do, you can just as easily turn on the television set and let him watch as go through the actions of remarrying.

As for what he can gain in knowledge of his own role from a new marriage, similar criticisms must be lodged. He cannot obtain a solid identification with a competitor, and this is exactly what a new father is. Had the new father come during the pre-Oedipal years, the competition then would have been minimal; and by now your child would have adjusted to his new father, able to use him as a perfectly natural father during these Oedipal times. But because of the autism of the Oedipal times, which emphasizes competition, your child feels additional pain and shame about losing to this superior man you have just married. He cannot in a short time identify with his new father, compete against him, and then re-identify; he can do only one thing at a time, each takes months to develop, and the choice is decided by his autism in favor of competing.

You also cannot help your child by trying to encourage his close involvement with any of your gentleman friends—platonic or romantic.

A friendship between your child and a man who is not regarding you with sexually-tinged, loving feelings, is only a "palship"; it provides none of the crucially needed tie between you and this adult man. From it, your child can learn nothing but the same knowledge all pre-Oedipal identifications can provide. Because the relationship essentially is beyond your control except through rational appeals to the man and your child, you cannot easily keep it from lending itself to your child's autism. He may, out of his quest for a repository for his Oedipal fantasies, easily develop a crush on the man; and you have no basis for emotional persuasion that can easily manipulate such a tie away from its dangers. Nor can you keep the man from inhibiting the necessary Oedipal fantasies; if your child is finally able to develop an animosity toward the man—remember that this is a necessary feature of usual Oedipal developments—the adult is far more likely to suggest they stop seeing each other than to tolerate and work with the hostility. Your child, therefore, can learn nothing new and good, although he can learn some new and unhelpful attitudes, from his tie to a man with whom you have but a platonic relationship.

And for every danger involved in a palship of this sort at this time, there are several involved in a friendship between your child and a man who *is* lovingly, sexually involved with you. (By this is not meant an affair; only the attitudes of love and sexual desire with overtones of realism and responsibility that characterize marriage and courtship are being focused upon as the vital elements differentiating this kind of tie from the platonic type of tie.) Your child can develop a harmful crush, he can be subjected to harmful rejections from the man, and in addition, he can feel all the problems a child feels with a new father at this time: the inferiority in the face of obvious competition for you and the confusion of the lover role with the husband role. Combined for him are the difficulties of a new marriage with the difficulties of a palship, as well as the hazards and pains of the risk or actuality of losing the relationship.

The major danger of any courtship is that the man may not marry the woman. Whatever she and he invest in forming the tie may be lost if a split occurs. Adults have a safeguard in that they seldom invest greatly in an emotional relationship unless they have evaluated its dangers realistically; consequently, adults do not wear their hearts on their sleeves and do not get hurt, often.

But a child cannot evaluate realistically; he does not have sufficient know-how or information; also, he does not want to have.

Instead, he needs to throw himself into a tie, wholly and completely; he has no use for caution. So he may over-invest, he may put more into a tie than he is likely to be able, without great pain, to lose. And if your courtship stops, your child is thus in a position of losing a great deal. He faces all the pain of ordinary mourning; he also faces the confusions and pains particular for the Oedipal time.

He may incorrectly conclude that he is the one who has beaten off the competitor. Or, he may incorrectly conclude that he has been rejected, that he is not good enough to be loved and accepted by this man you have liked.

And you, too, face added difficulties in precluding various possibilities: you must exert your will during the courtship to keep from trying to make your child be more pleasant and less troublesome than he naturally is, and you must exert your self-control after the break-up to keep from blaming your child for any contribution he has made to tensions during the courtship. To the extent that you fail to exert these controls, your child receives support in his erroneous conclusions that he is able to break up a potential marriage.

In short, neither remarriage, platonic ties with men, nor romantic ties with men afford the relationships your child needs to solve his Oedipal problems.

It follows, therefore, that *you cannot help your child solve his Oedipal problems.*

*All you can do is to keep him from settling on incorrect conclusions and keep him from additional problems because of the unsolved Oedipal problems; all you can do is help to strengthen him so that he can live with these unsolved problems until he is old enough to solve them himself in the course of real experience.*

### How to Help Your Child During His Fatherless Oedipal Development

The two potent forces in a complete home that solve the Oedipal problems are the parental relationship, which forces a child to develop a sense of realism about his own childish sexuality, and the presence of a father-husband from whom can be learned the adult male sexual role. Your child does not have the second element to gain help from—he must learn this by himself in later life.

But you, by yourself, *can* help your child develop his sense of realism about his own childish sexuality.

Everything you do is perforce artificial, not natural; but keep in mind that the artificial substitutes are effective and valuable. Like synthetic milk substitutes for infants who cannot nurse or drink milk, your artificial substitutes for the naturally occurring pressures still keep your child from pain and distortion.

The rule to follow is simple, though you must be extremely alert to remember to follow it, for you, too, have few pressures in ordinary events that naturally lead you to remember to follow this rule:

*Interpret reality to him consistently; stimulate his expression of his inner conflicts and Oedipal autism.*

Keep him from harboring incorrect, distorted, neurotic versions of reality; consistently remind him of the correct and realistic life around him.

Remember that you cannot just do nothing; whatever you do, your child is viewing life symbolically; in line with his current autism, he is distorting the meaning of your actions relating to him. So, even if you believe you are not responding to his Oedipal overtures, even if you believe you are not supporting his Oedipal distortions, you must still take deliberate action to interpret and express reality—else he remains unopposed in his childish ideas that he has truly won you for his own already, and that he is truly all that a man is.

You cannot make up for the lack of a father's loving him while loving you; but you can at least, by consistently exerting pressure on your child to pay attention to reality and to recognize his own unrealities, enable your child to come through this time having learned correct and useful ideas about himself.

Get the Oedipal fantasies out into the open where you can expose them to realistic thought. Throughout this time, deliberately and consistently stimulate and encourage your child to express himself. Exert all the pressure of your adult intelligence and self-control to back up interpretations of your child's fantastic ideas. You know from preceding discussions and from the books previously referred to what your child is feeling and thinking. You know as much as any well-trained psychologist can know observing your child; indeed, you know more. Use this knowledge to help your child.

As undramatic as this method may seem, it is the only method that does not corrupt the Oedipal period with additional problems. Expression and interpretation of his Oedipal fantasies permits your child to be open to the new experiences in later life that will finally finish up his Oedipal development, experiences that will finally enable him to form an image within himself of his sexual identity and role. At least his development is not damaged, as might be the case if he were stopped from all show of Oedipal sexuality, or if he were encouraged by your mistaken response to believe that his false ideas are correct.

Your child's inner attitudes during his later school years and his adolescence are necessarily not the normal, usual ones. His adulthood is a state that is attained with more trial and error, more strain and work, than it is for a child who has had the opportunity to work through all his Oedipal problems before he enters grade school. But, at least, as a result of your help, your child is able to go through his school years unplagued with Oedipal sexuality. And he can approach adolescence and adulthood with optimism and faith, ready to learn what he was unable to learn when younger.

Basically, your role is to encourage your child to be frank about his own sexuality and about the extent to which he has involved you in his sexual fantasies, so that you can correct his childish ideas that he is an adult. In order for you to succeed in your corrective strategy, you must steer clear of any open rejection of your child, while continuing to refer his sexuality back to himself.

Do not try to be fancy and involved; remember, your role is not to be a psychotherapist. You are just a mother forcing issues that a mother in a complete home more easily is pressured into clarifying.

Talk freely about how children grow up with time; remind your child of the fun children can have as children, running, hopping, playing, and exploring an ever-new, ever-growing world.

Emphasize the joy of childhood, without, of course, leading your child to believe that you resent being an adult. When he tries to do something grown-up, insist that he hear you out in your statement that this is what he is doing: "I know you want to walk on the street side the same way a grown man does when he walks with a woman, but I feel more comfortable having you walk on the inside. After all, even though you aren't a baby any longer, my job is still to be your mother and make sure you don't get hurt by things flying up from the street."

The more you reassure him you accept him, but only as a young child, not as a miniature adult, the less anxiety he must feel that he is required to act like a miniature adult.

Deal with his frankly sexual overtures in the same matter-of-fact way. He may complain that his phallus hurts, and ask you to inspect. If your child seems feverish, if his eating stops suddenly, if you see signs of blood, call your physician to check for physical illness. But if none of these gross signs of illness seem present, you must be careful to check for other signs of illness in a way that will not lead you to be seduced by your child into handling his phallus. You must remember that his complaints may be overtures to get you to pay attention to his phallus.

In checking for signs of inflammation and discharge, therefore, avoid touching him. Ask your son to hold his penis—or your daughter to hold apart the lips of the vulva. If you see no signs of inflammation, say so. Your child may demonstrate crankiness and irritability because you will not touch him; this is often an indication that the complaint was an effort to gain attention. Without condemnation or annoyance, comment openly that you think he wants you to touch him, and that you can easily understand how much he would like you to; but remind him that a child his age actually can obtain the same pleasure from touching himself that he can get from being touched by his mother.

Many other opportunities to call his attention to masturbation arise when he is bathing or toileting; seize on these opportunities to comment on the acceptability of masturbation only under the particular circumstances of his being alone in safe privacy and with his hands clean. If, for example, he masturbates as you are washing him, ask him to stop until he can be alone: "Please stop masturbating until after I've finished washing you, and you can be alone, because people are not supposed to masturbate when others are around."

If he accuses you of trying to make him stop masturbating (the Oedipal autism may lead him to try to project his inner struggles on to you), clear up his confusion immediately. "I have no objection to your masturbating, because I know that all children like to, because it feels good. When you're grown-up, you'll be able to get married and enjoy another kind of good feeling, very much like masturbating, but different because you'll be enjoying it with your wife. But for right now, so long as you're not grown-up, I want you to remember that you are supposed to masturbate only when you're alone."

If his anxieties about masturbating lead him to worry that he has hurt himself (again, the Oedipal autism can cause this reaction, even though you have been careful to avoid condemning masturbation, and even though you have never terrified him with false cautions that masturbation will harm him), deal directly with his complaints that he is worried or sore; reassure him: "If you think your penis—or 'gina—will feel better if you leave it alone for a day or two, how about not masturbating for a while? When you get your clothes on, come on and let's read a story together. After all, I want to have the fun of reading with my child and being a mommy for you."

The more you enable him to accept his sexuality, the less need he has to re-assure himself of it by masturbating. Thus the less trouble he promotes within himself by the fantasies that accompany his masturbating. He can gradually comprehend the uselessness to him, at the time, of his masturbating; so he can put it away.

If he tries to sleep with you, remind him that he is a big child with his own bed that he knows he likes, and that you are a grown woman with your own bed that you like to have privacy in. Remind him that when he grows up, he will marry and probably sleep with his wife together in one bed; remind him that married people sleep together and make love and babies together. But point out that he is not able to do this now because he has not yet grown up.

Often a child proposes marriage to get around such obstacles. If this happens, do not ridicule, do not shame, but be sure to straighten out the misunderstanding: "Darling, it's very nice of you to want to marry me, but I'm a grown woman, and grown women only marry grown men, not young children. When you grow up, you'll love a grown-up woman and marry her and sleep with her and make love and babies with her. But by that time, you'll think I'm too old for you, just as now you are too young for any grown woman."

Be ready, not only during this time, but also throughout the forthcoming school years and during early adolescence, to offer your child plenty of solid reassurance about himself. Comment proudly to him about how much he knows and is able to do as a young child. Whenever possible, tell him how happy you are to think that he is going to grow up to be a much wiser adult than you.

The more openly you accept his desire to become an adult, but point out how much you also accept his state of being yet a child, the more he is reconciled to his reality, and the more optimism he develops about his future.

Be sure to exploit the many helps provided by the vicarious outlets available through books, movies, and television. Not all the images these media provide are derogative and distorted, so provide your child with the opportunity to identify with the many wholesome and fairly comprehensive characters in good literature and drama. (Probably, many works of art have continued to live and be enjoyed by many generations just because their characters do permit a well-rounded extension of the self through identification. Like the universal appeal of certain games that provide well-rounded challenges to different aspects of the body, the universal appeal of many good books rests on the well-rounded challenge to sympathies and identifications they provide.) Though no literary character, however extensively and realistically portrayed, can serve as a complete vehicle for your child's identification, he is better off with some of these images, however marginal and flimsy, than he is if left empty of any idea of how adults regard each other.

Keep in mind that interpretation tends to destroy, so concentrate your interpretative remarks on the behavior you wish eliminated because it merely represents Oedipal, autistic fantasies. Encourage open expression of the fantasies based on progress toward realism; accept this behavior and speak out your approval of it but do not necessarily interpret its roots. For example, you may note that your child has started to act toward you the way some favorite television character behaves toward his wife; this is not the kind of tie, remember, that ought to be promoted. So mention your awareness and interpret your child's motives: "You know, I've just realized you're the spitting image of Mr. Smith in that funny program about that silly family on television. But I hope you don't think I'd like to be as stupid as his wife is. I'm much happier the way I am; and I certainly think you're a much nicer boy than their son is, he's always poking his nose into things that are none of his business. I wouldn't want either a husband or a son like them; and I'm sure when you grow up, you'll be much nicer than Mr. Smith."

Be careful to avoid comments that increase self-consciousness about identifications that indicate progress toward reality. For example, if you notice your child becoming nicer to his pet after you have read one of the classic children's animal books to him, you can store away this fact for your own comfort, but do not call his attention to it. Let him keep his strengths below the level of his consciousness, so they provide impetus to his spontaneity and self-confidence.

If you are a divorced mother and your child sees his father relatively frequently during the Oedipal period, be sure to avoid any interactions with your former husband that implement and support your child's Oedipal misconceptions. Analyze and interpret all your child's efforts to turn on one of you and make accusations about not being loved and about having been rejected. If, for example, your child says his father does not want to see him, because his father does not really love him—or if your child says he only wants to stay with you and not visit his father—get right to the heart of the matter: "I'm very happy you want me all to yourself, but that really has nothing to do with how you get along with your father. I don't think it's so much a question of whether or not your father likes you; I think all that it is is that you don't like him, the same way you don't like me half the time. But I'm sure your father loves you as much as he always has, maybe even more, because you're growing up so much lately. I've got other things to do, so I'll leave you alone with your father, now. I'm sure you'll figure out how to get along with each other."

It helps if you and your former husband have an occasional word of praise for each other. But do not let yourself be deluded into hoping that you can replicate the ordinary household and so help your child solve the Oedipal problems. However much tact and forbearance you and your former husband practice, you still do not present the necessary picture of two adults cleaved unto each other; without the marriage to observe, your child still cannot develop his adult masculine sexual identity.

Your child's grandparents often serve as the source or focus of extra problems at this time. Your child may return from a visit with his father's parents to report to you that they—who may be less reticent about their feelings than your former husband is—have told him his daddy would be a happy man, still married to you, if you had only been less foolish, more patient, and more loving. Be sure to interpret your child's desire to promote friction, competition, and generally to manipulate all you adults. "I think you're just trying to stir up trouble, and I think your grandmommy is just trying to avoid thinking that your daddy has ever been naughty. That's how mothers are with their children. But even though I don't like to think that you want to cause an argument, I still think that's what you're doing. After all, you know as well as I do that your father is a grown-up man. Do you honestly think an adult would marry someone who was foolish and impatient and unloving? Now why don't you just stop trying to figure out about my divorce and tell me what was nice about your visit with your grandmommy."

In a similar way, if you are a widow, deal with second-hand accusations passed by your child from his grandparents that his father would still be alive if he had not worked so hard to support you or if you had taken better care of him.

Death brings intense feelings of guilt at this Oedipal time; your child can easily conclude that the reason his father died was that he wished his father would go away. The consequent guilt can cause extreme reactions, ranging from a strangely intense kind of goodness in your child to equally intense delinquent behavior like running away from home or being destructive. Reassure your child that he had nothing to do with the death; point out that most boys his age often wish their fathers would die and leave them alone with their mothers. If his behavior indicates that he is still reacting severely to the death after the passage of a few months, consult professional psychological help for specific advice that takes account of your unique circumstances.

Your child is now likely to ask why he had no father during the earlier years—if this was the case. Include in your response that the absence is not due to your child's behavior or wishes. Remember that his Oedipal autism colors even his view of his own reactions in the past; competitive now, he assumes that he was always competitive. So he can feel as much anxiety, apprehension, and shame about nonexistent past attitudes as he might if everything were happening in the here and now. Remind him of this, and otherwise stick to the simple, factual answers advised earlier.

If you are an illegitimate mother, be prepared for some special troubles with neighborhood children who are your child's age at this time. Remember that other children are also going through this time of heightened interest in marriage, babies, and sex. Parents of other Oedipal children may not be so careful as you are in their reactions to their children's Oedipal acting out. They may prohibit masturbation, for example, by telling their children, "You'd better stop that, or soon you won't be able to control yourself, and then you'll have to have a baby without being married, like the people down the street." They may answer questions about marriage and babies by saying, "The only children who don't have daddies are kids whose mothers we don't want to associate with."

Your child may come to you and say the other children called him a bastard and said they would not play with him. In your reaction, pay attention to both important aspects: the social pain of being rejected and the confusion about his parentage and origins.

Remind him that these children and he have had lots of other arguments in the past. Reassure him that you and he both can count on everybody starting to play together again in the near future, particularly when they see that they cannot tease or hurt him with this particular name. Tell him to play with other children or by himself until he and his friends can play together nicely.

As for the bastardy, explain to him that a bastard is not a bad child or a child who has done something wrong; tell him it is just an old French name for a child whose mother and father were never married. Point out that the way people get married is very different in different parts of the world: "In America, parents get married first because it is believed to be the best way to be sure that they really love each other and want to live together to bring up their children. But in other parts of the world, where adults have different ideas about marriage, almost every child is a bastard, for almost no parents are married."

Tell your child that the whole idea of being a bastard is much too complicated for any children to understand, so there is little point in his arguing with his friends about it. Tell him you and he will have more time to discuss it with greater understanding when he grows up.

In short, do not get involved in his fight with his friends—or in a fight with the parents who have provided the ammunition your child's friends are using—just reassure your child that he is not bad, and that he must claim his friends as always, by refusing to interact with them except as an equal.

If your child has suffered some injury to the phallus, has been molested, or becomes accident-prone in other ways at this time, reassure him that his phallus is still good, and that he is not being punished just because he gets pleasure from handling it. If behavior-changes lasting for more than a few days follow a sexual attack, be sure to seek professional advice. But be equally sure that in a matter-of-fact way you point out to your child his own contributions to provoking or permitting the sexual attack. Remind him that he was pointlessly curious about how the penis or clitoris and vagina look and feel, for he already knew all there was for a child his age to know about them. Point out that until he was hurt by the other person, he was probably feeling very excited and happy, even though you had told him that a person who wants to have sexual contacts with a child is really very angry about sex and very likely to get hurtful and frightening. Remind him that in the future, until he is completely grown-up, you expect him to follow your instructions to have nothing to do with strangers or friends who want to touch his genitals or have him touch theirs. And he is also to report to you or a teacher or a policeman immediately whenever anyone offers to take him for a ride or a walk when you have not told him he may go with that person. Keep in mind, however, that sexual molestation is not the "worst thing that can happen," and that most of its unfortunate effects are eliminated if a child is helped to accept his own share in and his own feelings about the seduction.

If you notice your child spending a great deal of time with another adult in circumstances that suggest they are not operating innocently together, put a halt to the visits. Remember that seduction is not always openly sexual. Any chronic interaction that is titillating promotes troubles. An elder male boarder, for example, can confuse your daughter and hurt her development as well through spending hours weaving overstimulating stories for her as by open sexuality. Apply the same yardstick you use for yourself: an adult who is truly adult does not care to spend hours with a child, alone, unless they are spending their aggressive drives together in creating some genuine product, not just talking and dreaming and walking together. Your child must not be treated by anyone as if he or she were an adult.

Whatever the special problems may be that crop up, deal with them all by the same efforts directed toward realism. However challenging your task at this time may seem, remind yourself that your child is probably better off with a good mother, alone, than watching a poor marriage of an unhappy set of parents, thereby getting harmful, wrong ideas of what marriage is like and what adult men and women are like and what he, as a child, is like.

## Grade School Years: The Latency Period

With the capacity developed during the Oedipal period to view abstractions, to accept knowledge that he cannot himself test out and prove, your child typically approaches the information set before him during these grade school years with active curiosity, but in a non-emotional way.

However, your child is not so likely as are other children from complete homes to have matter-of-fact friendships; he still needs to form a sexual identification, so he tends to over-identify during these years. His identifications, of course, are not heavily tinged with sexuality (if they seem to be, by all means seek out psychotherapeutic help immediately); but they are more emotionally intense than ordinary friendships of other children might be. Your child is more likely to copy and imitate closely his friends' likes and dislikes; he is more likely to be seriously depressed when he has an argument with or other separation from his friends.

Your primary task throughout these years is to keep your child's attitudes open with regard to sexuality until he can be additionally realistic and concrete in adolescence and during young adulthood. So, though parents are ordinarily not advised to tamper with friendships, in your case it may be necessary if you see your child chumming around with a child whose Oedipal development obviously has not been good, who is rebellious, seductive, or passive, for example. Weed out the identifications you think are valuable from the ones you think are likely to inhibit the later development of the final stages of Oedipal growth; do this by using the tool of interpretation. Whenever possible, strive to avoid attacking the friendship, just attack the features of the friendship that you believe are not helpful for your child. For example, let your child continue his friendship with a rather tough and independent child, but comment: "From the way your friend Charlie acts, you'd think he still figures he's the only important person on earth. I wish he were more like you and were happier just being a child, because I certainly don't want you to start getting silly ideas like his."

Friendships, like a creative occupation and a love relationship, are major sources of pleasure in adult life; but your child, like an adult, is better off relatively lonely than involved with friends who can offset his constructive approach to life. Your child, less certain of his own identity, has fewer automatic, inner guideposts and strengths; he needs support from you as he relies on his capacity to think objectively and clearly; as always, reason and intellect are weaker forces than emotion.

Though the child from a complete family is able to wall off his emotions during the latency period if he has had good experiences in the Oedipal times, your child is able only to put them behind a heavy curtain. If you see signs that the curtain is parting overly often, letting sexualized emotions interrupt school concerns and friendship activity, seek psychological consultation.

The latency period is an excellent time to take stock and seek help. Keep in mind that it is a long stretch of years during which your child must fortify himself with intellectualized skills he will need in adulthood; he must not, therefore, be allowed to stumble through these years, making less than full use of them because of problems from earlier childhood. The pre-Oedipal difficulties which you can note all require attention and cure. And Oedipal difficulties must be helped. (Consult previous chapters and the books previously recommended for more information on how to recognize signs of serious disturbance.)

*Do not expect psychotherapy at this time to "cure" or solve the Oedipal problem; it can only remove the impediments for future solution by your child.* A therapist is no more able to provide to your child the example of a happily-married-to-you man than is any other man, save a husband. But you can confidently expect that treatment *will* enable your child to have an open attitude regarding his sexual identification, an attitude that will permit him in adolescence to use realistic choice and trial-and-error and practice to develop his ideas of who and what he is.

## Puberty

Sexual excitement is no new sensation to your adolescent; he felt intense sexual excitement at the Oedipal times when he was about six years old. Affectionate regard for another person is no new emotional attitude, either; he felt altruistic love both before and after the Oedipal period.

But never before puberty ensues has he felt the flicker of sexual desire for a person whom he sees objectively and whom he loves. Always before, desire was self-centered—with images of other people only brought in to explain his feelings to himself— or affection devoid of sexual attraction was felt for people.

Thus the new task of adolescence, the major problem he grapples with, is integrating his sexual excitement and his emotions. He must contain both so that he does not lose his emerging independence, but test them and practice them so that he is sure of having control over them. All this is going on in the context of a new body, new social roles, and new privileges and responsibilities.

In general, the task of restraining and practicing control of new emotions is not new, of course; your child spends his childhood doing exactly this. His initial approach to every new drive in the past has been to start to experience its need, then feel anxious because it is new, then draw away from it for a while to muster his control forces; later on, once the impulse is less new and the controls have been readied, he has been able to permit some additional release of the impulse but not feel overwhelmed, awkward, anxious, or worried about being hurt by the drive.

In adolescence, his response to his genital sexuality is much the same. So the initial pubertal period is spent by restraining, constraining, and avoiding open elicitation of his sexuality. Both a boy and a girl react to puberty by emphasizing all the non-sexual, latency-period relationships. Although their bodies are now capable of adult sexual activities—orgasm and procreation—their emotional and social reactions are conservative, withdrawal responses. Only a renewed experimentation with masturbation indicates the awakened sexuality of puberty. With no shame about his own bodily impulses, so long as they do not involve other people, your child can relieve occasional sexual tensions quite completely through masturbation; he does not face the Oedipal problem of having fantasies that make him anxious—he takes a realistic attitude of curiosity toward masturbation.

After the early pubertal period, your child starts to come to grips with the question of his social role. The increased impetus of his now not so frightening sexuality directs his social activities into boy-girl relationships. And he is finally face-to-face with the problem he could not solve in the Oedipal period: he is faced with the problem of playing a sex-differentiated role. Remember that your child has still no well-founded, secure, firm picture of himself playing an adult "sexual" role. (Do not concern yourself with concrete aspects of this role as related to activities in bed;

by "sexual role" is meant only the over-all social posture that an individual of a given sex is expected to play in this society.) Your child must be additionally alert to the ways of man or woman; he has to substitute an intellectual observance, appreciation, and understanding for the less conscious kind of identification and understanding that takes place in the child of a complete home at the Oedipal time.

Your child must also tolerate an extra amount of tension while testing out a particular aspect of his role. He did not have the chance to try out many aspects with you (assuming that his father was absent during the Oedipal time) and he must still go through the Oedipal stages previously discussed, the he-man stage, the esthete stage, and so forth, outside the relative safety of his home. His experimentation must take place in his own peer group, in the social context of a group of children who are likely to be extremely competitive and intolerant. If he is to have the courage to seek out his own individuality, he must not be faced with side issues that take attention and energy away from his main task. He needs additional guidance and support and limits from you; he needs reassurance that he is not being expected to conform to the general social image before he has tested himself out in individualistic ways; and he also needs protection from some of the hazards that might put a crimp in his style before he has a chance to test it.

One side issue that *must* be avoided is open temptation to act out sexually. Although a healthy young adolescent shies away from sexual intercourse—for the reasons described above: it is overwhelmingly anxiety-provoking—not all adolescents are healthy. You must help your child reject friendship ties with children you can observe as being sexually provocative. Just as you worked to keep his friendships helpful during the latency times, you need to work to support his healthy tendencies during early adolescence. Interpret the reactions of friends that do not represent healthy role behavior. Of course, avoid being heavy-handed, or else you will provoke rebellion and competitive resistance in your child. But by tactful, casual conversation, comment on how friends behave; when natural, discuss possible motives your child may have for being attracted to a particular friend you worry about.

Your daughter, for example, may be trying to be sweet and ladylike with a tough character of a boy who derides her for such behavior; she is then unable to decide securely and clearly that the roughneck is out of line; she may decide instead, in her confusion, that femininity is outmoded. She may thus get herself into a very confusing position regarding her own role as a young lady. You can help by asking, "Why are you putting on your new dress to go to the party with Aleck? Isn't he the one who says he can't stand a girl who gets dressed up and who wants to be treated differently from a boy?"

This is not a condemning statement, so your daughter is not tempted to defend her friend's attitude; rather, she is likely just to deny that this really is his attitude: "Oh Mother, you know he's just saying that. He doesn't really mean it, and anyhow, I like my dress and I don't want to wear slacks."

You can easily call her attention to her motives, forcing her to recognize that she is confusing several different reasons for going with this friend, and forcing her to sort them out: "I suppose there must be some special fun in trying to make a boy admit he's posing, but if all the boys aren't that resentful about girls' being different from boys, why don't you date a boy who honestly admits he likes girls instead of saying he wants a buddy?"

It may not be pleasant—but it is necessary—for your daughter to admit it to herself if her major reason for going with Aleck is not her genuine pleasure while with him, but is instead her desire to get him to admit that he really does like her when she's girlish. It may not be pleasant—but it is necessary—for her to admit it to herself if she is going with Aleck because she senses he may provoke her to play another role, one she believes she owes herself the chance to try out, the unfeminine pal role. Being brought to face her real motives before they pull her into trouble and confusion is necessary. Her inner personality is strong enough to stand whatever pain is felt as she deals honestly with herself; remember that she has far greater inner resources than a child of six, with whom, rightly, such exploration and confrontation is both unnecessary and harmful. So call to her attention those reactions that your experience and wisdom tell you are likely to be productive of confusion or added difficulty.

Do not, of course, make her self-conscious about behavior

that is based on progress-making efforts or successes in assuming new dimensions. Only a spiteful and jealous mother comments, "Oh, I see you're getting all dressed up for the Smith boy. You must be feeling pretty proud of yourself. I suppose you think he's quite a catch."

And do not seek to spare your child all suffering and trouble. If some time she inappropriately decides to be sophisticated when she ought to be folksy, let her suffer the minor social difficulties she may experience. Remember that as your child nears adulthood, she must be helped to take responsibility for minor errors in judgment. Only interfere if she seems to be crossing the line that divides sophistication from being predatory or lascivious, or that divides being sweet and folksy from being helpless and falsely dependent. And avoid regarding early adolescent dating with the same attitudes appropriate to steady dating in late adolescence or young adulthood. Early adolescent dating is not selection of a marriage partner. Do not worry about your daughter's dating a boy whose parents are not in a class similar to yours (money, education, or descent are usually the distinguishing features of different social groups) unless you note that the boy-girl relationship is not one of mutual regard.

Because any boy's appreciation of his adult sexual role is less nebulous than a girl's, guiding and disciplining a boy at early adolescence can be less constant. If your son has no erroneous beliefs about himself and about sex, you can be less attentive to his early adolescent role explorations. Because boys spend a longer time in the palship stage of early adolescence, too, the onset of puberty in your son does not call for such prompt attention as is required for a girl. She matures earlier and more quickly, so her troubles descend more closely together.

You need to take the initiative in explaining to your child the tangible proofs of sexual excitement. Although your child is accustomed to masturbation, he is not sure of the new presentation of the ejaculation, and he needs reassurance that this is a normal accompaniment of the ripening of his sex glands. Point out to your son that when his night dreams are sexually exciting, without his waking he may have an orgasm, a nocturnal emission, and that during the daytime an erection accompanies erotic day dreams. Your daughter, too, needs this explanation, so that she is not confused or frightened when a boy she is dancing with, for example, develops an erection. She also needs to have explained the flow of thick liquid secreted by the glands at the vaginal opening when she thinks erotic thoughts. Information about hygiene during the menstrual period needs to be accompanied by information about the general body happenings during the menstrual cycle, from ovulation through menstruation to ovulation again.

This information is appropriate, not only for a child of a single mother, but for all children, of course; but you must be explicit and deliberate in discussing it, for you may otherwise be led into delaying such information because you are influenced by your child's general slowness in social development. Whatever rate of social maturation your child shows, he or she still needs to have the facts that are pertinent to puberty explained at puberty. Although having no father affects emotional development, it does not alter the reality of biological development.

You need not worry about the possibility of being provocative while discussing these facts of life; your child is much less likely to show embarrassment than impatience that you doubt his store of information.

## Late Adolescence

By the time your child is fifteen, or so, many changes take place in his attitude regarding sexuality and love. The two are more closely connected by your child. At puberty, sex was seen as proof of having become a man or a woman; any acting out of sexuality that a disturbed pubertal child engages in is usually an effort to prove having become an "adult"; it is the same as Oedipal demonstrations (though admittedly more dangerous because of the possibilities of disease or pregnancy).

But by the middle teens, sex is viewed as proof of the maturity of emotions. Even though your fifteen-year-old is still, actually, incapable of making a wise love-choice, there is a great deal of adolescent pressure leading him to believe that he can prove by feeling sexually demonstrative how wise he is in the choice of someone to love. Dimly conscious that a specific choice of partner for dating steadily is not exactly perfect, yet unwilling because of the impatience dictated by mid-teen autism to back down and admit that dating experience still has not led to his being able to make—or claim—the perfect choice, your teen-ager can often drum up a tremendous amount of false positive emotion. He sells himself on his choice, then makes it doubly imperative by focusing his sexuality on the choice. Without conscious volition, he ends up choosing this person as his steady date. ("Dating steadily" means taking one person to important affairs but still dating other people occasionally. "Steady dating" means being exclusively tied to one person for all dates.)

Whatever else can be said about the practice of steady dating—that it demonstrates a negative reaction to the insecurity of modern times, or that it demonstrates a creative approach to the problem of competition—it has been shown to accompany a testing of sexual responsiveness. Surveys show that only one steady couple out of ten leaves such sexual experimentation on the level of kissing and hand holding. Three neck and pet; and the other six couples either engage in sexual intercourse or believe that they ought to be free to do so. (These studies are limited to couples who go steady. Teen-agers who date different people have been shown to have relatively greater self-confidence and inner restraint, and are less likely to engage in sexual intercourse—or advocate it—at this time of life.)

Because there is a reduced pressure within your child to avoid sexual acting out, compared to the anxieties and pressures he felt when sex first arrived at puberty (or compared to the thorough assurance and self-knowledge combined with realistic idealism that prevails in young adulthood), the middle teens are years when it is easy for a child to promote trouble for himself by failing to control sexual acting out.

He does not, certainly, regard sex as cheap. He thinks it ought to be an expression of love. But he cannot bring himself to grant that he spends his dating time with one particular person, not out of love, but because of other forces. In the effort to prove to himself that he is not yielding to community customs, that he is not just taking the line of least resistance, he can often argue himself in over his head, feeling forced to engage in sexual inter-course, although it is still not comfortably enjoyable, although it is still overwhelming and anxiety-provoking.

Although it might be pleasant if the dating steady custom were discarded, this is not reality. So, in helping your child, you cannot prohibit going steady; you must resort to relying on other outside helps.

No effective force that you can bring to bear on your son, directly, is helpful; every direct pressure you can bring to bear on him makes more resistance and more difficulty. As the mother of a son, you provide most help to him by encouraging him to date girls who seem objective about sex. You, in short, need to rely on his girl friends to provide most of the restraint that keeps the couple from the unfortunate experience of intercourse.

As the mother of a daughter, your role is more direct. Like any wise parent, require that she limit her necking to her own home when you are elsewhere in the house; she is thereby sup-ported in her restraint tendencies by the reality circumstances surrounding kissing and necking. The tangible environment re-minds her of the emotional support she has received from you in the past, it helps her regard herself as a sensible person who does not jeopardize her welfare for the sake of instant gratification. And she can resort to pointing out the surroundings in order to avoid heavy petting or intercourse yet still enjoy kissing and neck-ing. Without much artistry, she can extricate herself from too hot a clinch just be reminding her boy friend that you may appear at any moment. With the information about sex that she has, she can set limits on sexual intimacy with her boy friend, sensibly and reliably, for she knows what she is talking about. She is not in the vulnerable position of an uninformed girl who breathlessly mum-bles, "Nice people don't do things like that," "No good man will want to marry me if I do," or "I'm scared I'll catch something or get pregnant."

An impetuous boy friend can easily knock apart each of these arguments, but he cannot successfully tear down her insistence that she is not curious or interested. She is not tempted to experi-ment because she knows what there is to learn and experience— her own masturbatory experiences give her a good idea of the pleasure she can obtain from intercourse—and she also knows what she may have to pay to provide pleasure to her boy friend. The balance weighs in the direction of avoiding the risk of infection from heavy petting and intercourse and the risk of pregnancy from intercourse.

Once she reassures herself that a boy friend will still date her even if she has refused to "put out," she no longer is likely to be seduced by supplication or threat. She can tolerate even an angry reaction or rejection; she can pride herself in being acceptable even when she does not "prove her love."

And the boy who is healthy receives needed support from these actions of his girl. He becomes free to take her or leave her; he is provided with a rationalization for staying with her, if he wants, to prove that he loves her "even though" they avoid intercourse. Or, if he is not ready yet to take over this kind of role, he can travel on to another girl. As a healthy boy, he may make progress toward maturity by deciding to keep things from getting to a fever pitch with a new girl; he may support his healthy tendencies even by melodramatically spending the next few years nursing his broken heart and staying away from pain.

Surveys show that a higher percentage of teen-agers in father-erless homes go steady than teen-agers in complete families, and at an earlier age. So, though the dangers of acting out sexually are not different for your child from those for any child, the likelihood is greater that a provocative force, dating steady, is present and dangerous. Consequently, you must strive harder than the mother in a complete family to keep your child's sexual attitudes open and approachable by reason. To do so, you must avoid all suggestion of condemnation of sex, all suggestion of ridicule of your child's emotional convictions about the steady date, all suggestion of competition with your child for the coveted role of being considered mature. You must simply stick to insisting that your child learn and keep in mind the realities involved in open sexuality. The same concepts discussed in Chapter Six with regard to sexual acting out for the adult woman apply to your adolescent.

Do not hesitate to speak frankly and honestly about sex and emotion because of your desire to avoid shattering your child's idealism about love and marriage and sex. Remember that if six out of ten teen-agers who go steady know enough about sexual intercourse either to indulge in it or to believe that they ought to—if they can even answer questions about it and know what the question is about—their idealism about love exists in the midst of a great deal of confused "carnal" knowledge.

Do not hesitate to speak frankly and honestly about sex and emotion because of your sensitivity for your child's emotional reaction to the subject, itself. Keep your child's autism separate from your realism. Your teen-ager may talk about sex with his friends in order to titillate himself; he may talk about sex with his girl friend in order to "go on the make." But keep in mind that you have no such motives. Clearly announce to him that though you know he is angered or embarrassed by your concern, you insist on talking with him. Your job is harder than that of a mother in a complete home, especially with a son, for his father might otherwise talk with him about contraception, for example, without risking great emotional difficulties. But do not, because of this, seek to shift the responsibility to others; your child is as likely to be troubled by the family physician as by you—and in addition, he is likely to develop the well-founded notion that sex obviously is not as open and acceptable a topic as you have told him it is since you cannot even talk to him straightforwardly about it.

If your child is not separated from his father until this time, of course, many of these problems are reduced. Keep in mind, though, that you may react to being single in a way that is out of the ordinary for a woman who loses her husband at other times. Your natural tendency to think of remarriage, in the face of the fact that you are probably still in the child-bearing age but no longer young, may lead you to emphasize your efforts to conquer your despair by convincing yourself that you are still quite marriageable. You may unconsciously take on the attributes of your teen-ager, almost as if you wanted to be taken for his sister, not his mother. The troubles this promotes for you have already been discussed in Chapter Five; you must be alert, however, to the troubles this kind of behavior may create for your child.

Already facing the difficulty of losing his father, he has no resources to spare in defending his privacy from you. By this age, he is less self-centered and so less able to rebuff your intrusion, your needs; yet he cannot easily tolerate feeling that you are

crowding him, refusing to let him have his unique place in the
sun as a member of a generation absolutely different from yours.
However tender toward you he may feel, he is frantic that you
may cut down on his mobility and freedom and independence.

So be sure to provide him reassurance that you intend to lead
your own life, that you will not intrude into his except to protect or guide him.

It is highly unlikely that your child will react to the loss of
his father at this time with morbid reactions. If evidence of
deeper emotional disturbances does come out, ask your child to
consult a professionally trained worker for help with his problems. This is the time of life when your child is forced to make
many far-reaching decisions about college training or occupation,
and he needs support in making wise choices as well as help in
integrating the loss of his father.

If you are an illegitimate mother, and events have not opened
up the subject before, you must bring up some discussion of your
child's background; entrance into military service or college or
later application for a marriage license are sure to uncover a well-
guarded secret, otherwise, and it is easier for your child to understand you than to be confronted with an impersonalized
fact. Do not engage in a true-confession session, of course; just
be objective and willing to take responsibility for your past role.
Describe simply and without apology the web of circumstances
of your own making that you and his father became emmeshed in
and tore yourselves loose from, unable at the time to find another
solution because of your anxieties. Your child is likely to be
moved by his sense of your tragedy, and he can thereby avoid
feeling harmful self-pity or resentment toward you or his father
for your failures.

Your marital life or your sexual activities, of course, are subject to questioning by your child, for his autism makes him in-
trusive and curious. It is seldom helpful, however, to provide him
with any information about your marital sexual activities, as such;
answer only in general terms about your marriage, whatever may
have been the role of sexual difficulties in promoting a divorce
or separation. Say only that when other aspects of a marriage are
not pleasant and good, the sexual relationship usually reflects this
and can seldom offset it; then discuss whatever you feel comfort-

able about with regard to the general difficulties and faults of your former marriage.

If you are a mother still legally married though you have been separated from your husband for a long time, your child may be confused by the continuance of your marriage. He may have many questions about loyalty, many practical and ethical doubts. All you can be responsible for, of course, are your own reactions. So point out to him why, if you have, you have remained sexually loyal or in love.

If, however, you have not remained sexually loyal, or if you face no claims on your loyalty and you have had sexual affairs your child knows about, an explanation is also due him. If you only attempt to cover up, your alert and sensitive adolescent who can unearth sexuality miles away is disturbed in his trust of you and in his regard of himself. You can risk attempting to hide your sexual activities only under highly unusual circumstances: if you have searched for or accepted sexual adventures only when on vacation by yourself or on business trips, or if you have confined meetings to places away from private homes and popular hotels or motels in a large city. But your secret is likely to be known to others, and so likely to be learned by your teen-ager, if you have been having an affair at a motel where you may easily have been seen by others, or, of course, if you have been having an affair in your home when your child is away for the day or when he is in his room for the night. In order to avoid the distrust you may promote, be truthful, not rationalizing or evasive. He may otherwise decide that his own mother is not worth respecting if she cannot respect herself at least enough to be honest about what she is doing; and conclude then no other girl or woman is. Or he may discard you as an authority of any sort and, before he is truly capable of it, seek out total independence for himself.

If the affair is still continuing, tell your child you know you are probably doing something foolish, something you wish you could make less foolish, but that, though it is very likely to end without producing lasting pleasure or even more pleasure than pain, you need and want some adult closeness and intimacy, and you are willing to forget, temporarily, that you are being irresponsible and self-deluding. Explain past affairs in the same way.

Whether your child then thinks you are a fool or envies you, he cannot in any way dismiss your explanation as insincere or hypocritical or cowardly. He can draw from your example some reassurance that lessens his possible envy, as he realizes that he is not so insecure as you and so does not need to despair of ever having greater completeness, joy, and hope. Support his considerations by telling him that if you were younger and had more hope for another chance to find a person to love and marry, you probably would not choose this poor substitute. Remind him that he has all the chance in the world of being able to enjoy the fine feeling of being confident and hopeful, convinced he is in love and sure that he is loved in return, combined with and expressed through sex. Remind him that, by settling for anything less at his age, he alters possible future pleasures and also risks not achieving them.

If your marriage ended because of your adultery, it is likely that both you and your child need help in re-cementing the bridge between you. He is likely to forgive you only if your former husband were an exceedingly difficult person to live with; and even so, he is likely to be confused because you did not seek an honest divorce. Your child needs to be able to honor you, not just blindly defend you; and although you may not choose to apply the term to yourself, your activities can be accurately described as cheating on your husband. Your child cannot easily honor cheating, for his values do not permit him to. In order to clear up the multitude of confusions, therefore, this particular situation cannot be left to time alone to heal.

These many different, special situations can all be used constructively by your child for help in answering the one most important question he asks himself through most of middle and late adolescence: Why shouldn't I express my love for my steady through sexual intercourse? He is able to recognize that love is not only sex, but responsibility as well; it is constancy of companionship, common fulfillment of shared aspirations, and respect and liking for separate goals and for individuality.

If your teen-age child reacts to his insecurity by wanting to marry, come to grips with his central argument—that he believes he is old enough to know what he is doing. Tell him flatly that you do not believe he is any better equipped at his age to make the wise decision he believes he is capable of making than you were or than any other person of similar age is. Remind him that he knows he is not unique just because he is in love, and that he must remember he is also not unique and so capable of avoiding the difficulties early marriage brings. Point out all the old saws which remain, however old, still valid: a majority of marriages occurring during adolescence are broken, many after a first child is born, many before the new mother is more than a year older. Suggest that he and his girl friend therefore reconsider and take a temporary vacation from each other while they date other people.

He may have been impelled to consider marriage by the natural temptations of going steady and by his tendency to overidentify with his loved one; so this desire, by itself, cannot be viewed as a sign of deep disturbance. But if he is unable or unwilling to consider the realistic aspects you point out, if he does not chance a separation that gives him time to cool down, insist that he accompany you to consult professional help. Admit that you cannot communicate with your child's good sense and realism; do not abdicate responsibility for finding someone who can. A professional worker, trained and experienced in working with teen-agers, can usually uncover the anxieties that are leading to your child's defensiveness and irrealism. With help, you can cement friendly relationships with your child again, later.

By all means, keep in mind that the facts are facts. It is highly unlikely that your child can make a good marriage on the strength of adolescent love and experience. Do not be led astray by his fierce hatred of you for standing in his way; do not be led astray by romantic idealism that young love is true love. It may be; but it seldom stands the test of time. You would not permit your child to cross a street if his chances of escaping injury were only fifty-fifty, so do not let him marry in the face of similar odds that the marriage will break up and cause lasting trouble.

## Problems and Judgment

All additional problem situations, whether having to do with sexuality or with the other aspects of living, can be analyzed in the same way. So long as you are alert to signs of your child's complicated and autistic attitudes, you can arrange corrective circumstances and offer corrective comments. When you are very wrong in your views, your child can easily reject your suggestion; when you hit home, his behavior gradually changes from being acting-out in nature, to becoming expressive and constructive. When you are right, but your relations with your child are so strained that you cannot communicate, you can seek professional help.

Throughout, by your use of the same realism, courage, and strength that you apply to your child, you can reassure yourself, judge yourself, and govern your actions to insure your child's continued well-being.

Generally, having experienced a good relationship with you during his childhood, your fatherless child has an understanding that is deeper and broader than that of another child of equal age. Though his view of himself is bound to be less firm until he is well into young adulthood, his tolerance for delay is likely to be stronger; so, without giving way to his discomfort, he can stand the added tension he feels as he tries himself out. Even as a young adult—in school, working, or married—some of these tensions have positive values, however; they enable him to be additionally delighted as he discovers himself.

By enabling your child to be a responsible person and a responsive person in his activity patterns, sexually, and intellectually, you have done all that a mother can do. You have helped your child find and give a maximum amount of pleasure in his life. Alone, you have conquered the difficulties of raising your child in a fatherless home.

# Index

Accusations from child, 201
Acting out, 9, 42, 284
  effects on child, 11
  guilts about responsibility, 48
  hostility, 64
  insecurities about standards, 57
Activity, 120, 139
Adolescence, 139; *See also* Childhood development
Adolescent rebellion, 287
Adolescent roles, 322
Adrenaline addicts, 66
Adult needs, 12, 14
  and satisfaction, 78
Allowances, 281
American Hospital Association, 89
American Medical Association, 89
American Orthopsychiatric Association, 89
American Psychiatric Association, 89
American Psychoanalytic Association, 89
American Psychological Association, 88
Anal stages, 120; *See also* Childhood development
Anger, child's, 267, 276, 296
Anger, mother's
  over desertion, 39
  over divorce and separation, 18
  over illegitimate motherhood, 35

over insecurities, 63
over irresponsibility, 51
over widowhood, 30
Anxieties, mother's, *See* Career; Divorce and separation; Illegitimate motherhood; Loneliness; Remarriage; Safety precautions; Sexual excitement; Standards; Visits with father; Widowhood
Apologizing, 239
Authority, 45, 122
Autistic stage, 116
Autism, 142, 171, 239, 259
Automobiles, 214

Baby-sitters, 170
Bastardy, 316
Behavior and feelings, 42
Birth, 297
Biting, 117
Boarding schools, 255
Bossiness, 282
Bragging about problems, 217
Bribing, 271
Broken friendships
  after desertion, 39
  after divorce and separation, 24
  after illegitimate motherhood, 34
  after widowhood, 32
  in extended absence of husband, 40
Brother and sisters, 157

Care
    of child, 112
    of possessions, 272
Career, mother's
    and divorce and separation, 28
    and irresponsibility, 52
Career choice at adolescence, 140
Carelessness, child's, 199, 271
Cars, 214
Child's needs, 108, 115; *See also*
    Childhood development
Child-rearing guides, 114
Childhood development, 106, 109
    anal stages, 120
    autistic stage, 115
    oral-aggressive stage, 117
    oral-dependent stage, 115
    typical, in complete home, 115
Checking on care, 174, 222
Client-centered therapy, 96
Clinics, 87
Clothes budget, 213
Common sense, 87
*The Common Sense Book of Baby
    and Child Care*, 114
Competition with other women, 72
Competitive activity, 142
Community Chest, 103
Community Referral Service, 103
Consideration of others, 118
Constriction, 57
Constructive behavior, 270
Consulting medical help, 174, 178,
    235
Cooperative frame of mind, 115
Counseling, 96
Courage, 7, 121
Creativity, 117
Curiosity, 117

Dating, 143 145, 284, 321, 325
Day dreams, 125; *See also* Autism;
    Fantasies
Dependency, child's, 176, 190
Dependency, mother's, 15
    in absence of husband, 40
    in desertion, 38
    in divorce and separation, 22
    in widowhood, 30
Desertion, 38
Despondency, 16
    in absence of husband, 40

in desertion, 38
in divorce and separation, 23
in illegitimate motherhood, 35
in widowhood, 29
Destructiveness, 268
Development, *See* Childhood de-
    velopment
Discipline, 112, 256
Discomfort, 293
Discrimination, 229
Divorce and separation
    and immaturity, 81
    and neurosis, 81
    and situational pressures, 17
Dreams of glory, 125

Egotism, adolescent, 140
Embarrassment over being father-
    less, 210
Exhaustion, 16, 48, 172
Exhibitionism, 143, 311
Expectations, 108
Expenses, 163
Explaining mistakes, 155
Explaining singleness, 243
Exploitation, 218
Exploration, 182
Expressing emotions, 9, 42
    anger, 65, 238
    goals, 71
    insecurities, 63

Fads and fanaticism, 58
Failure to provide stimulation, 225
Faith, 115
Fantasies, 125, 141, 309
Father's remarriage, 252
Father's role, 302
    in adolescence, 143
    in anal stages, 123
    in autistic stage, 116
    in latency period, 137
    in oral aggressive stage, 119
    in oral dependent stage, 116
    in phallic stages, 133
    Victorian, 123
Fatigue, 267
Fears, 15
    of mother, 239
    in reaction to loss of father, 199,
        273
Feeding problems, 187

Femininity, 119, 127
Fifth and sixth years, 124
Flirting, 303
Force, 263
Foster homes, 170, 255
Freedom, 112
Friendships, 204, 307, 318
Frustration, 57

General goals, 3, 4
Genital sexuality, 145
Gifts and possessions, 160
Grade school age, 136
Guidance, 183, 192, 195, 259
Guides for child-rearing, 112
Guilt, 16, 239, 272, 275, 315
    about absence of husband, 40,
        199, 202, 275
    and baby's irritability, 173
    and behavior, 48
    about divorce and separation, 26
    about illegitimate motherhood, 35
    and rejection of child, 189, 240
    and shame, 70
    about widowhood, 33

Habits, outworn, 48
Hand-me-downs, 162
Handling arguments, 197
Honesty, 7, 67
Hope, 15, 115; *See also* Despondency
Hospitalized husband, 39
Humility, 135
Husbands
    hospitalized, 39
    imprisoned, 39
    in military service, 39
    in out-of-town employment, 39

Illegitimate motherhood, 34, 330
    and immaturity, 82
    and neurosis, 82
Idealist, 303
Ideals, 47
Identification, 124, 167, 181, 229, 250,
    253, 265, 303
Imagination, 125
Immaturity, 77
    and divorce, 81
    and illegitimate motherhood, 82
    and marriage, 79

and nonmarital sexual intercourse,
    84
Independence, 15, 45, 184; *See also*
    Dependency
Individual characteristics, 113
Infants, 115
*Infant and Child in the Culture of
    Today*, 114
Infantilism, 304
Insecurity over weaknesses, 200;
    *See also* Anxieties
Instructions, 234
Interests, 244, 282
*Intelligent Parents' Guide to Raising
    Children, The*, 114
Intruding on privacy, 225
Intuition and femininity, 134
Irresponsibility, 66

Jobs, 218, 288

Kindergarten child, 124

Latency period, 136
Laws, 260
Lawyers, 103
Learning, 137, 279
Listlessness, 270, 288
Logical thinking and masculinity,
    134
Loneliness, 16, 282
    and absence of husband, 39
    and discrimination, 61
    and divorce, 24
    and widowhood, 32
Love, 15, 54
    and divorce and separation, 18
    and illegitimate motherhood, 34
    and widowhood, 33

Making amends, 239
Manlike strivings, 304
Marriage, 80, 300, 332
Masculinity, 119, 127
Masturbation, 126, 206, 311, 321
Material needs, 15; *See also* Care
Mealtimes, 190, 212
Memory, 120
Menstruation and activity patterns,
    139
Mercy, 124
Momma's boy, 303

Money, 281
Mother's remarriage, 251
Mother's role in complete family
   in adolescence, 143
   in anal stages, 123
   in autistic stage, 116
   in latency period, 137
   in oral-aggressive stage, 119
   in oral-dependent stage, 116
   in phallic stages, 133
   Victorian, 123
Mourning, 30, 163, 219, 246, 265

National Association of Social
   Workers, 89
National Psychological Association
   for Psychoanalysis, 89
Necking, 143, 144
Needs, child's (*see* Childhood development)
   effects of precocious stimulation,
   151
Negative feelings, *see* Anxieties
   and parental failure, 151
Neglect, 175, 183
Neurosis, child's, 299, 303
   and parental failures, 150
   and single mother's behavior, 152
Neurosis, mother's
   and common-sense action, 87
   and divorce, 81
   and illegitimate motherhood, 83
   and immaturity, 77
   and marriage, 80
   and nonmarital sexual intercourse,
   84
   and singleness, 76
Neurotic attitudes toward psychotherapy, 100
Neurotic conflicts, *see* Neurosis and
   acting out, 9, 42
Newborn infant, 115
Nightmares, 239
Nonmarital sexual intercourse, 84
Nudity, 297
Nursery school, 274
Nursery school child, 120

Oedipal problems, 302
Oedipal stage, 126
One-year-old, 117

Optimism, 115
Oral-aggressive stage, 117
Oral-dependent stage, 116
Overactivity, 235
Overdressing baby, 177, 186
Overfeeding, 175
Overidentification, 318
Overprotection, 196
Overrestrictions, 237
Overstimulation, 225, 293

Pain, 110; *See also* Reality; Sexuality
Pals, 306
Parenthood, 110
   the good parent, 111
Parents without Partners, 103
Passive, receptive child, 115
Passivity, 303
Personality types and acting out, 74
Pets, 207
Petting, 143
Phallic stage, 124, 142
Physical development, *see* Child-
   hood development
Physical punishment, 183, 261
Playing with child, 225, 227, 237
Playtoys, 205, 207
Pleasure, 110; *See also* Reality; Sex-
   uality
Praise, 233
Precocious training, 151
Prejudice, 66
Pre-school child, 120
Pretence, 63
Pride, 15, 67; *See also* Shame
Prison, 39
Privacy, 13
   for child to develop interests, 54,
   245, 329
   during visits with father, 249
Private sex life, 330
Problems, general, 5, 6
Problems in providing stimulation
   and freedom, 220
   during adolescence, 247
   during early infancy, 224
   during fifth and sixth years, 242
   during fourth and fifth years, 236
   during latency period, 244
   during Oedipal period, 242
   from weaning through third year,
   226

Problems in stimulating realism about sexuality, 292
  in late adolescence, 325
  in latency period, 318
  during Oedipal stage, 298
  during pre-Oedipal stages, 292
  in puberty, 320
Problems in stimulating responsibility, 256
  in adolescence, 284
  in fifth and sixth years, 275
  in fourth year, 270
  in grade school years, 278
  during Oedipal stage, 275
  in second year, 264
  in third year, 266
Problems of material care and protection, 171
  in adolescence, 211
  in early infancy, 171
  in fifth and sixth years, 201
  in first and second years, 180
  in grade school years, 208
  in Oedipal stage, 201
  in third and fourth years, 193
Protection, 112
  from playmates, 195
  from school authorities, 208
Psychological development, *See* Childhood development
Psychological help, 88
Psychiatrists, 94
Psychoanalysis, 95
Psychobiological development, 108, 115; *See also* Childhood development
Psychologists, 93
Psychosexual stages, *see* Childhood development
Psychotherapy for child, 320
Puberty, 139; *See also* Childhood development
Punishment, 227, 285, 295

Questions about mother's past, *see* Divorce and separation; Illegitimate motherhood

Reactions to loss of father
  absence during infancy, 180
  bizarre behavior, 205, 288
  carelessness, 199, 271
  confusion, 218
  dependency, 190
  fears, 199, 273
  guilts, 199, 275
  indifference, 242
  listlessness, 270, 288
  over-maturity, 190, 219, 272, 288
  problems about money, 281
  realistic mourning, 219, 246
  social difficulties, 210
  tendency toward tantrums, 235
  transvestitism, 205
Reality, child's, 109
  in anal stages, 121
  in autistic stage, 115
  in latency period, 136
  in oral-aggressive stage, 117
  in oral-dependency stage, 116
  in phallic stage, 125
  at puberty, 140
Reality testing of Oedipal fantasies, 141
Recognition, 233
Regression, 191
Rejections, 165
Relaxed frame of mind, 115
Religious leaders, 103
Remarriage
  after desertion, 39
  after divorce and separation, 24, 27
  after illegitimate motherhood, 36
  after widowhood, 32
  followed by birth of new children, 254
  of two single parents, 253, 305
Responsibility, child's, 109
  in anal stages, 122
  in autistic stage, 116
  in latency period, 137
  in oral-aggressive stage, 118
  in oral-dependency stage, 116
  in phallic stage, 125
  at puberty, 140
Responsibilities, mother's, 45
Roles, parents', 110
  bad, 150
  *See also* Father's role; Mother's role

Safeguards against trouble, 221, 327
Safety precautions, 160, 178, 192

School problems, 208
Self-confidence, 198
Self condemnation, *see* Guilt
Self-control, 7
  and acting out, 8
  and problems of divorce and separation, 21
  and problems of widowhood, 29
Self-defeating reactions, child's, 156
Self-respect, 55
Self-sufficiency, 58, 185, 187, 190, 196, 219, 255, 272, 288
Sex differences, 298; *See also* Father's roles; Mother's roles
Sex education, 324
Sex life, mother's
  after divorce, 22
  after widowhood, 33
  past, 35, 59
Sex play, 297
Sexual excitement, 320
Sexual inhibition, 294
Sexual intercourse, 322
Sexual molestation, 206, 317
Sexuality, child's, 110
  in anal stages, 122
  in autistic stage, 116
  in latency period, 136
  in oral-aggressive stage, 118
  in oral-dependency stage, 116
  in phallic stage, 125
  at puberty and adolescence, 139
Shame, 68, 304
Siblings, 157
Situational pressures, 17
  after desertion, 38
  after divorce and separation, 17
  during extended absence of husband, 39
  in illegitimate motherhood, 34
  in widowhood, 29
Social events, 210
Social workers, 93
Solving problems, 154
Special needs or talents, 167
Special treats, 161
Spontaneity, 10, 15
Standards, 15, 54

Stealing, 277
Stimulation, 112
Strength of character, 121
Submissive behavior, 65
Success in school, 137
Supervised play groups, 240
Symbolic thinking, 136

Tact, 124
Talents, special, 167
Talking, 120, 122
Tantrums, 235, 269
Taste, personal, 54
Teachers, 103
Temper tantrum, 234, 238
Three to five years of age, 120
Timidity, 121
Toddler, 117
Tolerance for delay, 262
Tolerance for long-term goals, 137
Tolerance of frustration, 118
Toileting, 268
Traveling husband, 39
Treatment for emotional disturbances, 87
Trust, 15, 115

Under-dressing, 178, 185
Unhappiness, child's, 156
United Fund, 103
Unwed mothers, *See* Illegitimate motherhood

Vicarious outlets, 313
Visits with father, 161, 165
  after divorce, 249, 314
  if imprisoned or hospitalized, 166
  if prohibited, 165
Visits with grandparents, 250, 315

Weakness, 121
Weaning, 117
Widowhood, situational pressures in, 29
Working mother, 169

YMCA, 103
Young adulthood, 145

301.427
J77